The Blake Library

Martin County Library System
2351 S.E. Monterey Road
Stuart, FL 34996-3331

American Poets Say Goodbye to the Twentieth Century

edited and with an introduction by
Andrei Codrescu and Laura Rosenthal

FOUR WALLS EIGHT WINDOWS
NEW YORK / LONDON

ANTHOLOGY COPYRIGHT ©
ANDREI CODRESCU AND LAURA ROSENTHAL

PUBLISHED IN THE UNITED STATES BY
FOUR WALLS EIGHT WINDOWS
39 WEST 14TH STREET, SUITE 503
NEW YORK, NY 10011

UK OFFICES:
FOUR WALLS EIGHT WINDOWS/TURNAROUND
27 HORSELL ROAD
LONDON N51 XL
ENGLAND

LIBRARY OF CONGRESS CATALOGING-IN-PUBLICATION DATA

AMERICAN POETS SAY GOODBYE TO THE 20TH CENTURY/EDITED
AND INTRODUCED BY ANDREI CODRESCU AND LAURA ROSENTHAL
P.   CM.
ISBN 1-56858-068-1 (PAPER)   1-56858-071-1 (CLOTH)
1. TWENTIETH CENTURY—POETRY. 2. AMERICAN POETRY—20TH
CENTURY I. CODRESCU, ANDREI, 1946– . II. ROSENTHAL, LAURA,
1958– .
PS595.T84A83   1996
811'.5408—DC20   96-2033
                                                         CIP

10 9 8 7 6 5 4 3 2 1
PRINTED IN THE UNITED STATES

NOTE & ACKNOWLEDGMENT

M OST of the work herein was written in response to the title of this book. These are original poems, published here by permission of and copyrighted by their authors. A few poets felt that some of their earlier poems addressed the subject adequately: they are reprinted here by permission of the authors. The places where these poems first appeared are acknowledged below their poems. We are deeply grateful to the more than one hundred poets who heeded our melancholy yet hopeful call.

PROLOGUE TO AN EPILOGUE

WHY THE TWENTIETH CENTURY and not the millennium? Gary Snyder suggested that we call on poets to say their farewells to the millennium. The twentieth century, it seemed to him, was only a speck in the millennial tide and the millennium itself was no more than a blip to the earth, the living entity that sets its clock by rocks and stars. It's a tempting perspective: in the 1960s the cosmos briefly intersected the twentieth century. The cosmic debris has remained imbedded more or less firmly in the flesh of a number of poets. Michael McClure was left with "shells of silicon and waving pseudopods." Will Alexander minds the alchemy of "blinding glycerin seas." Antler recalls that "500,000 years ago sleepy chipmunks/ snuggled in their burrows." Lawrence Ferlinghetti, reaching forward, surveys the century from a zeppelin and arrives in "endless eternity."

The only anthologizable millennium carvable from such duration is the one beginning in original sin and ending in utopia. But, for the most part, such millennial perspective is willfully absent here, deliberately excised. And when that isn't possible, it is dissolved in the acid bath of irony, a native twentieth-century substance. "god's very/ possibly way outta here," says Jonathan Williams. Faye Kicknosway writes that "God is a dimwit." And Maxine Kumin wonders, "And what terror awaits those among us/ whose moral priorities are unattached/ to Yahweh, Allah, Buddha, Christ." It's hard to say adios when God's gone.

The truth is that the twentieth century, the American century, matters far more to these poets than the Christian millennium. There are few calls for redemption. Tom Clark asks what will become of the "lyric spirit." Robert Creeley affirms that in his lifetime "Yet I loved, I love." And for Edward Field, hope attaches to "poetry, fantasy weapon for non-fighters." There is no hint of the Messiah, not one welcome sign. Embarrassment escorts the end and denial greets the beginning.

The twentieth century is where we have lived our lives. Where we were compelled to embody modern differences. We were constituted to be utterly unlike the centuries that came before us. At times, this was a great hope, all that revolutionary newness in a stale world. Watch Apollinaire and Marinetti, before the first World War, greeting the aesthetics of steel girders and engines. Theirs was an ambiguous enterprise: an attempt, on the one hand, to partake of the bounty of forms bequeathed by the future; on the other, a futile effort to humanize the machine. Happily, and necessarily, irony was born again at the same time. Tristan Tzara could declare, while the utopian machine of the Russian revolution was being deployed: "I am still charming." Thank God. (In whom no one trusts.)

Later, it appeared that what was universally human had to be defended against what was not: vast warring ideologies, war itself, genocide. This vision sustains a number of what may be called citizen poets. For Sam Abrams, the incendiary necessity to scourge the polis asks "And how are we better than the good Germans, the so civilized French/ who stood by, who averted their eyes?" In her "Note from Memphis," Lucille Clifton knows that "history is chasing you, america,/ like a mean dog." Carolyn Kizer lists the victims: ". . . Armenians, Jews,/ Gypsies, Russians, Vietnamese,/ the Bosnians, the Somalians . . . /" Elinor Nauen, quoting Freud quoting Heine, declares that "One must forgive one's enemies/ but not before they have been hanged."

All the poets in here can be said to affirm their citizenship in this century, but there are degrees of awkwardness. Abrams, Clifton, Kizer, and Nauen do so with a straight face and thus make the strongest connection to Walt Whitman's nineteenth century. For others, such certitudes become either hedged by absurdity or qualified by powerlessness. One of the poets in this book, Eileen Myles, ran for the presidency on a poetry-lesbian-feminist platform. Her seriousness was not compromised by the knowledge that "100 years of the naked emperor/ is more than my eyes can stand." Looking back, Keith Waldrop notes soberly, "horrors of/ blood and state."

The clearest and, for that matter, the least utopian views come from the grand elders who have lived in, seen, and questioned this century, having seen, as well, the shipwreck of presumptions big and small. The century belongs to them by virtue of their having survived it. Speaking of his "impending demise," James Broughton, born in 1914, notes: "Some kind of cold comfort to know that/ one will be lying about in the ruins/ with Ozymandias Mussolini/ and all the other residue of the millennium." Robert Creeley asks only, sensibly: "But couldn't it all have been/ a little nicer,/ as my mother'd say." And from Carl Rakosi: "the state of the world . . . flaky."

Anselm Hollo, born in Finland, was a child during the second World War. Looking back, he sees that "whatever it ever was/ fights among *capos*." The century's history was but a gang fight, a clash of mafiosi egos. Who the *capos* were and what they stood for is a mystery that everyone would like to solve. Who did it? is a question asked often in this book. The "who" and "it" change, but the belief that there was a crime and that someone or something did it to us are unchanging. The *capos*, or those *capo* forces that Marxists and Neomarxists tagged and tag, are the object of many a poetic volley. Racism gets it in John Yau's aesthetic, moral, environmental, ironic, trivial, and, ultimately, political question: "Will this spill finally bleach me?" Jonathan Williams delivers a moralist's blast at the enfeebling of the American mind, from "lorena to tonya." The antiseptic utopia of space salesmen gets it from Terence Winch, "cursing Carl Sagan." Even amnesia comes in for a whacking, the result of overstimulation and excess: Paul Auster regrets losing the details of his life through an American life-riddled brain. And Anne Waldman finds that she ". . . forgot/ I forgot something/

amnesia of holocaust/ amnesia for war & war & more war . . ." She has forgotten precisely that which is unforgettable. What we would like to forget, if only it were possible.

None of these culprits, to be sure, stand shelled for long. The more abominably obvious sins of America are not so much excoriated as noted in their complex interplay with the poet. It is Allen Ginsberg who most completely identifies himself with his time and place. He accuses America of poisoning the world's air and water, but it is his own body that is America. "Fire Air Water tainted," he laments, followed by "poor circulation, smoke more cigarettes." Four decades have passed since the poet's curse, "America, go fuck yourself with your atom bomb!" In that time, Ginsberg and America merged. He, no less than the rest of us, stands no longer outside because the outside, like clean air and water, has vanished, another fin-de-siécle casualty.

One can hear a harsh urgency now in the work of those whose bodies have become the organs of a new American politics. Here, in an arena circumscribed by the body, even Judeo-Christianity gets a new job. "The Voice kept tugging at my ear," declares Jack Anderson in the persona of Noah, ". . . nagging and ordering me/ to tell the people of the city, 'Because of your wickedness/ this place will be destroyed.'" The place *has* been destroyed, in the ravaged bodies of Michael Andre's friends: "the tragedy of the homosexual today—all I can do for/ such friends is make this hello to the magnetic/ pole of death that draws us like the years./ I made few prayers while this cold Pole is pope/" William Burroughs takes on Christianity in the flesh: ". . . what about the Inquisition, that stinks of burning flesh, torture, excrement—its stultifying presence imposed by brutal force." The meek, for whom Christ apparently died, are all but forgotten. For Charles Bukowski, it's not worth living in a future where "hospitals are so expensive it's cheaper to die."

Bukowski is one of the few poets here—Tom Dent is another—to speak on behalf of the truly downtrodden in a manner not checked by self-consciousness. From the 1930s to midcentury, such paucity of proletarian sympathy would have been shocking. Even more shocking to those distant ages of humanism would have been the radical doubts some poets have about the nature of humanity itself. Bruce Andrews produces an alphabetical list of words defined randomly by vaguely familiar found phrases. Rae Armantrout's faith is retained only by a question mark: "No one home/ in the 'Virtual Village'?/ Between the quote marks,/ nothing but disparagement." Jack Marshall notes, with remarkable understatement, "Earth's not cherry anymore."

A shattering malaise has entered the world and left its signature in fractured language, a medium no longer transparent, and badly suited for carrying understanding. All that remains are the shards of what we thought or had been made to think, shards that are vastly outnumbered by the things we make and buy. What did we think? What were we made to think? Whatever it was, it is late. "Ditto the caveat, ibid the scam," writes Bill Berkson. For all that, the elegiac calibrates even the densest texts, the most telegraphic notations. For some, here Charles Bernstein, the multiplication of products induces regret at having done anything at all: "The goats pass/ from view, the boys/ skip stones from/ melancholy hydroplanes./ I should have wasted my life."

Without irony such sentiments would be tragic. But not necessarily. The world of bright, shiny, American-made objects has its fans. David Trinidad's American century is the movies. And Joe Cardarelli in "Against the 21st Century," disdains the coming age of antiseptic living. He has loved his time and the abusive pleasures of his world. And there are ways of relishing the mess, as Pat Nolan suggests: "acquire a taste for the bittersweet/ it soothes that sinking feeling." Jim Gustafson celebrates "not getting caught." Still, an American *De Natura Rerum* is missing from this book, which is a mystery. In saying goodbye to their century, our poets were careful to note the "noise, blood, suffering," as Janine Pommy Vega put it, and to keep their distance from even those objects that fill their other poems.

Oh, but there is hope. The women keep it. Some of them, anyway, are able to see the future as something they will give birth to, something to nurture. "O Century of Ceaseless Labor!/ Drop by drop the blood-streaked columns thicken/ and our fire is glowing still," says Janine Canan. Bernadette Mayer prays for better men and women to inhabit the planet: "so therefore war father, mother, let me be & leave me/ I know how to propagate the race for slightly peace that is/ to only give birth to women: or to sweet loving boys who have in their builds/ no desire to make us war or crazier." Sex receives its *hommage* but not as lyrically as was once the norm. Summer Brenner reports some "naked Doric gals on Emerald Hill" who have no regret for having whooped it up.

Make no mistake: the sacred that enters the world of these poems has gotten here the hard way. It has made its way through beliefs and discarded beliefs. It has survived loves and Love. It has stared Death in the face. It has burrowed through the postmodern fragments of poetry and through the shopping malls. It has outlived the death of the twentieth century, a harsh father. It has asked, who will pay the century's "karmic debt"? In "Désamère," Alice Notley journeys through the desert, confronts Evil and evils, and finds, in the end, a commonality that transcends everything. "'Brother,' says Amère, 'Why are you and I/ Like this . . . soldier, widow,/ Why aren't we cars?'" This is the reply, in the voice of Robert Desnos: "'Because we grieve like animals . . . / Behaving as your species would/ If it hadn't turned into cars/ You're still the animals.'"

Here it is, all the tragicomic grotesquerie of the spent century. It's not a fond farewell. No one seems to have liked the deceased. And yet everyone suspects that the convention of the artificially designated "twentieth" century held something profoundly significant. While it is true, says Jack Anderson, that "there is never an end/ . . . / of treachery, lies/ stupidity, arrogance,/ brute force, and lost causes," there is also, as Arthur Sze puts it, the "moment when a child asks/

when will it be tomorrow?" Elaine Equi gives us the possibility that you can ". . . sleep now, gentle/ reader, and dream of comets trailing blood and/ planets exploding. When you wake, it will be spring."

That would be nice. It would be nice, that is, if like the old movies, this narrative had a happy ending. It might have been possible if it had had a happy beginning. But, as Eileen Myles says: "the first thing we learned/ was the world would end/ in our time." The editors of this book, born respectively in 1946 and 1958, learned that. In 1946 the beginning and the end were one the year before at Hiroshima. In 1958 the end was happily one with the beginning of rock 'n' roll. "That's the human song," says Notley, "from the past to nowhere."

In compiling this book, the editors avoided deliberately the customary fault lines in American poetry. We approached poets from all walks of verse and included all those who responded. Some poets were too superstitious to be in a book so definitely framed. James Laughlin, who published the twentieth century, stayed out of it. Others, like Charles Bukowski and Joe Cardarelli, said their goodbyes just before they left us. They didn't see the end of the twentieth century. We might. *Enivrez-vous!*

Andrei Codrescu
Laura Rosenthal
Baton Rouge

GOODBYE TWENTIETH CENTURY

> *You've been a good old wagon,*
> *but Daddy, you done broke down.*
>   traditional blues

I am looking at the Twentieth xx from under my desk
    waiting for the all-clear signal miniature Mouseketeers
    dancing past suicides & headcases child actors all
    smiles I draw cartoons of them in pencil Boy
    Mouseketeers drooling over Annette's & Cheryl's breasts
    Girl Mouseketeers trash talking about guys & makeup &
    shoes and delayed gratification under my desk my dipshit
    teachers didn't notice *that* died too

Under my desk Ray Charles shouting *Tell The Truth* our theme
    song while cars spazzed into mushroom bulbous pubic
    beards (just like me) chromed & slathered & pointy it
    was thrilling beef dripped down a golden tube into my
    arm until I stepped out in front of 777 Haight St. with
    a lunch bag in my hand going to Pan American to release
    mail to Vietnam an Army truck rolled by with eight
    assault rifles trained on me RACE RIOTS IN THE FILLMORE
    Thought Lunch Was Bomb subhead I didn't know that I was
    waiting for the end of the 20th xx but I was & it didn't
    come then and

Also forgot to mention had to get to the disco
    so I ran my truck over a railroad crossing sign to
    create an impromptu parking place & the next morning a
    station wagon full of Serbian nuns and Kuwaiti gas
    attack victims and Somalian sick children and Panamanian

war orphans died there hit by the assassination of John
Fitzgerald Kennedy I was guilty & sorry but I wasn't
serious couldn't be trusted I was a secular humanist in
the waiting room where Bill Burroughs strongly advised
me to turn necrophiliac so Vietnam remained only one
word without an I in it Thanks, Bill!

The 20th xx where I played with F-86s rifle butts cracked
bucktoothedjaws and endless villains who were physically
challenged by bad complexions acid baths mole breaths
dysfunctional hooks snags Ugh genetic codes later
showing up as an Armani draped chorus line highkicking
Whoever dies with the most toys wins

But then it was Inventory Time:
A trinity of peepholes under my desk labeled Duck and
Explain Yourself and Coming Back T'Getcha
Two starry telephones labeled Love It/Leave it
One saffron toilet labeled You Stink Dualistic One!
How annoying hand me my fuzzy logic floating above
aisles of deodorants douches powders perfect body hairs
installed while you wait and you better at the Park 'n'
Pay Congregational Synagogue Ball

Waiting for the 20th xx to end Euro-Disney shares were
falling ding-a-ling! what a great ride you're kidding
you come here often that was sexist racist ageist
Oooooh! The Feast of Saint Fellatio! Yow! Pussy
Upside-down Cake! Oops! Herpes Donor! Rump titty rump
titty rump rump rump! Look: The Lone Ranger versus
Virusilla!

But the blackberry vines talked intelligently to me
   the wall dissolved we conversed telepathically
   compassionate sunbeams smeared on tangled up in blue
   bread it was better than the book better than the big
   screen yes in virtual deniability we were waiting always
   waiting for the 20th xx Goodbye

OUR HOLOCAUST: 2 HOURS FROM HEATHROW

I thirst for accusation.
    William Butler Yeats

All the fine words ever said in Europe, lies,
All the poems, all the songs of Europe, lies,
All the fine theories, all the philosophies, lies,
Bloody, beshitted, refuted in Croatia,
In Herzegovina, in Bosnia, in Bosnia, in Sarajevo.

Voltaire a liar! Goethe a liar! Garibaldi bugiardo!
Dostoyefsky, Tolstoi, Checkov, Solzhenitsyn liars!
Erasmus mendax! Shakespeare a liar! Dante a liar!
Foucault and Lacan big liars! Dickens a liar! Kant a liar!
Spinoza a liar! Wittgenstein, Russell liars!
Manet and Picasso blind! Verdi deaf! Nijinsky lame!
Bach a liar! Mozart a liar! Byron, Keats and Shelley liars!
Hugo menteur! Marx and Freud and Einstein lugnerin!
Madam Curie menteuse! Balzac a liar! Flaubert a liar!
The Beatles, the Stones liars! Gilbert and Sullivan liars!
Florence Nightingale a liar! Sarah Bernhardt a phoney!
Mallarmé liar! Sartre and Beauvoir and Camus liars!
Charlie Chaplin and Diaghilev liars!
Plato a liar! Aristotle liar! Socrates big liar!

Only Stalin told the truth! only Hitler! only Himmler!
Only Beria! only Dzerzhinsky!
Only Treblinka told the truth! Auschwitz told the truth!
Katya Woods the truth! Warsaw Ghetto the truth!
Dachau the truth!
The Quai at Smyrna the truth!
The Trail of Tears the truth!

Andersonville the truth! Wallabout Bay the truth!
Hiroshima the truth! Nagasaki the truth! Dresden the truth!
My Lai the truth! El Mozote truth!
Buchenwald the truth! Gulag the truth!

Are those who slaughter the innocents
From mere cowardice or inertia
To be ranked above the slaughterers
Who kill from rage and hatred?
How are Major, Bush, Clinton, Kohl, Mitterrand—that set—better
Than Dzerzhinsky? Eichmann? Stalin? Hitler?
And how are we better than the good Germans,
        the so civilized French
Who stood by, who averted their eyes?

How are we better than the worst?
This is not happening somewhere else.
This is happening in the "European Home" now,
Two hours from Heathrow!
One from De Gaulle or Orly!
One hour from Frankfort, from Fiumicino!

The bombers of the Uffizi are right!
Why preserve the relics of these scum?
These worse than nazis!
These murderers by inertia, by sloth!

If there was ever a cause worth fighting for
It's peace in Yugoslavia.
If there was ever a cause worth dying for,
It's law and peace in Europe.

SAM ABRAMS

But you will die in your bed, for no cause,
Meaningless lives, meaningless deaths,
Automobile freaks, image junkies, weaklings, mere lumps,
Hypocrite readers, my brothers, my sisters, my peers!

These are the fruits of winning the cold war: cowardice and sloth.
These are the fruits of materialism: cowardice and sloth.
These are the fruits of consumerism: cowardice and sloth.
These are the fruits of multi-media: cowardice and sloth.
These are the fruits of the global economy: cowardice and sloth.
These are the fruits of mtv: cowardice and sloth.
These are the fruits of cnn: cowardice and sloth.
These are the fruits of the autobahn: cowardice and sloth.
These are the fruits of victory: cowardice and sloth.
These are the fruits of the victory of capitalism.
These are the fruits of the victory of democracy.
In our time. Our holocaust.

THE DAWNING ZONE / THE ERUPTING PARALLEL SPECIES

> *. . . a planetary system has been*
> *found about 1,500 light-years*
> *away in the Virgo constellation.*
> John Noble Wilford
> *The New York Times*

Crossed beyond the zones of the Piscean, meandering like a sand demon, shedding the old human stupors, falling into each blank hysterical revery, each chant turned around into a ceaseless totemic of splitting, of intrusion, of sullen binary gulfs, released from one's laws by lean amorphic telepathy, amassing a fount of green kilometer ravings, become spoors, devoid of culmination, leaking, with vicious ambulations, the turquoise, drained of each declivitous nuance, each devious magnitude, which both strengthens and annuls, which eradicates yet unseals its fate, the hounded walk, the suicidal instant, as in a circumstantial dosage which both hampers and blurs with the sudden stereopsis of overwhelming acuity, which eats up the ruthless, divested of each animal ruin, of each slaughter as vapour, of each pouring cimex balance, thrust through blinding glycerin seas, being the omega and its preferential rivers, by means of spells, by means of shifting multitudes and scorn, of sundered dialectics, as if the blood inside the galaxy had shifted, as if in the cruel declamatory reason for being there were trekless amalgamations focused upon a new symbolic physiology, with a newly declared wattage, with an intense and cerulean cometary mane, as if, the former century had been scorched and transmuted to an occulted fever within the psychic ambit of the curious Trogan planets, or in the Hottentot aura of the protean Virgo constellation, as in the anomalous resurrection of a stormy ice volcano, brewing its strange and perilous gentian greens, its first true electrical ammonias, as to liminal flight, as to the coming protospecies, there exists only strange aphotic measuring bursts, defeated parallel founderies phantasmic with delay, with the kyphotic rays of calamitous insurgency, which again is motion to every parallel star, which ensnares, which seasons a mythology amidst a darkened psychic obligation, bespeaking a terminal lunar obligation, as if the mind could model and colour a new abstract to be subsumed in a former scintilla of torment around the flair of a poisoned monsoon fatigue, never knowing if one is miming the demiurge, or transfixing the skull inside a new or more shadowy logos, with its nerveless embers at the peak of a wild and deceptive conflagration, yes, there are ideals which shadow themselves, which disrupt their original rhythm, without taking as virtue a supreme and melancholy rubric, only to fall into the hauntings of a darkened sunbeam tree absorbing a blank delusional treatise on being, therefore, the erupting species, lightless, darting, its confusions intemperate, like blazing dunes in the void, emitting sounds from reticulate muzzles, as if it could evolve and receive dimensions of a dazed and horrified scarification, as a soaked and glandular velocity, as in a clandestine moat, as in genetic revival as error, therefore snares, multiple and occluded explosions, as in a liminal fleece corrupted by enzymes, by monarchical aggregates as in a maniacal forum for diseased expression, for monomial branding, for a future tense of antediluvian hemorrhage, as a thesis stamped upon the voices of the neurons, voiced and re-voiced through aggregation and millennia, the poise with its scarobs, with its beleaguered testing counts, with its deep and omnipotent deficiency as beacon, with its alien form of progressive strychnine inclusive, discovering its source by means of accursed ironics, the future ideal burned into the leaves as flameless mining dots, as locales which incinerate like a convulsed and shadowed stone bringing forth auras, as one addresses a decibel, or foreshadows a scope in a neutered washing grain, in this incinerated future maps condoned in hierarchical plague, in steaming sphinxian moss broken into parts by mensuration, by error and warmth, its geologies living with incommensurate curses so that each geo-physical reaction exists as an internal pointing threat, as accursed base for existence, basing its dread on a neoteric spawning order, on palsied integers which burn, which hold a proto-chaparral in the form of a neodymium shrieking, as if the buds of the species evolved from horrific incline tables, of hydrogen and shale, from divisive turpentine atoms, surviving instinctive malice by means of frayed and immaculate singeing, because the heat from its landing coast like the heat from its partial and scorpion neutron star, which erupts with irregular blinding, as in a brand from old symbolical Assyrias, in the musics of a cradled lightning germ, there exist wings, of the fiercest, most inevitable rookeries, evolved from the zones of shattered iodine rays, of salt, of plummeting mixtures of torment, bereft, dazzled by a music of circles, as logos seethes in neither trajectory or foment, there is only the marking, with its sundered want, with its cataclysmic crystal, merged with the substance of vistas.

WILLIAM ALLEN

FOR THE DARKLING THRUSH
(December 2000)

This time we have to hope: green Cockaigne and truck stops
overgrown with mammoth, radiant radishes,
bent-cripple roadsigns hawking stuff like gall-
stones' bitumen, radioactive breadfruit,
fluff of catatonic Presidents, each morning's
sobbing of daughters at the turnstile plots
where their fathers turn the other cheek,
roll-over-play-dead for the arty-appetite of 'possum,
patois come up to Okeechobee. Pythagoras
has a dike-and-copse where we can go
and meditate, those of us who think there's
just one corpse that cardiograms a soul.
Beware the moribund throng of bridesmaids,
choughs, Little Leaguers: they speak too soon.

All of our past *ménage à trois?* Wall-to-wall
Osterpandemonium, on a sweltering Parsee moon
of swallows. For now, the Ukraine-orthodox
church bells rankle us down to Third Street,
kindling household TV fireblow, tangled bine-
stem cable spool and cardamon, spewling
out Hardy's old pulse of germ and birth,
this sky a crypt of clouds a century old still,
Oh to see you shirtless out at Rockaway again!
I pluck at bass strings for all of Pleiades:
advise their twinkling oars pull faster, past
solar mid-career, a thousand points of light
I aim at specters of the universe, at the dog
who snaps at flies but eats the sandfleas.

SOME WORDS, STORIES,
AND PEOPLE FOR AN OLD CENTURY AND A NEW

1. *The Bewilderment of Noah*
What amazed me
about those people
was not their sins.

No,
it was seeing them
just standing around gawking
while the rain kept falling,
their mouths open wide
like empty buckets,

and if they did
say something, they sighed,
"Oh dear,
what can we do?"
or "Well,
that's how things are."

And they just kept standing there
until the waves had covered them.

But did no one
—didn't even one person—
have a boat,
could I have been
the only one?

What bunk!
Of course
there must have been boats:
fishermen would have had them,
and merchants,
and yachtsmen,
there must have been ferries and liners.

But no one used them;
they just stood around sniveling,
getting soaked, getting drowned.

Okay:
maybe even the best of those boats
would have been no protection,
would have gone under at last,

but at least they'd have tried
to challenge their condition.
They, though, did nothing,
they just stood around.

No,
what pisses me of
about those people
is not their great sinning,
but their god-damned stupidity.

2. *The Dudgeon of Jonah*
And after all that,
nothing happened.

The Voice kept tugging at my ear,
hissing in my head,
whispering, barking, meowing, hollering,
ordering me
to go to the city and tell the people,
"Because of your wickedness
this place will be destroyed."

But I can't preach,
so I didn't go,
I went the other way instead
and got thrown overboard
and landed in the whale,
and there I was
trapped in its belly
with that awful Voice again
lecturing me, hectoring me,
nagging and ordering me
to tell the people of the city,
"Because of your wickedness
this place will be destroyed."

So, after all that,
I did go
and I preached to the people
as the Voice commanded,
and when I was through
they said, "We're sorry,
forgive us,
we didn't realize,"
and I laughed to hear their pathetic squeaking,
for I knew that judgment was at hand.

And then,
after all that,
nothing happened.

Yet I kept waiting,
I planted myself behind battlements of scowls
while they organized committees
to end corruption
and promote reforms,
I stayed on, a glowering fortress,
while their generations came and went
and they took their puny measures.
I waited to be paid
for having gone through so much
to learn how to preach,
to gain the courage to prophesy,
I waited for the reward
of seeing that great city
go up in smoke and flame
and topple to the ground
while its citizens gnashed their teeth.

But nothing happened:
after all that,
after all I did and endured,
THE CITY WAS SPARED.

And now,
as one last affliction,
the Voice is ordering me
to settle in this city
and live among its people.

3. *The Radiance of a Woman in Milwaukee*

Those who'd been staying
were well on their way,
what had to be done was done,
things were in order
as best they could be,
and now that she was
by herself, the city
—this city she grew up in,
this city where she lived—
stretched out about her
like someplace new
which she could explore
just as she wished.

And, this morning, she chose
to get up early
and watch the sun rise
over Lake Michigan
as she'd wanted to do
for so many years,
yet never had managed
to be there to see it,
and away she went then
all on her own.

It's rather exciting
at that time of the day,
it's almost still night,
though streaks
the color of peaches
are showing in the sky,

and as she sped along
the empty avenues
the stop lights winked yellow
and there surely weren't more
than two other cars
between her house and the lake.

The rise of the sun
is really not
a slow thing, she discovered,
and she didn't take
her eyes off it
until it had gotten
all the way up—
and what a dazzle it was:
she could even feel it
under her skin.

And after she'd marveled,
she got back in her car,
and again as she drove
no red lights stopped her,
and soon she was home,
with every room filled
with sunlight and forever,
and she drank some hot coffee
and ate a cheese Danish
(and liked how they tasted)
and, checking the clock,
she saw with surprise
her whole trip had taken
almost no time at all,

but it was so rich,
it gave her so much,
and she was ready now
to wonder
about the rest of this day:
what it would bring her,
what it would ask.

4. *The Poet Speaks*

However long
I shall live, I know
I now have lived
most of my life.
If no catastrophe
intervenes, I
shall probably see
the century's turn.
How my friends and I,
when we were kids,
would sometimes talk of it,
about how lucky we were
that we had been born
in just the right years
that we could be
still alive and well
when the new age dawned,
whereas others would be
senile or dead then
and still others so young
they couldn't appreciate
the change in its glory.
Now the time is at hand.

The end is near.
But there is never an end,
I've lived long enough to know,
of treachery, lies,
stupidity, arrogance,
brute force, and lost causes.
But I also know,
or I'd not be writing this,
that there is never an end
of aspiration
and stumbling good will
and that I am not
alone in thinking so,
or otherwise why,
whoever you are,
would you bother to read
and go on reading,
whenever you do,
all this stuff
about Noah and Jonah,
who are surely only mythical,
and a woman in Milwaukee
you probably don't know,
but who is real (and who knows
if she's mythic as well?),
and on to these last words
by someone who
is also real,
as real as you are?
But what else could be said here,
given the occasion?
Think of something.

Make it good.
Then let us join hands
as best we can
while we face the truths
that all works worth accomplishing
must somehow be begun,
that few great things
are ever brought to pass
in any one lifetime
and seldom by anyone
acting alone,
and that we need to be
here where we are
with both a wonderment
so wholly ours
no one else can know it
and a trust that unites us
with whoever else lives here,
forgiving them
and ourselves,
and staying alive
if only because
we still remain curious
about what will come next,
curiosity being
a shy kind of hope
and a trembling faith
that, whatever may happen,
things are never quite finished.

MICHAEL ANDRE

ELEGY FOR A CENTURY OF AIDS

Although the Germans in their wars
shot my uncle and grandfather

and the Holocaust and Vietnam perturb,
AIDS kills my friends:

Brian my collaborator
Tom my editor   Jorge the horizonatal

Jimmy my photographer   Paul my sculptor

Andrew my harpsichordist. My
ink is no ocean. Pine at the tree line vanishes, today

my cold country turns colder, September, spring and summer
for me this year has been a long

dying. Bear season on James Bay opens
in a few weeks, I'd like to turn

the page, kill, why not
deal death? The Blue Jays in the paper are in first,

as a kid, I shot
a jay with a 22, game called

for bullets. The sands of diamond seduction tick white.
"You're with the press

and you don't know what that is?"
Looked like brains and sangria to me.

Bury me in: the R.C.
cemetery

Kingston: no
headstone against the snow.

Murder in the streets
or a clock by the bedside, acknowledging

the tragedy of the homosexual today—all I can do for
such friends is make this hello to the magnetic

pole of death that draws us like the years.
I make few prayers while this cold Pole is pope

DEFINITION

A—on how—
Abandonment—publicity—
Abbreviations—magnolias—
Abrasion—profit at bay—
Abrupt—ripe—
Abstraction—indifference—
Abuttal—your skull—
Action—cuckold—
Active—neural—
Actor—avidity—
Admixture—to the fuzz—
Adoration—adoption—
Adore—to pretend—
Adultery—"a slice off a cut loaf is never missed"—
Adventure—their plurality against directness—
Affidavit—potentiometer—
After-life—up my anus—
Ageism—documentary—
Agnostics—to foretaste—
Air—as nausea's competitor—
Akimbo—desweatering—
Aladdin's lamp—shock troops—
ALIAS—BIGS—
Altruism—habit's—
Am—his was the—
Ambition—1. then near 2. unproof station
America—a Beautician—
Anchorage—redness of—
And—to make reasons worse—
An Angle—supposes—

An Animal—rule—
Antipathy—by wonder—
Apart—swerve—
Ape—fiction—
Aphrodisiac—interval—
Apparatus—self-love—
Apparel—a night itself—
Appeal—drink the blood—
Appease—defaced—
Applaud—command—
The Arbitrary—re-outfitted as cotton candy—
Arclights—on the gerund—
Arms—as clichés—
Art—confuse distributive—
Aside—feminizably—
Ass—mousse—
Astrology—viceking—
Astronomy—for masturbators—
Atmosphere—gift for commerce—
Atmospheres—vertical—
Atom—bullethole—
Attention—fruit of the evocative—
Attitude—missiles—
Attracted to—reference to specifics, at least—
Authoritarian—the present tense itself—
Autism—gappish—
Autokinetic—taxes—
Autonomiʒe—bursting twitch—
Autonomy—1. any care 2. promiscuity—
Avocational—propaganda—
Aware—prosperity—
Awkwardness—listens hard—

AMERICAN HISTORY IN CONTEXT

500,000 years ago sleepy chipmunks
   snuggled in their burrows.
400,000 years ago doe
   nibbled ladyslipper.
300,000 years ago
   dust on tiger swallowtail wing.
200,000 years ago
   whirligig beetle whirligigged.
100,000 years ago
   blue heron still as a statue.
50,000 years ago
   male seahorse belly-pouch
     swollen with herd of
   perfectly shaped baby seahorses.
25,000 years ago
   leopard frog on lilypad.
10,000 years ago
   male wasp stroking female wasp antennae
     lightly with his mouthparts
   as they copulate on the wing
     from flower to flower.
Right now hippo shitting and pissing
   while whirling its tail like a propeller
     scattering the mess in all directions.
10,000 years from now
   opossum scurries across
     overgrown road.
25,000 years from now
   lobsters grappling lobsters
     with giant chelae.

50,000 years from now
    alligator snapper huge mouth agape
        wriggling pink worm-like tongue
    to attract unwary fish.
100,000 years from now
    female praying mantis clasps her mate
        eating his eyes and head
    causing headless corpse to writhe and kick
        till it inserts penis and pumps
    as she continues eating him
        till nothing's left
    but his penis still ejaculating
        in her ovipositor.
200,000 years from now
    yellow pollen-hung anthers
        of a red columbine.
300,000 years from now
    a white pine in spring
        smells just as good.
400,000 years from now
    a black bear sighs
        in her hibernation den.
500,000 years from now sleepy chipmunks
    snuggle in their burrows.

EXTRATERRESTRIALS TO COME

Just as People of the Future will know
    what we could not,
Extraterrestrials to come will know
    what they could not;
And just as People of the Future's technology
    will exceed ours like ours
        exceeded Paleolithic Man,
The technology of Extraterrestrials to come
    will exceed theirs;
And if we think we're so smart because we know
    the entire Universe was once
        contained in a space the size of a dime
        and is now expanding majestically speed of light
            outward across dimensionless space,
What will they think they're so smart for knowing?
What will they think they're so smart for knowing
When we already know a zillion solarsystems
    with planets that will have life on them
        are created every nanosecond?
Extraterrestrials to Come,
Thinking of you makes you exist.
You are present in my mind.
When you do arrive, Welcome,
Welcome O Cosmic Sojourners from Afar!
Welcome from one long dead
    who received this signal from you
        that you would come!

AVE ATQUE VALE CENTURY OF XEROX
(sehr langsam und mit sehnsucht)

which is unwinding
far from the BOOM of the collapse
winding down through soundless fern
winding down into lightless backwaters
to areas where breath has no commerce
little concordance with the light
what has been a marvelous air
a winding through the context of air
a twisting in bending in the play of air
great and variable in all registers and keys
the solo of air   the polyphony of air
and who admits of downwinding
into the mind's dead sea
where no seeds grow
                              the mind's dead
where breath has no commerce
beyond the ephemeral shining
of the crown of matter

beyond what cannot be conceived

and I saw Milton in eastern ward asylum
eating his own lime-soaked fingers

beyond what cannot be conceived
to where things cannot be
and no ideational content informs them
                              the mind's dead
the river styx   the river lethe

consumed in the chasm of no-thought
where the upper realms were

and where fire and the other elements
spoke to the numinous ones
in language of pure metaphor and allusion

suggestion that man is a terminus
                              the mind's dead
only to enter lands withered and sere
where the dead prop up the dead in commerce
                              the mind's gone

who the strangers are and
who the strangers are looking for
are the same

the fatal burning deep within
that spells the most profound enigma
unapprehended

inversion of light
                    in sheaves
in order to distinguish night
the dark downslide curving
the battery's cold, mother
I can't feel for crying winding down
like this
            and mourn the noetic city gone
and the toy fair where I bought
my first japan

and could see them bereft of masks
confused in the smoke guessing
which was agamemnon
                        once in a lifetime

the going down the under going
the west gone   in a blink of the eye
the west is gone
                    only the language of flowers
only the language of flowers closing themselves
to sleep an earth asleep
the west is gone
                    BANG
only the unconscious language of flowers
that soft dewlike lisping of light
                        becoming green
which is the theme of the urge
in earth sleep enigmatic riddled

                    I grieve
                    the battery's cold

                    I grieve
                    the battery's cold

                only the language of flowers
the mind's gone

Untergang des Abendlandes
                        at eventide in dewspeech lisping
    once in a lifetime
                    each dark sleep the sound
unwinding winding down the gone the last speaker to whisper a lisp
listen   lisshen   I can't no more
                        I've gone noddy
    no thought
the gone mind
    it's music of soundless water
        not even echo's echo   ever again

silver's rust the gone
    west is gone   brain dead
deserts where once rain forests
                not gentle enough
gone the sound that once was
and spent the fuse that rent the wave that poured the sound

falling sleepy sound the plunging overdoom
and the stones the stones talking
with their unseen eyes the sound of rock
"the west is gone"
                in one intake of breath at the toyfair

not plastic the real but gone
an under a sound the reel a fold the air
my page!   my page!

the west is gone
       not even a whisper of organization
bankruptcy of air
              total as air
who grieves?
        the rain   the ancient rain

and what is under the downwinding?
the spiral staircase of sand/sound
no language but a tomb
            the mind's end
            the mind's end
a language of flowers deposited in the deeptomb
no sound but flickerends and the snuffed taper
the carriage of relics lumbering slowly over the carpathians
the carriage of relics

the mine's dead end

rocketfire of pure silence

into the BOOMspook   shout   shout

the peace of the absence of the sky

at last

when music is gone

the alone an avatar feels the spookspeech doomed

twisted around a single copper filament

and thrust into the absent sky

forever flown gone again for all

language of flowers dimsound around the spool

the crazy wind has blown away

the dimsound the old unwinding down

I am

dear reader now a gone sound

that's gone to numb

no round

a cleft the inch

no inch left

the mind's end

and who will never

and who will never

I take thumb

mother

I take thumb

in mouth for mother

not blessed not blessed

the book is old

the hills are dim the heather

the hills are dim the heather

I light the fuse

how many times have I

how many times have I

                        west is no more

          was it a cyclotron?

                            man the mix

and fold tenderly each remaining page

so it may say no more

                   and hush silent one

the sea   hear the sea

a wavesound silent duncolored humussleep adown gone

               no city here

a single one-wingéd angel I saw

enter a perfect block of carrara marble

it was endless noon

              the end of matter

              the end of time

the music was no more

mind's end

dead west the rust opaque the ear died in sound

of nothing

             the tale is told

aloft

      the thing was

             a sign to sign

THE TURN

A plane drags its banner,
"Modern Oldies,"

to and fro
in the distance:

the relatively calm lake
in which we see ourselves

shrugged off
steadily, every which way,

without suffering,
seeming to thrive

on succession now
as decades do. They

don't exist
until they're caricatured.

With nonstop
exits and appearances

to reflect on,
any attribute

looks like a running gag
as well as a splashy

sales pitch. "United
Colors of Benetton"—

the increasingly rare
Cedar Wax-Wing?

RAE ARMANTROUT

BETWEEN

The sky's ribbed
vanishing act
and solidity's encryption.

Gasping had always
conjured voyeurs;

now even shrinking
and shrivelling didn't!

No one home
in the "Virtual Village?"

Between the quote marks,
nothing but disparagement.

from IN THE COUNTRY OF LAST THINGS

You see what you are up against here. It's not just that things vanish—but once they vanish, the memory of them vanishes as well. Dark areas form in the brain, and unless you make a constant effort to summon up the things that are gone, they will quickly be lost to you forever. I am no more immune to this disease than anyone else, and no doubt there are many such blanks inside me. A thing vanishes, and if you wait too long before thinking about it, no amount of struggle can ever wrench it back. Memory is not an act of will, after all. It is something that happens in spite of oneself, and when too much is changing all the time, the brain is bound to falter, things are bound to slip through it. Sometimes, when I find myself groping for a thought that has eluded me, I begin to drift off to the old days back home, remembering how it used to be when I was a little girl and the whole family would go up north on the train for the summer holidays. Big brother William would always let me have the window seat, and more often than not I wouldn't say anything to anyone, riding with my face pressed against the window and looking out at the scenery, studying the sky and the trees and the water as the train sped through the wilderness. It was always so beautiful to me, so much more beautiful than the things in the city, and every year I would say to myself, Anna, you have never seen anything more beautiful than this—try to remember it, try to memorize all the beautiful things you are seeing, and in that way they will always be with you, even when you can't see them anymore. I don't think I ever looked harder at the world than on those train rides up north. I wanted everything to belong to me, for all that beauty to be a part of what I was, and I remember trying to remember it, trying to store it up for later, trying to hold on to it for a time when I would really need it. But the odd thing was that none of it ever stayed with me. I tried so hard, but somehow or other I always wound up losing it, and in the end the only thing I could remember was how hard I had tried. The things themselves passed too quickly, and by the time I saw them they were already flying out of my head, replaced by still more things that vanished before I could see them. The only thing that remains for me is a blur, a bright and beautiful blur. But the trees and the sky and the water—all that is gone. It was always gone, even before I had it.

It will not do, then, simply to feel disgust. Everyone is prone to forgetfulness, even under the most favorable conditions, and in a place like this, with so much actually disappearing from the physical world, you can imagine how many things are forgotten all the time. In the end, the problem is not so much that people forget, but that they do not always forget the same thing. What still exists as a memory for one person can be irretrievably lost for another, and this creates difficulties, insuperable barriers against understanding. How can you talk to someone about airplanes, for example, if that person doesn't know what an airplane is? It is a slow but ineluctable process of erasure. Words tend to last a bit longer than things, but eventually they fade too, along with the pictures they once evoked. Entire categories of objects disappear—flowerpots, for example, or cigarette filters, or rubber bands—and for a time you will be able to recognize those words, even if you cannot recall what they mean. But then, little by little, the words become only sounds, a random collection of glottals and fricatives, a storm of whirling phonemes, and finally the whole thing just collapses into gibberish. The word "flowerpot" will make no more sense to you than the word "splandigo." Your mind will hear it, but it will register as something incomprehensible, a word from a language you cannot speak. As more and more of these foreign-sounding words crop up around you, conversations become rather strenuous. In effect, each person is speaking his own private language, and as the instances of shared understanding diminish, it becomes increasingly difficult to communicate with anyone.

USELESS KNOWLEDGE

I am reading
    "From Hegel to Nietzsche;
    German Spirit
    During the 19th Century."
The elevator operator
is reading
    "Christ
    and Redemption of the Human
    Spirit."
Sequestered in the Swiss Alps
a year before Heidegger was born
Nietzsche wrote:
    "The highest concepts"
    of Western Metaphysics
    are nothing more than
    "the last wisps of evaporating
    reality."
Panhandling around the gates
of Jerusalem
2000 years before Heidegger was born
Christ said:
    "Turn the other"
    evaporating
    "cheek."
But neither the elevator operator
nor I
empathize that we are terrified to face
a world of ceaseless change
and eternal Becoming.
Eternal Becoming Gone.

And so
both of us eye the other's book
with civilized smugness
absolutely convinced
of our individual approach—
its Spirit of correctness.
Perhaps the most that can be said for me
is I
armed with the knowledge of our mutual
self-deceit
can be less smug than he
If I want to
which
I don't.

VOLUNTEER BASIS

From few beginnings,
as when a thunderclap be furled,
slop air wedges a light hail

to resistance and scandal in parts.
Ditto the caveat, ibid the scam.
One to 15 years at K through 12 issues a monograph in the blind
      door slanted.

Here in the city, full-throttle realism
sings clangorous empowerment of next-move years
(a dribble-glass tone, leastwise) apropos alternative paths.

Reevaluate thrush concept:
if we only knew, chaos dynamics would shower a Garden of
      Delights,
fanning the useful toehold flange.

But when shades impend
the sticky hand goes home
to the new inference paints.

CHARLES BERNSTEIN

LOW REGRETS

> *Oh rain me down from your darks that contain me.*
>   Sidney Lanier, "Sunrise"

"The marsh, my marsh"
stumbles out of
bound and usually
reliable whistle stops
of comparison or
follow-me-to-the-stars-but-not-one-step-into-my-backyard
flutes their way to
second-hand accounts
of what, in another
life, might be
thought. The slow
caboose, with its
weary
resignation, shuffling
behind flights of
untenable gestures, aspirant
irregularities,
"counting the seconds
in dozens,"
blinking in jags
like the elevator without side
effects, or inaugural
stunts
bouncing off the scrawls of
(don't
ask me again)
fomented momentum.

Till the toast is cold
Till the baby finishes its bottle
Till you buy me a harp
Shuddering in the bright sum
of midday, smoltering with
ice cream and frumpled sodas
sipped through a straw
composed of one hundred percent
carrot product. Beating my rugs
until the dusk becomes
storm clouds,
Kona coffee beans from Honolulu,
ziplock packagettes,
The Club antitheft device.
The goats pass
from view, the boys
skip stones from
melancholy hydroplanes.
I should have wasted my life.

JOHN BRANDI

FOR THIS WE COME

Obedient to the luminous ray
that evaporates the time-stopped edge,
we begin our stroke.

Inside the hypnotized eye
we empty the boulevard and multiply
into a kingdom of waving trees.

I am your offspring, you the ultimate sea.
A mantra of silent pirouettes
that informs the dream.

In a heatwave, love burns without shadow.
Along a moonstruck outline
we swell and become thin.

Under the tea kettle are flames,
every essence hides in steam. The world
isn't exactly seen.

For this we come:
to breathe and stop still, to find form
behind our names.

from *Shadow Play* (Light & Dust, 1992)

JOURNAL ENTRY, WEST OF RENO

Not such a bad day.
Won seventeen twenty in the slots.
Received hard cash for old Gurdjieff books.
Offered blue flames to a smiling virgin.
Bought gooseberries in a Paiute smoke shop.
Pressed Johnny Jump Ups into new notebook.
Decorated stone with ribbons
for meditative shadow flutter.
Raised kitchen window to sound of silence
between bird calls.
Read about swallowtails and genebanks.
Discovered it's not just the tip,
but the whole fingernail that grows.
Bathed in hot springs with a highway patrol officer.
Polished shoes for potential marriage feast.
Scrubbed candle holders with s o s.
Made thermos of tea instead of coffee.
Prayed to sunflowers for rain.
Read real estate terminology to Mozart.
Laughed at my face in someone else's mirror.
Listened to history evaporate inside a mirage.
Remembered skeletons and Buddhas
side by side, Thai monastery.
Picked mums, stole tulips from senior citizens' home.

Saw who was meant for me.
Recognized the curve of her spine underwater.
Heard bells, heard the striker empty its sound.
Dreamed that once beckoned I could not be refused.
Heard the blood of my love drumming, heard a gallop.
Saw the children running up.

Hummed poptune ecstasy in falsetto freeplay.
Walked through walls, lay down with laughter.
Lit the nave with bare bulbs of desire.

Practiced truthful genuflections and thankyous.
Dressed the altar with sheets and pillows.
Faxed home intricate floorplan of roofless house.
Received letter stating "Cancel Resistance, Listen!"
Looked to the stars for an end to my poem.
Flipped through pages of water inside my head.
Realized world leaders should hold dialogues
in nautiloid floating position
rather than sitting at tables.

Spoke long distance my inner reality.
Received a Yes.
Broke down on way to supermarket.
Returned with pancake batter instead of asparagus.
Watched snails migrate in sudden rain.
Called again to say hello.
Woke from trance dream of wrap around rivers.
Woke into her arms through high voltage life lines.
Began latest journal entry without using "I"
Drove record distance with tank on empty.
Recovered Mystery from the Great
& All Bountiful Vacuum.

Said Good Night, turned off the light
to illuminate sleep.
Said Good Day, remembered gratitude
Remembered praise . . .

from *Shadow Play* (Light & Dust, 1992)

THE FESTIVAL OF INSTINCT

Infection is one way to describe discovery, although it only shows on the north side of the Aquiline Fault. On the south is island vegetation where the Festival of Hairlines is taking place right now. The women are holding hands for the occasion of the flight and the men are preparing the International Variety of Crackers. And it isn't only the past we're leaving behind like Hansel's clever crumbs, but a wind blowing through a stray harp which plays on such occasions when we're all together at the Festival of Lips, and the favorite game is "Leave It to Your Imagination."

On the eve of the Festival of Cheeks, Begonia is crowned queen of the Occasion. Cosmology returns as the other bookend, and cosmetology is our fastest growing industry. A sanguinary smear sneers from coast to coast, while belly to belly some still can dance. Outer limbs arrive to attend lectures on grafting plant tissue to human epiderm, and operations are scheduled after the noon parade. Then the mongolian lambs are rounded and hacked up. "Just like in the olden days," those naked doric gals on Emerald Hill conclude.

How does a fall guy become a hit man? That is a lover's question and the contests for answers occur annually at the Festival of Hands whose attendants sit around and grope. "Blindness in the light of truth." Nowhere is the housing shortage more apparent than in Paradise, and the lines for the Dimension Ride stretch from Eureka to the border. Everyone wants to come here AND everyone wants to leave.

By the end of the century we're exhausted by an insane parent or even two who took us to the First Festival of Brains where scrambled eggs was a big joke for lunch. And children like myself and you—and you and you and you—sat by the silly stream and watched our faces waver.

It was the discovery of fiber sculpture in our own backyard that led each of us to support our local pine. Let's rush back to that Definition of Harmony again, the one on the pyramid in the sandbox.

I've never been able to live with a sax or without, for that matter. Nor do I know whether to subtract bodies or GNP. Nevertheless, I take precautions for Discovery as days' light whiles upon us. Grass is also proven to grow through shoes, and a terrific clamor can be heard thundering for return.

ON THE WAY TO THE EXIT

I am glad of one thing.
In my impending demise
I won't be going out alone.
For company I can count on
   the passing of the twentieth century
   the closing of the American mind
   the lowering of the common denominator
   the disappearance of the rain forest
   the decay of individual morality
   the disintegration of the social fabric
   the deterioration of the economy
   the decline of the West
   the end of the age of Pisces
   the collapse of civilization
and the termination of any number of
grandeurs   follies   and hopeless causes.

Some kind of cold comfort to know that
one will be lying about in the ruins
   with Ozymandias   Mussolini
and all the other residue of the millennium.

from *Special Deliveries* (Broken Moon Press, 1990)

DINOSAURIA, WE

born like this
into this
as the chalk faces smile
as Mrs. Death laughs
as the elevators break
as political landscapes dissolve
as the supermarket bag boy holds a college degree
as the oily fish spit out their oily prey
as the sun is masked

we are
born like this
into this
into these carefully mad wars
into the sight of broken factory windows of emptiness
into bars where people no longer speak to each other
into fist fights that end as shootings and knifings

born into this
into hospitals which are so expensive that it's cheaper to die
into lawyers who charge so much it's cheaper to plead guilty
into a country where the jails are full and the madhouses closed
into a place where the masses elevate fools into rich heroes

born into this
walking and living through this
dying because of this
muted because of this
castrated
debauched

disinherited
because of this
fooled by this
used by this
pissed on by this
made crazy and sick by this
made violent
made inhuman
by this

the heart is blackened
the fingers reach for the throat
the gun
the knife
the bomb
the fingers reach toward an unresponsive god

the fingers reach for the bottle
the pill
the powder

we are born into this sorrowful deadliness
we are born into a government 60 years in debt
that soon will be unable to even pay the interest on that debt
and the banks will burn
money will be useless
there will be open and unpunished murder in the streets
it will be guns and roving mobs
land will be useless
food will become a diminishing return
nuclear power will be taken over by the many
explosions will continually shake the earth

radiated robot men will stalk each other
the rich and the chosen will watch from space platforms
Dante's Inferno will be made to look like a children's playground

the sun will not be seen and it will always be night
trees will die
all vegetation will die
radiated men will eat the flesh of radiated men
the sea will be poisoned
the lakes and rivers will vanish
rain will be the new gold

the rotting bodies of men and animals will stink in the dark wind

the last few survivors will be overtaken by new and hideous diseases

and the space platforms will be destroyed by attrition
the petering out of supplies
the natural effect of general decay

and there will be the most beautiful silence never heard

born out of that.

the sun still hidden there

awaiting the next chapter.

from *The Last Night of the Earth Poems* (Black Sparrow Press, 1992)

LACK

November 1, 1993. Monday. Standing on the shore of a huge lake. The sky is overcast and the water a silver gray mirror. Looking straight ahead south, I can see the opposite shore: low hills, no sign of vegetation. To my left the lake widens, and I cannot see the far shore. The same holds for the view to my right; it widens and extends out of sight. The water is twenty feet deep, slanting down into darkness.

My separation from Christianity is not the banal stupid drivel of a secular humanist: "We must seek happiness here on earth . . . progress . . . higher living standards . . . better medical service . . . fold, et cetera . . . to bed with your ovaltine . . . ."

No, it is the total lack of any spiritual content, or any spiritual discipline leading to tangible gains, comparable to Zen Buddhism: Tibetan practitioners who, through rigorous and prolonged training, can spend a night in sub-zero cold with only a loincloth. The Shaman's Way to achieve the palpable status of the Impeccable Warrior. I fault Christianity for its lack . . . a lack that does not even have the vitality to ache.

And another matter: what about the Inquisition, that stinks of burning flesh, torture, excrement—its stultifying presence imposed by brutal force. The Karmic Debt is staggering, and not to be shrugged off with a few Hail Marys.

Why are evil spirits confounded by the name of Jesus? AND WHY ARE THEY SCALDED by Holy Water? As circus lions are sometimes blinded with a blank pistol, so they will forevermore cringe from the sound.

JANINE CANAN

A WOMAN MEDITATES ON THE TURNING
OF THE SIXTIETH CENTURY

I. *Remembering*

Hasn't tenderness the sweetest scent?
Haven't you missed mothering
and being tenderly adored.
We forgot something—was it God

the Mother who gave birth to all.
On the crescent moon
She rocks her Child through the night,
in the day showering glorious sunshine.

Do you feel loved?
If not, how can you uncover that radiant jewel—
connected and reflecting,
open, aware and free.

In this conversation
of desire, suffering and loss,
we sing together in the all-pervading light
and our caring sounds—unimpeded, unending.

II. *The Passage*

A girl must speak for five minutes,
as her father glares at his watch.
"Not good enough," he snaps, "again!"
And so went your childhood.
After your brother's demise
your mother confessed, "I can't

be your mother anymore."
"You would have chosen my death?"
And like a knife she answered, "Yes."

This suffering, this ritual sorrow
of woman—by adding yours to mine
can I lessen our pain?
Outside the airplane cobbled clouds pave the sky,
but no one walks there—oh,
where are we going?
This violent film on the screen—
men with fat muscles and guns shouting—
is this entertainment for Hell?

The world is whole, yet broken minds stutter and rave.
"Again!" the heartless tyrant mocks.
His story, however, is ending.
A song soars—burning, rich and dripping,
now soft and pure as snow.
Nesting in peace, finally it flies free!
The clouds part, revealing rivers that widen into azure seas,
forests of evergreen, and beings—
are they human?—of towering grace.

III. *What Woman Wants*

First woman does *womanly* things,
then she does what man does—only better,
but as she pushes against his metal—
cold, cruel with judgment and arrogance,
the more she wants to be woman,
softly sensing the world as it is.

Woman wants to touch the tender leaf,
speak in growing ripples of meaning,
blushing with joy at her thoughts
that come from so far away—
a miracle is what woman wants!

So come to woman and we will begin again:
Stars flooding the void with light!
Then the ceaseless flow of mirage,
one moment dissolving in the next—
yet always here, the joy of your heart.

Woman wants to plant the seed,
see the dream, sink into sleep.
She wants to breathe!—joy the song
she hums as she walks in love,
tuned to the Goddess in everyone.

First woman does *womanly* things,
then she does what man does—only better,
but as she pushes against his metal,
cold, cruel with judgment and arrogance,
the more she wants to be woman,
softly sensing the world as it is.

IV. *Oh Century, My Century*

Oh Century, my Century, from where have you come?
Cows and sheep once blissfully grazed
on Mother's millennial mounds.
Rivers chatted and berries bounded
past the pistachios and fat red apples.
Grasses fed the ovens with bread.
The villagers gathered into Her temple

to praise the Womb brimming over with life:
Red pots spinning with sacred design,
naked priestesses dancing in gold
and coaxing their lyres into grateful song.

Then, my Trembling One, six thousand years ago
Horsemen swarm from the distant barren steppes
upon Her beloved fertile land,
swinging their daggers, swords and spears.
Inventors of weapons and slavery
who worship the torrid sun
and wear strings of glaring teeth,
they raze and raid, rape and smash.
Crushing the rule of nature,
they establish the law of terror.
The Patriarch buries his own family in a tomb.

Twentieth Century—No!
You have never been a century of Christ,
that divine Child of The Mother,
who taught the sweet sovereignty of love.
The Metal Men nail his holy body to a tortured tree
and crucify his teachings:
Surrender succumbs to dominance.
Tenderness is shredded by violence,
generosity devoured by greed.
Innocence is twisted into guilt,
and beauty, Oh beauty mocked to shame.

Are you then, my maddened Century, to be the last?
Today Bully Boy rides on bulldozer, sub, airplane and missile
carrying ammunition to kill all life.
Land, sea and sky he inseminates with a million poisons.

What has he not raped? The ancient tribes,
woman, child, plant and beast rage in torment and grief.
Even the atom, seed of creation, bleeds deadly radiation.
Murderer of the breathing Earth!
Seated on his massive throne of guns
at his mechanical money altar, adoring
his own power, he chews on the heart of God.

Oh my Battered Queen, once voluptuously green,
do you remember still those caves,
dark and moist with mirth,
where hundreds of centuries past a birth began?
Walking through the white salt forests,
we entered the inmost womb of wonder.
We lit Her fire, and on Her crystal flesh
we rang Her bellowing chimes.
Then fine-footed great-bellied beasts
romped across Her surging walls,
bringing forth ecstatic life.

Oh Century, my laborious Century!
Drop by drop the blood-streaked columns thicken
and our ancient fire glows still.
Now is the time to strike our truest chord!
Her vast heart pounds—Her waters break.
And moaning, praying, She pushes us
down the narrowing canal
against the stiffening crimson door.
Her lips stretch transparent to the light.
Her moment arches: Sweet red petals flutter.
And into Her garden a lark is descending.

AGAINST 21ST CENTURY

From the news room upstairs
the view is tops
now looking out and up
in the new year air tenuous
shaky up here in the head
the cap cerebrally a stretch
down into the feet
heart beating over the roofs
of the city on the hill
helicopter appears whirling
rapid gun fire sound
through the trees just above
my eyes flying—

The poets of the 21st century
will not smoke or drink
wil not partake of dangerous
or unhealthy sex—maybe
no sex at all

they will not be fat
they will not induce visions
will not fall hopelessly in love
will not flirt with death—maybe
or madness

they will not eat sugar
meat or processed foods
they will not abuse drugs
will not indulge themselves—maybe
even not in poems

they will not practice chaos
or disharmony
they will not disarm right
and left and discern—maybe
capitalism & communism, both wrong.

Many poets of the 21st century—most maybe
will think time has actually changed
that this 200-year-old kind
of culture after Christ—the oily one
is really coming into its own forgetting

that for Judim, the Chinese, Egyptian
our year 2000 to them is just another odd number
say 4523 or something while for the Cheyenne
time doesn't exactly exist at all

while these 21st century poets will
be writing poems about CLASS
going this way:

We like the Yankees!
all here in black and white
and gray.
It is all right there
just like reading words
printed on the page.

Having looked once
more into the pits
it is good to be so alive
joyous American Sports Fan
this spring Saturday afternoon.

The idea that one terrible
century has ended so another
more hopeful one may proceed
is mistake on a major scale
born of a similar confusion
that daylight savings time
gives more useful sunlight
while actually trips psychologic rhythm
and rushes us to thinking we are late
nor do we gain an hour's sleep
falling back again to standard time.

If we believe so much in counting time
why not have a real Sabbath Day
when time empty of all striving
is indulged as a sanctified Princess?
In fact to observe this new century
let us have a Sabbath Year.
No work of any kind
no thought of work
no worry. Let us put on our best
to muse and feast for a year.

History of the Western World
some of our greatest
most eternal truths
to preserve them
have been written
and printed on paper

but just because
some assertion, some idea or thing

is written on paper
does not mean it's so
does not make it true.

This is not really the 21st Century.
Thinking it so profoundly so
only embeds our shortsighted
wrongheaded carelessness
continuing the coma the *progress*
imagined in the 18th & 19th centuries.

Time exists less than the air.
A year is not a line
but is a cycle.
In a few more years we should return
to the reality of dream-time
to make more poems
that say this:

It's too bad sometimes I think
too bad we can't see the air
too bad the air's invisible
too bad the air's not clearly there
say as it is with just a little smoke
we'd find ourselves new eyes
taken up by the shapes of air tides
the multi-layered, striated, tunneled
twisted rolling wave shaped
moving patterns the air makes

no more or less substantial
than one hundred or thousand years.

THE GLORIFIED GO ONE BY ONE TO GLORY
Follies of 2001

Before the century's oncoming end,
Or surely not long after, age unknown
From having been so many times writ false,
In wealth or poverty or mobile home
The last surviving Ziegfeld Girl will die.
Of all who lined the ever-recurring stair,
A final glory goes to what reward?
And, like a carpet when the bride has passed,
That time's grand staircase can be gathered up.
If in his will the bankrupt *Intendant*
Had funded, in the abstract, a reward
For this long tontine he could not foresee,
Would he have equalled in his fantasy
Such as the Girls attained to on their own:
San Simeon, Burke's Peerage, *Modern Times?*
Is their extinction some in kind revenge
Of ostriches and egrets? Nakedness
Exacts its vengeance too. A skeleton
Is bare essentials bared. But let us bring,
As funeral directors bring dyed grass
To cemeteries, tread and riser back:
Folly in its root meaning is what fools
Accomplish, and there is no fool like a fool
Who thinks that he can turn back time. More reason,
Therefore, Folly's archetypal stair
Should share its image with the gold access
To Heaven and Eternity. Once more,
Paulette, Lorraine, Mae, Gladys, Marion,
Descend on shining slipper to the lights
That separate you from the eager dark.
What comes down, Numbered Beauties, must go up.

MAXINE CHERNOFF

FRANKLY

I have a notion the skyline is false,
a rude set of gangster mugs of the century.
Sixteen years to go and counting, we'll call ours
the age of being succinct, represented by empty
quotation marks etched on our Aubrey Beardsley
mood-generators. In China a philosopher once
called his age, "Time of Ship Fallen into the Sea."
Ours won't be the age of Yul Brynner or of the dentist
whose plastic heart we've already forgotten.
I want to be around New Year's Eve, 1999, gray hair
and streamers, and proclaim like a Russian poet,
"Thank God it's over!" New century arriving
with its coffee can of pennies, immigrant worker
whose father hopes for the best. We want
the best too, poor old century, waning moon,
small sculpture in the shape of the genius' head.
We want shiny new life and permission to close
a slippery chapter of imprecision we'll call
"Falling Headfirst on Memory's Pier."

from *Leap Year Day: New & Selected Poems* (ACP, 1990)

ON THE BRINK OF THE COLD MILLENNIUM

1. *The Decline of the Love Elegy*

We're all sensitive people, giving yourself to me
Can never be wrong, Marvin Gaye anachronistically
Croons on the radio. In an age of universal suspicion
And mistrust, such sentiments, like fragments of a forgotten
Language, drift through the static constricted darkness
Of the Erebus of Oldies. Past is past. A tide of lying rises,
The craft of song lies beached on the rocky coast
Of an annulled human future. Old poet-ghosts
Flutter ineffectually at the mouth of Avernus,
Now just another computer workstation. By the terminal gates
Linger the unsatisfied ghosts of the last of the love elegists,
Propertius, Catullus, Tibullus, Donny Hathaway,
Otis Redding, Marvin Gaye, The Four Tops, Ovid, Sam and Dave.
Fretful they hover, victims of sacrificial wounds,
Their silken lyricism drowned in brazen attitudes
Of rote, automated anger. Revenge against lovers
Exacted by the thought police of the Academy
Of the Future interrupts their restless hovering
With a thoughtless mechanized rap din, and as
The dim walls of Malebolge close in the last we see
Of them is a thin wrinkle of obscurity in the grit-charged wind.

2. *The Power of Song*

The Republic falls and the Empire rises out of its ruins
With a glare of hype that extinguishes memory
Still we have to go on living somehow, thus
It was that Homer's sailors stuffed their ears with
Wax plugs, produced by bees of Ithaca,
To which place, having shut out the sirens

Of continuous bullshit, they hope upon
Regaining their sense of direction
One day after all their errant travels to return home,
Still it continues and Odysseus insists on listening
So involved is he with the power of song
That she who spends her time waiting there must stick
To her knitting beyond human patience—
And there is no more wisdom in this
Than in joining the voluntarily hearing-impaired,
No matter how much blood has been ceremonially offered.

3. *A Spore of Hope*

As cold and sweeping as it surely is, the current domination of the
lives of human beings by values derived from commodities and
machines still retains no real power over the lyric spirit in poetry. The
lyric impulse, even if present only as a flickering implication in a pass-
ing moment of language, continues to express the dream of a lost
world: a world in which things would be otherwise, a world of pleni-
tude and completeness. It is a world which we may no longer con-
sciously remember but which in the survival of the lyric voice always
lingers as a haunting potential, like a spore of hope suspended in some
remote galaxy, or the seed of some miraculous plant preserved under
the glacial weight of adverse times.

NOTE FROM MEMPHIS

history is chasing you, america,
like a mean dog. the only way
to tame it is to turn
and stare direct in its red eye.

old folks used to talk about this;
how if you keep running it will see
you are afraid, how if you take a stand
it will take one with you.

old folks have watched this longer
than you think, they have learned
how mean that dog is, and they know
it is your dog.

ANDREI CODRESCU

AU BOUT DU TEMPS

So late in the 20th century
        So late in the 20th century
            At the end almost of the 20th century
    I sit in my home
            In my modest and meaningless home
                And worry about my penis
    ABOUT MY PENIS FOR CHRISSAKES!

In praise of biology
        In praise of visions . . .
Only a few years ago it did not seem
                so late in the 20th century
                    it did not seem very late
                        in the 20th century
                this saddest of centuries
maybe the 14th was a very sad century
                fin de siecle
                    mal de siecle
mal de fin
            so late in the night
                so late in the century
                    in the 20th century

from *Selected Poems 1970-1980* (Sun Books, 1981)

CONTRAFACT: THREE WORDS ABOUT IT
[lines for more than one speaker]

—That's where it breaks down
—Is not concomittant
—Does it take an object?
—Like being able to see the image of the body
—Not the body
—In it for the long run
—Not the person *per se*
—But things associated with the person
—More coffee?
—A shadow ran past the window
—Affiliation radiates from you as the central point
—In dotted lines that go to eternity
—At least in one dimension
—Full stop
—The you and the it
—When I'm thinking
—There's a reader in my head
—I almost had a memory
—Autonomous remembrance
—The living anger
—The long hyphen
—Industrialism, vandalism, idealism
—What's new about it
—Or it's a misreading of . . .
—Still searching for the object
—They had it
—Just had it
—Let's try metrical overdeterminism
—For a change

—Now we have it

—*His* point is what was it trying to do and

—Did it do it?

—That it could be so loaded

—You have it

—If we work it together?

—In its not being useful

—Practical

—Or entirely meaningful

—Or the idea of it

—We see it asymmetrically

—Nostalgically

—("metaphysical homesickness," *Novalis*)

—Imagine it in the form of a cube

—That's the preposterousness of return

—Once you start speaking in prepositions

—Compositions

—Memory is a chemical compound

—Memories jutting out

—Promontories

—Migrating

—Writing is a distance

—Spirit is literality

—Arbitrariness of address

—And of the speaker.

OBJET TROUVÉ

The terrible famine and accompanying disease
which caused the death
of over a thousand people on St. Lawrence Island
during the winter of 1879
and 1880 was said to have
been caused by the use of whisky.
The people of that island usually
obtained their supply of food
for the winter by
killing walrus from the great herds of these animals
that go through Bering Strait
on the first ice in the fall.
The walrus remain about the island
only a few days
and then go south, when
the ice closes about
and shuts the island in
till spring.

Just before the time for the walrus
to reach the island
that season, the Eskimo obtained a supply
of whisky from some vessels
and began a prolonged debauch,
which ended only
when the supply was
exhausted.
When this occurred the
annual migration of the wal-
rus has passed, and the

people were shut in for the
winter
by
the ice.
The result was that over two-thirds of the population died before
spring. The
following spring, when the *Corwin*
visited the islands,
some of the survivors came
on board bringing a few articles for trade.
They wished only to purchase
rifle cartridges and more whisky.

During July, 1881,
the *Corwin* made a visit to this famine-stricken district,
where the miserable survivors were seen.
Only a single dog
was left among them,
the others
having been eaten by the starving people.
Two of the largest villages were
entirely depopulated.
On the bluff
at the northwest point of this island
we found a couple of surviving families living in round-top,
walrus-hide summer houses.
The adults seemed very much depressed.
Among them were two
bright little girls.
When I shot a snow bunting near the village
they called to me

and ran to show me its nest
on the hillside.

When I asked
one of the inhabitants what had become
of the people who formerly lived
on that part of the island, he
waved his hand toward the winter village,
saying, "All *mucky mucky*,"
being the jargon term for "dead."

I tried to obtain a photograph of the women and little girls,
and for that purpose
placed them in position and focused the camera.
While I was waiting for a lull in the wind
to take the picture,
the husband of one of the women came up
and asked in a listless, matter-of-fact tone, "All *mucky* now?"
meaning, "Will they all die now?"
He evidently took it for granted
that my camera was a conjuring box,
which would complete the work of the
famine, yet he seemed perfectly
indifferent to
the consequences.

(from *The Eskimo About Bering Strait* by Edward William Nelson, Government
Printing Office, 1900)

CLARK COOLIDGE

ONE MAN TO A CENTURY
for Andrei

Wake me when it's over. Nope, how
can that
be
when what of my life there is
was there in it?
Whitewashed sides of skull snare
in a heat-sought moment the moment
falls, dulls, digit-in-fizzle
its reach too crouchy and the foundry humans
they live but do not stream
There was no keen line to this time
bread-lit boom frames now told out
shrugland tires
Regret? Pencil in small
tides of the reagent moniker
they take them in spin and file under Fade
to look at the one hand and find it as fake
fuck
in drying their tones these moons their slouch bags
couples chalking their upstairs makings
This is the place where the walls, hung as ends
thought turned out in honing suns but now
there is no edge to the glow
and a tent holds falsities
So stop me before I hurl anew
tobaccos down the tawdry nebula pull
and that man starting up he is snapping so
rain him down, askew to eureka
the pill to end all waits

This century? It is swift pasts
along with my and your, their and its
junk spent pensive, welcome to this world
of jeans to tweak an angry fit
the hill of beans on repeat
to cinch all the stragglers apt
as much to chance as dare glance
It does stop being but
nothing stops being barely written
so all
as it is it ceases
to pin the circle on the time
Now is that
the new drain on anyone's dreams
I've been knocking to
a fuck-thee-well
a fair while
too? Goodbye

ROBERT CREELEY

GOODBYE

Now I recognize
it was always me
like a camera
set to expose

itself to a picture
or a pipe
through which the water
might run

or a chicken
dead for dinner
or a plan
inside the head

of a dead man.
Nothing so wrong
when one considered
how it all began.

It was Zukofsky's
Born very young into a world
already very old . . .
The century was well along

when I came in
and now that it's ending,
I realize it won't
be long.

But couldn't it all have been
a little nicer,
as my mother'd say. Did it
have to kill everything in sight,

did right always have to be so wrong?
I know this body is impatient.
I know I constitute only a meager voice and mind.
Yet I loved, I love.

I want no sentimentality.
I want no more than home.

THE STATIONS OF THE CROSS, NEWLY REVISED FOR AMERICA IN THE TWENTY-FIRST CENTURY

1.

Pilate condemns Jesus
to watch twelve straight
hours of television,
consume two six-packs of beer,
three bags of chips, and four
hot dogs on white Wonder buns.

2.

Jesus' side is pierced
by the dull rhetoric
of presidential candidates,
who drink his blood.

3.

Jesus falls the first time,
under the federal budget deficit.

4.

Veronica wipes the face
of Jesus with a handy, pre-dampened,
perfumed towelette
that stings his wounds.

5.

Jesus falls the second time,
under the burden of
National Security
and the New World Order.

6.
Japan offers to carry
Jesus' cross
at a very attractive interest rate.

7.
Jesus meets his mother,
who introduces him
to several members
of her Lesbian support group.

8.
The infrastructure
along the Via Dolorosa
having gone to hell,
Jesus falls the third time
but is rescued
by a political action committee
interested in
His Father's vote.

9.
Jesus, who carries no cash
in his small loin cloth,
is stripped of his credit cards,
which have no limits.

10.
Jesus is nailed to a cross
of wood from an old-growth forest.

11.
Jesse Helms,
wrapped in stars and stripes
against the cold Golgotha wind,
watches all night
to make sure no one
digs up the cross
and sticks it in a jar of piss.

12.
Jesus is taken down
from the cross
because 64% of the people
surveyed in a Gallup poll
approve of such action
while only 32% disapprove
and 4% don't know what they think.

13.
Jesus is laid
in a tomb
converted from
a defunct
Savings and Loan
vault.

14.
The Supreme Court rules
God is guilty
of reverse discrimination
in letting only a Jew
rise from the dead.

from *Farmer's Market*

FROM A READING

having the last word the erotic angel stretches its feathers
the celebrated shepherds recollected as pranksters
and one a thief in that light
whose wife is brought to bed of a lamb
and later suffers the ignominy of discovery

however in our world the twisted gates of the secular
opposed an earlier practice the lines down the wondering
shepherds no more our progeny than the little lamb
who made thee in an uproar of sacrifice
a cut above the others living to eat
our hearts out away there in a manger

the social fabric knit with nylon
the perfect everlasting triumph of
the *God-damned crook and fugitive Robert Hathall*
whose life of crime resembles our own
a spare part an elaborate dumb show

sheltering tough thought in exchange for the thickened plot
the deliberate colors of the fall from grace in a frosted glass
an eternal winter sunset qualified by artifice
by the hairs on her chin dowdy gray
by sexual ambiguity by the refusal to be the classic straight line
by prickly holly thorns below south the sun in the shape

of a rooster's foot inching toward Lapland
where the witches live

upon whom the sun has gone down

quoted on the bare bricks of Market Street
is it the end yet said my grandfather dying
darkness is all *Were*
proud? Of what? To buy

a thing like that.

lo where she enters the rubbishy unregarded field.

the aitch dropped
the weaving spiders come
the domed skull a seacave
the headlands the mouth of the river
filling and falling
crouched in the animal kingdom
to whom do we owe our lives
the visible pulse in the wrist
the waste of fields and forests
blooming in the market pages as *agricultural production*
as *development of natural resources*

the serious powers of old are now portrayed almost exclusively
as women and children; the masculine angel, fear not, is become
a cute fat infant, wingèd cherub

the descendent powers ours
tin horn
toy drum
but soft here comes my mother now
that moth stuttering across Rachel's page

what thoughts these are I think I know
 : here's a poetry lesson. what's 'unnatural' word order
   that Pound's always complaining about is what sticks in
   the memory, another mnemonic device which, until so
   recently, distinguished the poem from ordinary
   conversation
writ by hand: an archaism
I ate the plums: wrong tense
the drift of nothingness, the spectacular, each individual plank
whirling in the explosion, walking away from it, the history of
movies, the horrors of bourgeois life

lax-ear'd
father Ricci posing as a Chinese monk
persons of no definite employment given to bewilderment
outrage and terror over and over
we love to hate modern art
see what the boys in the back room will have
see what's here
another new year
tea roses
total allout apocalyptic destruction a cliché

a long white blank
the still point of the turning world

I marking time
the events of the past half century
o *unhappy century* the ruin of childhood
a bourgeois custom or invention
shot down in flames
the human universe behaving as if it had endured a prolonged
      unhappy
         childhood
         upon my soul

Ezra: those 'dim lands of peace.' yerse.

dim lands of peace. dim lands of peace. dim lands of peace.
sometimes the memory of something, place or room, returns so
vividly, unexpectedly, as if I were hallucinating the interior
of my father's car, say, in 1946, or when did he sell the old
Plymouth, the green one, 'going to see a man about a horse,'
earlier, making the trade for it, were we really to have a
horse? and where would we keep him and what would he eat and
shall we ride him and shall we have a buggy too

autobiography, memory and mechanisms of concealment
that fantasy or wish to sit up all night with her exhausting
one another with talk conceals
o *you* know what
lavish passion in the absence of a mother

impressing *conscripting* language into the service
of repression

Repeated
    evidence has proved that it can live
    on what can not revive
        its youth. The sea grows old in it.

from *K*, #5

TIDBITS, ORBITS, OBITS
(for the 20th

Look on the illuminated side!
The masses still
embrace mass production, the intellectuals
the intellect
the custodians their broomhandles . . .
Despite isolated outbreaks of dreaded Cubicle Fever
& a yo-yoing self-esteem index
we're maintaining
   Ah, there's the rubdown!
"BILLIONS NEUTRALIZED BY CERTAINTY!"
proclaims today's headline
   O essential nutria,
      paddling off toward Whatever . . .
As the century crosses it blackstockinged legs
my untrammeled cow pastures in areas
we desire
peace, harmony, perpetual contentment sprinkled all over
this glob
—make that glob*e*
Yet the script reads thus:
World Peace = World In Pieces
Massive Upset Stomach
Nausea Ad Infin
2 World Wars & the World Serious every Mr. October . . .
Mere bang
for your buck
O who'll ignore the conventional wisdom
the prevailing a la mood
It's Docility 101

out there
where the rubber fits snugly over the arching banana . . .
where the Sunned & the Stunned wait
for excrement to happen
Gravity won't stop
encoring: celebs, akas
unknowns, stars
strips, the very flag of my indisposition
to discordant strains
acidic rains
all devolving
while the Curious & the Faithful inhabit the tectonic
    dancefloor
turning handsprings a cinderblock's throw
outside of Palm Springs
while the bulk of us
    kinda
      sorta
wait for the promised telepathic jujitsu lessons
All tupperware
burped for the millennium

TOM DENT

at sunrise
you will look for work
work at sunrise in the
dying city
& there will be none.

you will explore the maze of entrails
entrails of destruction
like your brother who could only
carve beautiful walking sticks
only to find the city uninterested in
walking sticks.

possibly as you search under the burning sun
you wonder how it got this way.
is it not true that we stride through
generations washing away
trails
tracks
traces
the first link in our chains?
                our chain of memory
                broken long ago

long ago we forgot
how it got this way under the burning sun.
they tell you it is you
you they say you they say
& we don't really need you & when we do
you will assume a pose

so
as the sun recedes you
look for work in the
elegantly crumbling city
while those behind you
stare their need.

it is here
cold fingers of night
mate the museum city of indifference
it is here
links of chain leap
through sleepless nights
enveloping you in the anger
of sharp thrust.
those who lose interest in carving walking sticks
sharpen their skill
on the acrid salt of dried tears.

there is no memory

there is no memory.
at sunrise you will look for work.
the sun falls.
the dying city.
america.
the full moon

Beyond subject, verb, and object an open phrase keys a field similar
To any type or stage. An integral part of the study
    of the soul. Starting
With allowance, cured by discipline. Label vague terrain
    and shadowy
Spacious grounds. Sooner or later in the latter part
    of the century every
Breath becomes good-bye. Coupled by conjunction
    refusing to accept
The eminence of a ruling type. Clauses deny a hub,
    strangle dismissal.
The principal parts of speech or written language a template
    for the governing
Body. This is license taken. This is a token, memory and praxis,
    decoding
The treasured deeds that litter the streets.

A few kids on a corner create themselves with words
Or made words in which clicks and whistles
Make sense in the same manner as reflexive verbs
    or auxiliary verbs, native,
A nice distinction where my finger is now suffixed to you,
    syllable or syllables
Way up high aspirated, not susceptible of British influence
    nor greased by guilt.
Arbitrary, with a different reason. Your Puerto Rican self
    way up inside me.
I'm a Paddy and proud with sensitive skin and tender
    flesh and muscles
That can pull the coat right off you if I'm not careful.

But I always am.
The Irish never err.

Who seeks recognition, who recognizes departure and success,
A cloudy day blurs borders and governing bodies, targeting
Various flattened *a*'s, verbs in the continual present as a gift on the
Ground where ancestors walk as I plan yet another memorial
    in a spoken
Language.

Dropped suffixes, an unemancipated minor, Standard English
As a second tongue. We make our mark. There was a
    permanent shift
To grasslands. Its forested habitat shrank.
    A tree-dwelling quadruped
Foraged. You can see it. It's right there in the family tree intensified
In a second cold pulse diverting cold air from one continent to
    another homeland
In the hominid line. Layers of dust bury the timing tightly.

A tangled forest. Climactic wiggle. Critical later periods.
    If she do right.
Fixed it, it wouldn't serve. Time collapses in the
    continual present tense
Once considered primitive. Now known as the quickest passage
To the provocative. Once Positive meant what it says,
    now it means "I have it" or
Entered the cell from the outside or making it accessible
    or stay far away
As witness to the days when a correctly fitting
    receptor cell embraced

Working in concert. Now work isolates the killer cells in the
    specificity of your
Skills, a job described devolving to barbarism. With so little time left
The daylight dims including proteins and peptides,
    big words for grouping
People according to their origins. Enabling the self to recognize
    the self in work.
He wrote about it years ago. And we still don't get it.
Women write about women to the lowest common denominator;
Shakespearean English preserved in the backwoods.
    I write as testament.

Hugger-mugger, hug me tight humanist hull or hell
    to supersede the ecstasy
Reserved for creationists a millennia later. Huckster,
    hawker, hue and cry, harking
Back to the last century for comfort. You'd never
    know it was a hundred
Years later. Bathed in blood, the menses serves
    us women well, dispelling
Denominations where "ignorant" is an affirmative exclamation
    pushed forward
By the MC as the band tunes up. Slumming.
In with the hood. Statistics tell stories for code
    when education is denied.

Pin hopes. Identificatory mechanism. Phallic phase.
    Personal perversion
Saves my life.

Benchmark symptom. Think I'll crawl into Not a
    Number and nap. Fill the classic

Screen, scree as if he knew, talus screw, scribble
    for transporting bulk
Across wires carving paths in air. The fractured sexual subject.
    Vlad, the Impaler.
Opinions blaze clinics. I tentatively tried to tell someone how
Scared I was. Genetic technology supplants description about what it
Might mean as if it could be called writing, but it is.

Appoint a commissar. Carry batteries in a sock as protection.
    Conception
Circumscribed by the sphere of immediate needs.
But we talk to their ghosts daily.

Punishment or reformation. Vehemence and violence subbing for
Cider. He took the plunge. Twelve-step programs
    proliferate in absence,
Like opium but worse. Rhetorically free, theoretically able,
    apothecary
Exclusion builds big chests. Commercial boundary, the simplification
Of flora and fauna, pots of purgative, the god we worship
    under a different
Name. High concept trains the night for normalcy. Just like
    the 14th Century.
They got scared or scarred. Can you blame them?

Relic in its senses: plural in the text,
Singular in the title. That bright delight called intention or thanks
From what state pride and glory. Despite the evidence,
    I refuse to give in.
Despite his admissions, I couldn't believe the warning voice,
    from cells
And of correctly fitting receptors, molecular, furious, our parents
    and our

Secrets. Devilish engines supplanted by silicon in that
    big continent just
As Blake said. Big as the mutating cell, infected
    and flourishing in the crass
Workings of envy. In sighs it begins, with fertile
Eden in view before service stills voluntary acts. The century
Is set in motion, marred by war, including the warring soul
    and stifled
Breath in cubes where make-work diminishes the senses, dulls the
Mind while need rules the roost for no reason but treachery
    bested by greed
Conjuring stars and signs, application of the will toward augury by
Precise operations for the few, splitting the word or world of
    would-be
Wealth. We call for mother and pray she never comes.

Lyrically at the limits of language's source: the first felt
Absence. Potential for a world of our own making. To dance
Like a truck driver or the common man or woman finding grace
In all causes, primary and secondary, knowledge and chance
For change without fear. The brightest of all luminous bodies,
Your voice inside me, sent to us by birth and passion in the flesh
Of our own human nature contiguous with plant life
    and mineral fire,
Dark and crude, deep under ground, dilated and furious, my flesh
Replies with the reasoning mind from the spirit
    with whom angels and
Energies break apart and rejoin for signs of love taking
    chances for trust.
Of corporeal nature. Good intent societywide divides as if forever,
Burns clean as if a virtue, but deep in the cojoining of body and
    mind

A rigorous mating lusts for diversity. From the
    coldest town in the country,
You call me, heat in the interior portion, differences as well
As different, confined in a cell or cellular structure of body or mind
For now. I wait for your call, but use the time well,
    as melting point with pressure
Dismissing use or augury, the vast heat discovered in the early part
Almost killed us in the middle called fusion or fission
    while we have it all
Already in the physical conditions of the Earth
    and aether informed and of
Form from words as physical things embracing visible process
    and the behavior
Of rocks at a high temperature within the sentence
    in its multiplicity of meanings
Way up inside in connection with distance, I can feel
    you already at that tiny
Point derived formally of rods and made of mercury
    at a constant velocity
Fidgeting with the future on the first warm day, late as usual.

RAY DiPALMA

BYZANTINE MOTES

Nodding through pendant marble
A weight feeds
Where the keys are hung

Gnarled and optically confined
A line draws a line
Keening a margin

Words go out
To win something
Even more
Ephemeral

Little more than the rhythm
Of particulars
A looking method
That had an intention
But no pattern

Between the persistent distance
And the spoken in common

THE FINAL WORD WILL ALWAYS
BELONG TO THE NIGHT WATCHMAN

I figure
That's what was
That was it
What was imagined
And what was
To be
Maybe
Seen

But chance tells after
It's had its go

Before that which
Is not seen
While it goes

Slow sudden last

LULLABY
for Stephen King

The zero of a yawn eclipses your face,
feeling drowsy, eyelids heavy:
goodnight, goodnight, blow out the light,
the century is going to sleep.
Goodnight, Adolf, you almost prevailed—
your dreams, little fellow, rose to fact
like a swamp beast from the muck, then
they settled back again: good luck for us,
bad luck for you, the century is going
to sleep. And Uncle Joe, your musings
tried to duplicate the density of concrete.
Should we add up the dead millions squeezed
like dry leaves to make your diamond?
But then, oh happy day, you passed away.
Dead brutes, dead bullies, the tyrants
totter past to forgottenhood, the century
is going to sleep. But also the heroes:
Babe Ruth, General MacArthur, Gypsy Rose Lee.
The stages you danced upon are compost now,
the newspapers headlining your exploits
pack the landfill. You imitate your shadows.
All the radio broadcasts have been silenced.
Hush! The century is going to sleep.
Erza Pound, are you still grinding your teeth?
Robert Frost, is your brick-like heart
the only solid chunk left in your coffin?
Thelonious Monk, are you still bopping
someplace down below? Lady Day hums the tune:
lullabies, lullabies, the century

is going to sleep. And all the objects:
the Model T Fords, the 45 rpm records,
eight-track tape players—see them drowsing
in cobwebbed warehouses. Even the rats put a paw
to their lips. The century is going to sleep.
Maybe in another world John Kennedy was never shot,
maybe John Berryman lived a few years longer,
wrote a villanelle before downing seconal.
And John Lennon, maybe in another world
the madman missed and more songs got made.
All the Johns, all the Janices, all the Sylvias—
blow out the light, the century is going to sleep.
Dead best sellers, dead Nobel winners,
dead academy award winners, dead football
heroes, world series champions, Kentucky
Derby winners: all tucked between warm sheets,
sweet dreams carouse across their brains.
My father, my grandparents, my cousins,
your faces slide away in the vapor. How
difficult to see you in memory anymore. You
are the frames from which a photo was stolen.
Or my friends, I have left behind too many—
their stories stopped before mine, their
straight lines banked up at black conclusions:
goodnight Ray, goodnight Betty, goodnight Dick
the century is going to sleep. And those ideas,
the glad ones, the young ones—integration,
human rights. Goodnight, goodnight. The twelve-
tone scale, abstract expressionism. Sweet dreams,
sweet dreams. A chicken in every pot, two cars
in every garage, three TVs in every house.
Sleep tight, sleep tight. We are retreating

to books, electronic texts, some get paragraphs,
some sentences, some footnotes, most get silence.
Shouldn't we walk on tiptoe, shouldn't we whisper?
Do you have sand in your eyes, little fellow?
Let's take a breather. A baby's about to be born.
I won't see much of this one. Maybe a morsel,
if I'm lucky, of its infancy. This next one
belongs to my children and their children. What
Auschwitzes and Hiroshimas are already being
prepared? What will be the carnage of tomorrow?
What dumb ideas will be used to erase human breath.
But also the good stuff: what jokes, what
laughter, what kisses, will there still
be kisses? Better not know, better let it come,
like always, as a surprise. Feeling frightened?
Are you scared? Blow out the light, goodnight,
goodnight, the century is going to sleep.

ONE HUNDRED FRAGMENTS
FOR THE TWENTIETH CENTURY
(including fifty-two by Dante,
allowing the traces of his voice to serve as conductor)

They came towards us, each crying, "Stop, you who by your dress seem to
us to be from our degenerate city!"

And I saw him dressed in a small house, or a barrier of cardboard. It
stood as a greeting card in front of him, just at his height as he sat,
contracted, pulled into his misery as a core or flower, as the film of a
flower running backward in slow motion, and retreating into the bud.

The poet waited a little, then said to me, "Since he is silent, do not lose
time, but speak and ask of him, if you would know more."

He's collapsed in his seat, looking at his hands, receiving his head
falling into them, startled to be the owner of the head and the hands,
to be receiving and to be falling. He's looking at the heel marks and
imprints on the subway floor, without pretending they are not there
(we are not here), to be reduced to this anonymous mark of a person,
contracted but knowing his appearance as any stranger might.

"Love moved me and makes me speak."

It's raining, the night scene like a film of itself, the river without a
surface except where the drops are falling and on the highway red and
green lights in the distance, streams of traffic blurred or smudged.
The sky is a deep field of black with a purple blotter behind it, satura-
tion of these colors the information of the clouds. Streetlights, white,

new-fangled sulfur, reflect in the river, dancing multiply in the square even windows of the giant buildings, live chips or screens of memory.

We did not cease going on because he spoke, but all the while were passing through the wood, I mean the wood of thronging spirits; nor had we yet gone far from the place of my slumber when I saw a fire, which overcame a hemisphere of darkness.

The fire destroyed this community of squatters, and one man died of the cold. They had built these places for seven years. In this newspaper photograph, the man in the foreground, trying to get through, is his brother.

Some call it the Helicopter Flower and others the Passion Flower, for the Passion of Christ, it is a green bud, tight even as it swells and opens and then inside this precise architecture, a purple cross flanked by yellow and pale green, the cross of stubborn pollen, I think it was orange. And after they opened, the whole vine in bloom, caterpillars consumed it overnight and within days the green cellulose skeleton of flowers and leaves was shaking beneath these butterflies, big as birds.

While the one spirit said this, the other wept, so that for pity I swooned, as if in death, and fell as a dead body falls.

No one has seen them, it must be circumstantial, although their plot had been apprehended before the bombing there was no interference, as if it were purely mental. The blast was felt as a quake but shorter and not communicating itself along any fault lines. There was repeated mention of hydrochloric acid, and hundreds of small fragments of metal, paper, cloth and twisted wire were introduced as evidence. For weeks before the final body was discovered cranes filled the road, lifting out slabs of the parking garage, split by the blast.

Cars were lifted out too, covered with a thick black soot and melted into themselves, contracted. It was a vast pit, three stories deep, and around it cordons of guards, ribbons upon their badges.

No green leaves, but of dusky hue; no smooth boughs, but gnarled and warped; no fruits were there, but thorns with poison.

And when I arrived there I went to the river and stood on a rock. A swarm of bees lit upon me, and I stood in horror as they bit me before I realized they were a different kind of bee than I had known, and the stings did not kill them and were not fierce, but were like the small bruises made by lips on skin. After this a flock of creamy butterflies as small as dimes covered my turquoise shirt. I could feel the sun beating through the cotton and their tiny but definite weight. They were like visible emotion, they were not my idea of insects. Beating their wings they circled my head and I felt I would soon be carried away.

Within sight was his plane brought down a number of years ago, resting on its side in the river. The women will come in their canoes from time to time and cut themselves a piece, out of which they will make earrings.

"Before the shore comes into view you shall be satisfied."

Now the shore rarely comes into view. Buildings, cars, people in the street come and go, seen through doorways, up staircases, out of windows, in winding lines leading into planes. Shapes fill the space in front of our eyes, from which depth has vanished through crowding. The shadows of buildings extend across rivers and bridges are so enormous we rarely find ourselves beneath them, contemplating them as structures, unless we are homeless or specialists or in love.

Then he said, "Now it is time to quit the wood; see that you come behind me: the margins, which are not burning, form a path, and over them every flame is quenched."

He was forced to move about the city, and from the city to the country or to another city, never having rest. He was one of the many dispossessed, a great train of people, the dispossessed, left without the fragrant leather library of his biography or the novel, plot of his life. For in the nineteenth century, he explains, one life mattered, but now one's life can be plucked away at any moment, like a ball from a billiard table. He claimed to be a creature of the nineteenth century, shipwrecked on the coast of the twentieth.

That which you tell me of my course I write, and keep with a text to be glossed by a lady who will know how, if I reach her.

The girl recognized the name, Felicity, calling it the doll from the seventeenth century, and when her father corrected her, saying it was the 18th, the 1700s, she said that's what I said, the seventeenth. He explained that she thought we were living in the nineteenth century, although he'd told her over and over that this is the twentieth and she is very bright.

"tell us if courtesy and valor abide in our city as once they did . . ."

The best lack all conviction, and the worst—or is it the worst lack all conviction, and the best—

They have been blown up, words and the people, they have come to think they are only these resemblances or images of themselves, in the line into the palace of art they watch themselves on the video monitor, there now to let them see themselves but usually mounted for security. The big balloons where the words are written in comics appear over their shoulders, and in these balloons the horizons that used to be in front of them, the shorelines that came into view appear. Here is the earth the teacher said, holding up the orange, and if you can imagine my finger as the mast appearing to Columbus upon the horizon, you can see that the curvature of the earth makes it appear not all at once but little by little as it comes closer.

Looking again, I saw a banner that ran so fast, whirling about, that it seemed it might never have rest, and behind it came so long a train of people that I should never have believed death had undone so many.

When he awoke he discovered the man who had shared his hospital room was gone and could not be found. The machines breathing for you after your heart is repaired are imperfect in the circulation of your blood and the uneven oxygen causes hallucinations. That is their explanation: the man who had shared his hospital room felt he must go to sleep, must sleep, and he pulled out all the tubes and apparatus and climbing down the stairs crossed the parking lot, scaled the fence, and fell asleep under an oak tree, where he was found in the morning.

Midway in the journey of our life I found myself in a dark wood, for the straight way was lost.

In every century did it seem that the ones before were surrounded by more space, or silence, or peace? Did people always count this way, thinking of the years as clusters of hundreds, sheaves of grain?

I was sitting in the field. I was sitting in the field, counting on my fingers, one two three four five six seven eight nine ten.

He goes swimming slowly on, wheels and descends, but I perceive it only by a wind upon my face and from below.

It was my daughter who discovered the path through the thicket of wild roses, planted recently, since we desire the native. The planting goes from the end of the esplanade to the edge of the river, where there is a clearing. Following it we were scratched, on her arms and my legs, the heights at which we wander about. It is summer, hot, bees surround the pink flowers, so open they lose their petals. Theirs is a stubborn pollen, reminding me of what is mental. The Hudson is bright blue, thick in the sun, the water a poster paint and the boats plying the river, the way Whitman described them.

Then he set out, and I followed after him.

I felt myself begin to lose the numbness. For the first few days after I began to rediscover my sensations, people had eyes, eyes in their heads, and they were looking at me, and looking all around them, and they were barely able to contain the curiosity they felt at being here, as I did. I felt that I was one of them, one of the surprised.

"By your words you have made me so eager to come with you that I have returned to my first resolve."

We are living on fill over the mariners' graveyard, men or perhaps some women, lost at sea, the Potter's Field. Fill came from the excavation of the World Trade Center, the Twin Towers, they dug the dirt out and dumped it in the river, and over the old bones. And when they built Washington Square there were many bones, whole skeletons, so it is not true that you disappear here without trace.

And I, my head circled with error, said, "Master, what is this I hear? And what people are these who seem so overcome by pain?"

They were singing the songs written in the fourteenth century, the songs of praise and the names of angels. Where one leaves off the other begins, and each is aware of the other in their silence.

. . . and I fell like one who is seized by sleep.

I saw a ship come sailing
sailing on the sea
and it was deeply laden
with pretty things for thee

. . . for I recognized that people of great worth were suspended in that Limbo.

The news came over the wire or through the air, or with the passengers who landed, here on business, here to do something and then return, bringing their report. The images spilled out of the monitor, faces, flesh, flowers so open they lose their petals. One story drifts into another; you can't stop the channel from changing and must just sit here with me and see everything with me. After this we'll walk over to the river, lean over the river, and watch things go by.

You have made you a god of gold and silver; and wherein do you differ from the idolators, save that they worship one, and you a hundred?

We pursue rumors of traffic in uranium, plutonium, and certain other metals by insiders in need of cash. It is true that a core was disassembled, the materials used to crown teeth in the small town. Enough has been sold to pollute the sea for a depth of a foot, but the amount is shy by far of what is needed for a bomb.

"Your city, which is so full of envy that already the sack runs over, held me in it, in the bright life."

I wore my warmest clothes against the cold, and only when, in the piles of filthy snow, a homeless man jumped out at me, crying, "Green with envy!" did I notice that everything I wore was green.

And if it were already come, it would not be too soon.

I was meeting her on the corner at the grocery store there, to go out of the city for a hike and picnic. She came toward me, carrying fruit and water.

We departed thence,

I planted the yellow rose bare root, so it was four stalks green and covered with thorns. But the very beginning of new leaves blushing green and transparent unfolded rapidly, and roses surrounded my window and climbed to the roof.

The poet waited a little, then said to me, "Since he is silent, do not lose time, but speak and ask of him, if you would know more."

Someone will take your young head in their hands and will stroke your hair, holding you in their lap and singing a song. Later you will be unable to remember if you imagined or dreamt this.

No green leaves,

at the very beginning it was not a beginning because the century had just turned. Thinking in centuries implies a kind of belief in magic, for at the start there is the feeling that later more will be known of what we are. At the very beginning it is a hint of what is to come, or what is imagined to be about to happen, or what we might already be implicated in without knowing. And then there was an excitement and a naivete, followed by an exercise of power, an extinction, a struggle, a resting, a complacency, a prosperity, a fecundity, a rigidity, a loosening, a wildness, an extremity, a violence, an absolution, a desire for peace, a restlessness, a desire to have the shore come into view, a getting into boats and vans, a driving, an exploration, a discovery, an accumulation, an exercise, an excision, an amnesia, an accumulation, gold and silver, greed, an absolution, a desire for peace.

They came towards us,

and the sense of the rest of the world? After we left we saw we were not the center, and our sense of being at the center was linked with dating everything and noticing time. But when we were not at the center it reminded us of our idea of the beginning of our own century. Patios, yellow roses climbing the window, dust, air, walking along a road somewhere.

the margins, which are not burning,

When we came back we noticed how many things from elsewhere we were eating—jam from England, butter and apples from New Zealand, and we are wearing clothes made in Hong Kong, Yugoslavia, India.

The poet waited a little, then said,

as the film of a flower running backward in slow motion, they begin toward the end to wear for costumes the styles of the eighteenth century, whose formality suddenly looks new. Exaggeration is modest before the turn

to me, "since he is silent, do not lose time,

and the century plant was fabled to send up a bloom only once in a hundred years and that is how long Rip Van Winkle slept but the century plant may bloom once every fifty or seventy years, pulling out with its heavy growth the plant from the hillside, and turning from that steely green-blue to an ashen soft mess. And Rip Van Winkle is a fictional character, and he had to encounter the departure of the king and we have not had any kings for long here although there are many kings in our century we didn't know them. When the snowstorm came the Prince of Denmark on his way to the exhibition of paintings had to go to Newark, this was toward the turn of the century, although the turn begins at the seven in my opinion and continues into the oval of the zero, use the numeral do not type o

but speak and ask of him,

the men were remote behind their glasses but became approachable and then were dapper, dancing, serious, wounded, took up arms, fought bravely, protested, sat with newspapers, worked nine to five, complained, cooked dinner but only outside, but this was only the idea of here, elsewhere it was quite different, we might really have been in a different time, and you notice that while travelling, that already you might be in another time, and if you go away for long enough, when you come back it's a new time.

Since he is silent

They were singing these songs from the fourteenth century, the individual voices composing the chorus in the manner of that century, which is the manner of Gertrude Stein when she says that in one hundred are one hundred ones

one and one and one and one

and in the paintings we will see a face in profile and a face facing us and this will tell us the sequence of events, when each one occurred

the words opened as the mouths of singers and within the composition time accrued within each one as a resin or sap, its history of meaning

meaning

do not lose time,

by breathing exchanging ourselves

but speak

with the atmosphere—take it

and ask of him,

zero or o
o or zero

and one
zero and one and one and
zero

two thousand in relation to Christ

the convention

if you would know more."

In this century the women are going to that cliff to carve out that special white mud and they are decorating themselves with it, painting themselves all over with this mud, this thin slip and it makes them hard to catch

"the longing that I had to gain experience of the world"

And it is, he said, that type of virtual reality, the type with the helmet in which you are within a landscape where a shore might come into view, but the light is new, graduated, like the light of the dawn, which is of course the dawn of the sun. You can get up to see it.

Consider your origin:

In many cultures the number twenty is synonymous with "human," for we count to twenty on our fingers and toes.

showing through like straw in glass

They have dug a vast pit in Brazil, into which they venture forth each day to mine for gold. And the rivers are full of mercury, but some of them must still be clean. Everything is coated with a fine layer of silt, fine as gold powder, only of a different color and weight.

Here it is morning when it is evening there.

someone will take your young head in their hands and will stroke your hair, holding you in their lap and singing a song,

you

who

by

your

dress

seem

to

us

to

be

from

our

degenerate

city!"

*Divine Comedy, Inferno, Charles Singleton translation

DEAR READER

When you read this paragraph about the end
of the world, things will happen in your life.
The old world with its pain, suffering and
sorrow will literally end, but a new world is
ready and waiting to take its place. It's a
world where there is exactly the right amount
of red, blue, green and yellow—exactly the
right amount of pollen, trees and flowers. There
comedians are always funny, mothers always kind,
and french fries never greasy. So sleep now, gentle
reader, and dream of comets trailing blood and
planets exploding. When you wake, it will be spring.

AT THE LOCKS OF INFINITY

When I genitalize my mind, any one or thing is a mine to be explored.

When I imagine my mind, the brain seems seminal, finite, keen on working its mine forever.

To imagine my genitalization is to know my self as a squid jetting by, or as a rock whose E, said to be unreadable, stares, a runic miss.

I used to think that there was only one missing story, in perpetual feedback, the gap between desire and its fulfillment, the stepping beyond, if only for an instant, onto that anvil heated beyond the grave.

In dream, as one ages, the dress rehearsals become more poignant than opening night. Let them continue to be interrupted by revenants passing, from eternity into dreamtime, across the Muladhara Bridge, starved to express their stories, dancing their realizations on the spongy stage.

Last night, I was in Mexico again, in an awesome half cave half cathedral, with an orchestra pit that flushed out stars. The scenery was organic. The baptism of a cockroach utter magic. Spellbound on my knees, my body still part of our sphere, my head peering beyond the encircling stars, I heard a voice command: "Now look back into that trough where god, cod, pod, rod, sod and nod once pullulated. Can you, using these od blocks, construct a cod-like sodpiece for god's nodding, pod-like rod?"

*

As at a gasoline pump, the scroll of numbers turns.

Suppose at this century's end, only the 3rd and 4th digits turn. We would be dropped back to 1900, on the eve of *The Interpretation of Dreams*, so as to be as we were, as if nothing but the passing of static time had occurred, as if we could not bear for all the digits to turn, for 2 to face—through the zero tube—infinity.

Indeed, what would it mean for 2 to face infinity?

2 might be living without the tombal influence of god. Then not only would the judgement of god be ended (1948), but his amoral, ventriloquistic umbilicus, rooted in any Bible or Korân without comparison, would be shredded apart—

a perilous moment, for then 2 would have to become a self-regulatory (homage to Wilhelm Reich) biune, a kind of double-backed crypt containing the history of laughter, all the vulva grigris, all the phallus jujus, in which the saint who pricks condoms is married to the bastard who imagines, the alchemical and perpetual wedding of Teresa and Sade.

The banquet of the ape's head projected through the earth's table center, held by a nuclear band, the skull top severed, entire populations with chop-sticks eager for live brain, could end—

but for maybe a hundred years the living would have to absorb and assimilate what god's rotting corpse has done to the earth, not knowing if the entire system had been made mortal, or if, once the oceans, ground, and air had been washed, a pristine impermanence, on which a dignified human mortality could be based, might be restored.

Facing this awesome roll call, the individual soul might look like a doll casing, the slash and burn of dream little more than a reflection of unlimited, human capacity for destruction. But it is precisely the imagination that must replace the social drama of reaction to god's rotting corpse. The corpse itself must be delineated, must be resolved within the double-backed crypt of 2 facing infinity.

Now Friedrich Schröder-Sonnenstern wants to say a word: "In the precious slime of vision, my mother's dear mouth became a toothed cavity, her flaccid breasts jetting peni. I painted the SS masculine displacement, how men everywhere raise their lower body that they cannot live with into a woman's upper body reconstructed as a Devil's Island."

Then a man with AIDS lay down upon me. His feet were huge, weighty, his head immense, his waist virtually nothing. Is he what is left of the Whitman man who received a plunged tongue in his bare-stript heart? How adhesively *and* romantically we must pay attention to beginnings and endings as the wrap-around of 2000 stares.

In imagination, one metaphor tries to grasp its amoebic split-off to hurl it forward into numerology, myth, any cosmic extension, while what it is anchored in, carnal, mute, as if a Covering Prefix, gestures earthward. Thus this flux, this stasis, this Kaaba moving at relativity with my death.

Reading deep into mortality, numbers curl obscurely. What *is* going on in that large, green, leather boot, its chimney fuming, with little windows and a stoop, in the childhood clearing? And the old lady, this grizzled, dog-headed gal, has she my report card? Is it written in Farsi? Am I all her children, the only and the many, in the aligator tunnel of that boot, "a boot full of brains," the heart goes forth, as if on elastic, to the other who gives it a good squeeze before releasing the sensation of the abyss back into its cavity.

In eternity—into which god's corpse is spilling oil—Rainer Maria Rilke and Francis Bacon are cleaning up our mess. Rilke curved into himself and stayed. Bacon curved into other men and left. Both found a main at the locks of infinity. Between black cracks the numbers shine!

A FLIGHT THROUGH TIME

Wearing Apollinaire's derby I am in a zeppelin with a
hundred dignitaries in tailcoats from all over the
world cruising about looking for a place to declare
peace looking for a soft landing for peace on earth
Gardens are sighted on the horizon and the airship
veers in that direction only to discover there is no
airfield and we veer off again The sky is lit with flames
A man in tails with wings jumps off the Eiffel tower
thinking he's a bird He plummets straight down in front
of his friends I am picking petals off a sunflower in
Provence It's midsummer A million crickets sound their
huge drone in the night A sunflower leans in a window
where I am a boy leaning out Loulou Loulou someone calls
I have picked all the petals They fall Loulou Loulou
Où es-tu It is hot in the dark room There are riots in
France and Italy The Americans killed Sacco and Vanzetti
I saw Lindbergh land The zeppelin sails on There is jazz
on the radio It's Sidney Bechet Paris 1930s the dignitaries
toasting each other in champagne and American cigarettes
The pilot sends a Morse code greeting to a ship at sea
The band plays on The Captain sends back a round of drinks
on the house sailing through the hot night an endless flight
around the world We gaze out the portals of the gondola
at the endless stars Night reveals the cities of earth
lit with leftover sun I am kneeling in short pants in a
cathedral somewhere in France Christ died on Friday and
rose on Sunday setting a world altitude record out of
sight in the dark firmament I don't believe a word of it
The wine doesn't taste like blood The dirigible soars in
the summit of heaven Where will it ever land The eternal

pilot pours over the charts The dawn is pointing On a lake
far below the wood boats knock together Life sails on I am
stretched out in a sailing-canoe in upstate New York An
eagle soars in the summit of heaven An opera hat lies on
a marble table in the lobby of the Paris opera High over
the city a plane searches the sky making a sound like a
gnat It's a plane it's a bird it's man There is a thrill
in the air We are walking down the Avenue de l'Opèra The
Metro entrance yawns with its art-deco mouth and swallows us
The zeppelin flies on into the twenty-first century The
zeppelin is life itself The zone we fly through endless
without borders without boundaries There are no more nations
Ethnic hordes sweep the earth in search of food and shelter
We throw down our champagne glasses The tv shows the endless
night sky We are watching an eclipse The universe endless
stretches away in the night There must be a place where
all is light Where then O Endless One in endless eternity
Where now We are heavenly bodies rapt in time hurtling through
bent space Flame-outs illuminate the landscape

THE SPIRIT OF 76

> *Time rushes like a madman forward . . .*
>   John Berryman

The first twenty-four years of this century
    were not mine,
and though at my age it's foolhardy

to assume survival even until tomorrow,
    by 2000 AD
I'll be an ancient of seventy-six.

So I'll risk a goodbye in advance
    to the century I was born in, an alien,
and lived through, a klutz.

The Depression made me, the saddest little Jewboy,
    then the War and the Holocaust.
I really want to leave him behind and exit laughing.

Goodbye, then, to my youth, and worse, my hair.
    Nice cock though, and still trim from yoga.
Anybody want a clean old man?

Forget it,
    who could have predicted AIDS. . . .
Goodbye, with regret, to all that stuff.

My parents have faded away at last.
    I survived you two sickos, so thanks,
but it's a relief to say goodbye.

And to the Cold War, and HUAC,
    which burned out our brains,
good riddance and feh!

It's the only explanation for the country
    falling for cadavers like Reagan
and Bush . . . Feh! Feh! The stink hangs on.

Trying to take in the stink of
    the collapse of the Soviet Union,
I wave goodbye with an ache

to all my crazy ideals and illusions,
    more fascinated than terrified
as monsters rise out of the wreckage.

I wish the worst would wait to happen till I'm gone,
    but if even the IMF is getting nervous
it's all-passengers-to-the-lifeboat-stations.

It's bye-bye time already
    as friends die off from age and AIDS,
so if I'm not ready now to let it go I'll never be.

Goodbye, then, to all my years on earth, mostly wasted
    except for dirty moments in the dark,
cooking for you, sweetheart,

and especially poetry, fantasy weapon for
    non-fighters, losers, and sissies.
I'll settle for it and Spanish brandy

to face the new century, which, like programming a VCR,
    no seventy-six year old twentieth century man
can be expected to understand a thing about,

and when anything I have to say:
    "Did I ever tell you about the time in the War. . . ?"
will produce a yawn.

BIRTHDAYS • & • HOLIDAYS

Mother • Father • Sister • Brother

All that hope • All that history

For many years I wanted to look like my father
People said I looked more like my mother
My mother thinks I look like her father

Scatter photographs • Summers at the beach • Dead Uncles

Dying Aunts • In a trunk • In a box • In a book

Birthdays • & • Holidays

Cousin's wedding • In Massachusetts
Chicago • No • San Diego • On who's side

Oh, yes!

Birthdays • & • Holidays

Do you want to invite them to your house?
They never visit me • Maybe we could go there

It's almost Mother's Day • What are you going to get Mother?
Father's Day is Sunday • What are you going to get Father?

Sister • Brother

Birthdays • & • Holidays

I stopped drinking • Why don't you change jobs

Yes, I'm learning to fly • Father doesn't look so well
As well as can be expected • The weather's getting better

Their Anniversary • Mother called

Birthdays • & • Holidays

I hate Christmas • I'm going home for Christmas

I don't think the relationship will change
Before I die I'd like to see

What did Mother say

There's not much more we can do at this point
Father said • Remember your dog • My dog

That was my room • We used to live there

Mother • Father • Sister • Brother

Birthdays • & • Holidays

FIRESTORM

1.

Pools of the almost unwarned clutching motions your mouth makes
From windows others' mouths lean across blue metal running exact
    strokes

As when you concentrate gone to this tongue make the glass
    come clean
Firestorms set the table with yellow linen rich who are still striving
    at the gates

They count bodies turning some suddenly glaring object lap lapping
    each other closely

Legs still wrapped in the long robe with delicate tightening
    torso shifting

Night moisture methodically hangs above us without mercy
    devours changes still in this second year of our watching in its
    path the form of everything

You were cleaning the flutter through my body a doorway
    seeing the muscles saying goodbye

Watching your body world without you as if fragile to sunlight
    but to each tongue asked to pay attention were ravenous motion

2.

The form of no stopping each other closely or houses
    watching your body

You concentrated your precision devoured it changed closely

They were asked methodically no stopping point no saturation
    to sunlight but to each striving

Tongue saying goodbye still still wrapped in your long robe

Firestorms heating souls with rubble doorway hanging

From the windows of others' mouths' blue metal motions your
    mouth flutters through my body
Still wrapped in your precision from the window of some suddenly
    glaring torso shifting

Concentration without mercy seeing the muscles unwarned
    the delicate tightening world without you above us

THE BLOWN ONES

We have blown by. Call us the blown ones. Write about us in those impressive alphabets designed during the period of Russian Constructivism. Busby Berkeley will provide movement, a waterfall, a bride, telephone operators at their switchboards. There's a collection here forming. Notice the ducks. Against the neat swing-set leans Brother Philip. He's a strong cigar smoker with a head that could have been a ball bearing in most cultures. "Hello Philip!" we say as we blow by. "We too could be like smoke."

After so much has been said, we can observe chemistry. It takes discipline and organization but singing will maximize our efforts. What carries us is an assortment of inhales. We know they occur though their directionality is still uncoordinated.

Across the school front lawn, a pink garage door. It might never in our lifetime open to reveal a car. Now imagine a subsidy. Of what in this instant will it be made. Would a kind relative suffice? I wonder.

You come across the threshold of my home. A lit wick floats in oil. The winter evening completely gray, simple and distinct, the air chilled around an old calendar picture of evening snow falling, moving as breeze through a winter grove. I look at you, sitting near a kitchen table that is motionless oak branches, so smoothed and angular—to have grown older than death.

GLORIA FRYM

HOTEL EXELSIOR SPLENDIDE

We washed our hands after reading the news
but we were never innocent bystanders.
Long ago, we pulled the plug
and the alarm continued to ring.
In a century of declining miracles
we tried to believe something enchanting could happen
as we lined up for all the box office failures.
Optimists stood at our door
fundraising for disabled batboys,
while doubt dragged us into a daily five-car pile up.
For years we received long distance calls
at midnight we couldn't bring ourselves not to answer.

But now the spearmint is high, the lupine regal
in the fields, the barrel pouring out of its sides.
Now the candied breeze of the Antilles is the same
that sways us. We hear of an old nun praying
before the shadow of a crucifix
upon her closet door. She drifts down our veranda
in this dusty pink, winking at our virtual desire
to believe.

Never mind that civilization is always collapsing
and we are always going to pieces.
There is a bleak loneliness across
the immense gulf of interstellar space
but an interesting character
waiting under the chandelier in the foyer
with a message from the front
that reaches us just in time.

FROM THE EDITORS

Dear Professor,
    Thank you for the lecture
on subverting the dominant paradigm.
    In our opinion, the writing writes out
the reader. If we catch you one more time
    mouthing the term *signifier*
you will be forced to roam the shopping malls at night
    then shot for hypocrisy at sunrise.
                              About that old blood
on your new syntax. Your experiment flopped
    like Democracy.
You'll have to take *twin diachronic*
    back to the cleaners. You might be asked
what *dialogic* actually means. You'll demure
    but it won't work this time. You'll shriek *Corrective*
at this insulting request for substance.
    Go back to the hotel and call all
your well-appointed ad men.
    They won't like the recontextualized qualities
of what's coming next, either.
                        Game's up! On account of
airless grammar, sexless nouns and tortured verbals,
    the house of art is off limits. You're not allowed
to chop down imagination's holy forest. It's as easy as
    We say so! We decided to dredge the murder weapon
out of the bay. It was a sad day
    for language. Assasin of our orchards!
Your speech never reflected the unspoken!
                              Granted
    you were in the right place at the worst of times.

But you gave up too easily
   on the beautiful and the unseen. You secretly pooped
on the prophetic. You ignored the consequences.
                                   So
no parole for you, just blackboard duty and complete
   sentences. From now on, quit the jive.
And write like your life
   depended on it.

MARIA LA O

In 1959, my cousin Chris and I
accompanied my Uncle Les
from Tampa to Jacksonville,
where he had business to do.
I was twelve, Chris sixteen.
Jacksonville was a small town
then, palms lined the street
where I bought a papaya drink
from a sidewalk stand.
We ate lunch in a big hotel.
I watched people through
a long, plate-glass window
behind our booth. After lunch,
Uncle Les passed out Havanas.
We lit them and puffed away
as the three of us left the hotel
and strolled down the street.
Passersby stared at me, a small boy
smoking a big, black, Cuban cigar.
I loved the taste of it, bitter
after eating sweet *flan*
for dessert, and breathed deeply
the romantic aroma of smoke
and tropical air. Thirty-five
years later I recall the smell,
the blue sailfish shirt
I wore, the Florida that
isn't there any more.

ALLEN GINSBERG

CALM PANIC CAMPAIGN PROMISE

End of Millennium
                    Earth's decay—
Fire Air Water tainted
   We're the Great Beast—
                    Dark bed thoughts,
Can't do anything to stop it—
Denial in Government, in Newspapers of Record—
Like watching gum disease & not brushing teeth
Getting heart failure, no rest much stress
Putting salt on your greasy Pork
Putting sugar in coffee you're diabetic
   Disaesthesia on foot soles
Poor circulation, smoke more cigarettes
Kick your son under the table have another beer
Need President who'll reverse the denial
                    The Calm Panic Party.
            to restore nature's balance.

from *Cosmopolitan Greetings* (HarperCollins Publishers, 1996)

THE TONGUES WE SPEAK

> *The human crowd has been the lesson of my life. I can come to*
> *it with the born timidity of the poet, with the fear of the timid,*
> *but once I am in its midst, I feel transfigured. I am part of the*
> *essential majority, I am one more leaf on the great human tree.*
> *Solitude and multitude will go on being the primary*
> *obligations of the poet in our time. . . .*
> from *Memoirs* by Pablo Neruda

I have arrived here after taking many steps
Over the kitchen floors of friends and through their lives.

The dun-colored hills have been good to me
And the gold rivers.

I have loved chrysanthemums, and children:
I have been grandmother to some.

In one pocket I have hidden chocolates from you
And knives.

Speaking my real thoughts to no one

In bars and at lecterns I have told the truth
Fairly often, but hardly ever to myself.

I have not cried out against the crimes of my country

But I have protected myself, I have watched from a safe corner
The rape of mountains, the eagle's reckless plunge.

PATRICIA GOEDICKE

Ever since high school I have waved goodbye to history:

I have assisted you to grow
In all ways that were convenient to me.

What is a block vote against steam shovels?

My current events teacher was a fine man
But his moral precepts were a put-up job and I followed them.

Well-dressed, in my new Adidas
At every gathering I investigated my psyche with friends

And they investigated theirs with me.

But whenever Trouble came in the front door I ran out the back
And fell into the pit of my bones.

Escaped from those burning buildings, the past,
What balance can any of us hope for?

I was comparing lipsticks
The day Nagasaki vanished.

The day Solzhenitsyn disappeared into the Gulag
I was attending a cocktail party.

Perhaps there are only ashes in my handbag.

A man at the corner of Broadway and Forty-Second Street
Tried to sweep me into a trash barrel and I almost agreed.

Already the dried blood was sifting along my wrists.

Already my own hands
Were tightening around my throat

But Sorrow saved me, Sorrow gave me an image
Of bombs like human tears watering the world's gardens.

How could I not answer?

Since then I have been planting words
In every windowbox, poking them to grow up.

What's God, that he should be mindful of me?

Sometimes I feel like wood
Waiting for someone to peel me.

Indeed I have been lukewarm
At heart, which is all that matters.

But I am afraid of disappearing
Into the wheat fields of a future

Of tiny bread-colored atoms,
Equal fragments equally dispersed

That love each other and are never hungry.

What have I ever ignited
That warmed anyone?

I have not followed the rivers.

Dangerous as a pine needle
Packed in among others, in the dense multitudes

And dry timbers of the West

I am afraid of greed,
The rich taste of it, the anger

Hidden in my pockets.

Columns of smoke on the horizon,
Pillars of green fire.

But I have arrived here somehow,
Neither have I stopped talking.

Numberless are the kitchens I have sat in,
Chewing my fingers, trying to say something,

Anything, so that the daughters of men should see
As many sides of themselves as possible.

Word after word my footprints
Have stumbled across deserts.

How should I escape them?
They keep following after me.

A little wind stirs itself,
Whisks across my eyelids,

And I know what it is before I say it:

What if the world really articulates itself
In the socket of a human knee?

God save me
From the swamps of hubris but it may be, it may be.

Before the idea, the impulse.

I feel it moving in me, it is there
Arthritic but still powerful, a seizure

Delicate as grasshoppers, a light
Gathering in the skull.

Between thumb and forefinger
And the ballbearing joints of the tongue

In soft, glottal convulsions
Out of no alien skies

But out of the mind's muscle
The hieroglyph figures rise.

PATRICIA GOEDICKE

The little histories of words
Cannot be eaten.

I know it, you know it
And the children . . .

But the images we make are our own.

In the cool caves of the intellect
The twisted roots of them lead us

Backwards and then forwards.

If only we could understand
What's in our pockets is for everyone!

I have a dictionary in one hand, a mirror.

Strangers look at themselves in it,
Tracing the expressions they use

From one family to the next
They comfort themselves, murmuring

The tongues we speak are a blizzard
Of words like warm wool flying:

In the shy conjugal rites
Of verb, consonant, vowel,

In the dark mucosal flesh lining

The prismed underside of the skin

Each one is a spark sheared
From the veined fleece of the spirit

Of the looking-glass body we live in.

It is the one I have been cherishing,
The one all of us speak from,

For the world as we know it moves
Necessarily, by steps.

Breath, pulse beat, ten digital stops.

At the foot of the mountains I look up. Does God
Lift up His hand to cover them?

Blinded by tears like rain
My bones turn granite, the spine of the hills congeals them.

Where is the eye of the storm,
Or where is the center of my seeing?

The wind of my breath is a hurricane:
I am locked inside myself.

Painfully, up the bald stepladder I climb,

But sometimes the light in my head goes on

PATRICIA GOEDICKE

More like the sun than a match.

Just as they said in Arabia

There's a huge pantalooned angel swelling
Inside the body's glass jar.

The white-haired thread of steam
From the teakettle on the range whistles

And sharpens itself into a voice

Bodiless as history, invisible
But still whispering in ears

That keep trying to hear it.

It is as if midgets were bellowing their names
Down sets of cardboard cylinders.

But we have not disappeared
Yet.

My friends, we have said many things to each other

In new combinations, seed upon seed exploding
And blossoming in kitchen gardens.

I confess I am ashamed of myself:

I have not tried hard enough to understand
Or listen to you speak.

But the Word is mindful of itself
And always has been.

Littering every street

In the sly eyes of tin cans,
Drops of water in the gutter

The world looks back at us

From every known language:
Yoruba, Hebrew, Chinese,

Arrogant English, the subject
Subjecting all to its desires,

Even the softer tongues, romantic

Self-reflexive, done to
As we would be done by,

Whatever life we cultivate
Out of the animal moans of childhood

It is all wheat fields, all grass
Growing and being grown.

With poisoned bread in my pockets, or gumdrops,
Or armies like Myrmidons rising

What I say is true
For a time only, thank God,

If I have arrived anywhere it is to look
Carefully, at all I thought I knew.

In living rivers of speech
The reflections I make are my own

And yet not:

Though the old growth rings are hidden from us
And the echoing tomorrows of the acorn,

The warm currents of the senses
Are a two-way street, my friends:

The palms of our hands are crisscrossed
With as many intersections as a leaf.

from *The Tongues We Speak, New & Selected Poems* (Milkweed Editions, 1989)

OUT OF TOWN

Everything in writing
Pure suit happiness
DC guitar head A / C'ed
Everything in writing
DC guitar head A / C'ed
In a manner of speaking
Everything in writing
Pure suit happiness
In a manner of speaking
Please look up Main Street
Brought back by tree demand
In a manner of speaking
Brought back by tree demand
Matter of actual fact
In a manner of speaking
Please look up Main Street
Matter of actual fact
Fold to believe
So easy, don't try on
Matter of actula fact
So easy, don't try on
The voice memorizes the night
Matter of actual fact
Fold to believe
The voice memorizes the night
With your body incorporates
Surrounds with mental woman tell
The voice memorizes the night
Surrounds with mental woman tell
Free at (shoe) last

The voice memorizes the night
With your body incorporates
Free at (shoe) last
Here's your door
You never know (auto) again
Free at (shoe) last
You never know (auto) again
Alive with bulbs (aflame)
Free at (shoe) last
Here's your door
Alive with bulbs (aflame)
Honk when you leave knees
Fortunate to be bordered
Alive with bulbs (aflame)
Fortunate to be bordered
(Don't) you know who you are
Alive with bulbs (aflame)
Honk when you leave knees
(Don't) you know who you are
Mind die suddenly
Expanding on what they know
(Don't) you know who you are
Expanding on what they know
Winner pieces save, goodness fit
(Don't) you know who you are
Mind die suddenly
Winner pieces save, goodness fit
Heart as a verb
More than needed
Winner pieces save, goodness fit
More than needed
Draw together to paint slope

Winner pieces save, goodness fit
Heart as a verb
Draw together to paint slope
Take requests oh dying embers
Understands *what* inner workings
Draw together to paint slope
Understands *what* inner workings
Reduce to a splendid more room
Draw together to paint slope
Take requests oh dying embers

AIMÉE GRUNBERGER

GOODBYE TO ALL THAT

it's hard to know where to stand
too close and the temptation
to straighten delint and groom overpowers

but admire from a distance
and the picture is mobbed with drainage
ditches ductwork and storm sewers

just say there arose a mania for invention
the patent office outgrew its premises
umpteen times and lexicographers ran
through all possible names for objects

young Freud swiped the dream
from a broken-down shaman
and Einstein put asunder
what God had so carefully joined

pale men in a darkened room
watch a pram endlessly tumble
down steep ceremonial steps
not one makes a move to stop it

just say people thought themselves
practical and hard-headed
in their dreams one centimeter
equalled one centimeter

each was labeled *actual size*

SPREE???

Crime spree? It wasn't any fucking *spree!*
It was a fact of life. When you say spree
you make it sound lightweight, like shopping.
Like one of those idiot contests where the chumps
have five minutes to rampage through a grocery
store and get to keep all the loot they can
haul to the cash register, all under the auspices
of a celebrity judge and the chain's regional VP.
That's a spree. A geeky husband and a porker wife
having free money fever as they round up
forty or fifty canned hams, a couple dozen salamis,
as many hundred pound bags of Puppy Chow they can lift,
and jar after jar of artichoke hearts . . . which they
don't even like but have heard are expensive.
Now that's a *spree.* What we did was more
like Attila the Hun paying a Scourge of God
courtesy call on Rome. Yeah, we blew in out of
the grasslands, confiscated all the Imperial geegaws,
set free the slave girls and lions, threw
a testimonial dinner for ourselves, and invented
pig latin. Up-Pay gainst-A the all-Way, otherfuckers-May!!
And sure, you can whine about your intentions.
You might as well . . . you whine about everything else.
And if you want to believe your intentions
were pure and hifalootin', and to live outside
the law you must be honest, and all that other
populist jive, go ahead . . . whine until you turn
a merry shade of tangled up in blue, but
I'm flat out telling you, that your real intentions,
were and still are *criminal*, with no ifs, ands,

or buts about it.
You artistes out there are more hung up on free money
and getting goodies without working than the poor stiff
who goes to the 7-11 for Huggies and in route
decides to pull a stick-up with a starter pistol.
The so-called authorities just haven't found a way
to prosecute you yet. And that's only because
you never score enough loot that anyone serious
notices it's gone. But this spree thing is utter bullshit.
You're either in it or out of it, and there's
no amount of weaseling or woosing or whining
in the world that's gonna change that.
FFF. Face the fucking facts.
Admit that you've lead a life of crime
and only by some malfunction of lucky
have you not been caught . . . yet.
Celebrate not getting caught, if you want,
and maybe concentrate for a second
then redouble your efforts not to be.
Keep writing those confessional poems
in the voice of a narco-terrorist
or drawing cute pictures of dinky murder scenes.
But at least admit that art is a crime
and you're a criminal, and start expecting
to get caught, just when you least expect it.
But more importantly admit
that it isn't just a *spree*,
for crying out loud,
it's a motive for existence.

IN TACOMA, SIGNE TURNS IOI
IN A BLUE VELVET DRESS

Can't visit on Mondays, I work
Mondays. Nursed till I turned
eighty. Now I quilt for new-borns, knit
lap robes for invalids. Tea?
Of course baked from scratch,
wedding-cake-white cake. I'll just have
hot water—slap my wrists two times
if I forget to turn off the kettle.
That photo? My hundredth birthday party.
Six children still living. You like my velvet dress?
Evening sapphire. My best. My oldest
sons were born on the homestead where
we raised fruit and grain and people paid us
five cents a pound for apples.
Moved across the Cascades
during slack times and don't miss
the rattlesnakes a bit. My husband
built ships. He's dead now and I'm sorry
things turned out like they did.
Tried to rent a place in town when
he left for good. But
no one would lease to a man-
less woman with six kids, so I sold the cow
and yearling calf for a hundred dollars, bought
my house on North Ninth. Scrubbed floors.
Didn't waste a living thing—saved
apple peelings for making vinegar.
Been cleaning houses since
I turned thirteen and North Star school

ended at grade eight. Been scrubbing
since I was tall enough to wash cups in a tub
Mama put on a chair seat in front of me.
My hands turned to lobster claws, we didn't
even have Bag Balm back then, though
washing isn't so bad if you don't have to haul water.
Which is why I liked my house on North Ninth.
One night before Pearl Harbor,
my youngest girl and a friend went out and
didn't come back. At midnight I scoured
the neighborhood, at two I found them
swinging in the park! Fifty-three years ago
and I'm still not over the fright. Do you think
those girls would be found alive today? That one
became a ballerina. After I put the others
through college and technical school
and got myself a nursing certificate, I bought
a nice dress. Elected two terms as Worthy
Grand Matron of Rebecca Lodge Number 6 and
wanted to look the part. My last
twenty-five dollars, an extravagance in 1952.
But I couldn't resist a dress the color of the sky
the night I found my daughter safe.
Wore it to my hundredth birthday party. God willing,
I'll wear it to the next and the next.

TIME SUITE

Just seven weeks ago in Paris
I read Chuang Tzu in my dreams
and remembered once again
we are only here for a moment,
not very wild mushrooms,
those cartoon creatures that are blown apart
and only think they are put back together,
housepets within a housefire of impermanence.
In this cold cellar we see light
without knowing it is out of reach;
not to be owned but earned
moment by moment.
But still at dawn
in the middle of Paris' heart
there was a crow I spoke to
on the cornice far above my window.
It is the crow from home
that cawed above the immense
gaunt bear eating sweet pea
and wild strawberries.
Today in the garden of Luxembourg
I passed through clumps of frozen vines
and saw a man in a bulletproof
glass house guarding stone,
a girl in the pink suit
of an unknown animal,
lovers nursing at each other's mouths.
I know that at my death bed's urging
there'll be no clocks and I'll cry out
for heat not light.

. . .

This lady is stuck
on an elevator
shuddering
between the planets
. . .

If life has passed this quickly,
a millennium is not all that long.
At fourteen
my sex fantasies
about Lucrezia Borgia:
I loved her name, the image
of her "renascimento" undies,
her feet in the stirrups
of a golden saddle.
She's gone now
these many years.
. . .

Dad told me that we have time
so that everything won't happen at once.
For instances, deaths are spread out.
It would be real hard on people
if all the deaths for the year
occurred on the same day.
. . .

Lemuribus vertebrates,
ossibus inter-tenebras—
"For the vertebrate ghosts,
for the bones among the darkenesses."
Quoted the great Bringhurst
who could have conquered Manhattan
and returned it to the Natives

who might have continued dancing
on the rocky sward.
        . . .
The stillness
of dog shadows.
        . . .
Here is time.
In the crotch of limbs
the cow's skull grew
into the tree
and birds nested in the mouth
year after year.
        . . .
Human blood still fertilizes
the crops of Yurp.
The humus owns names:
Fred and Ted from old Missouri,
Cedric and Basil from Cornwall,
Heinz and Hans from Stuttgart,
Fyodor and Gretel in final embrace
beside raped Sylvil,
clod to clod.
        . . .
The actual speed of life
is so much slower
we could have lived
exactly seven times as long as we did.
        . . .
These calendars
with pussy photos
send us a mixed message:
Marilyn Monroe stretched out

in unwinged victory,
pink against red and reaching
not for the president or Nembutal
but because, like cats,
we like to do so.

    . . .

Someday
like rockets without shells
we'll head for the stars.

    . . .

On my newly devised calendar
there are only three days a month
all the rest is space
so that night and day
don't feel uncomfortable
within my confines.
I'm not pushing them around,
making them do this and that.

    . . .

Just this once
cows are shuffling over the hard rock
of the creekbed.
Two ravens in the black oak
purling whistles, coos, croaks,
raven talk for the dead wild cow's
hindquarter in the grass,
the reddest of reds,
hips crushed when lassoed.
The cow dogs, blue heelers,
first in line for the meat
all tugging like Africa.
Later, a stray sister

sniffs the femur bone,
bawls in boredom or lament.
In this sun's clock the bone
will become white, whiter, whitest.
        · · ·
The soul's decorum
dissembles
when she understands
that ashes have never
returned to wood.
        · · ·
Even running downstream
I couldn't step
into the same river once
let alone twice.
        · · ·
At first the sound
of the cat drinking water
was unendurable,
then it was broken by a fly
heading north,
a curve bill thrasher
swallowing a red berry,
a dead sycamore leaf
suspended on its way to earth
by a breeze so slight
it went otherwise unnoticed.
        · · ·
The girl in the many windowed bedroom
with full light coming in from the south
and the sun broken by trees,
has never died.

...

My friend's great-grandfather
lived from 1798 until 1901
...

When a place is finished
you realize it went
like a truly beloved dog
whose vibrance had made
you think it would last forever;
becoming slightly sick,
then well and new again
though older, then sick
again, a long sickness.
A home burial.

...

They don't appear to have
firmed up their idea when time
started so we can go it alone.
"From birth to old age
it's just you," said Foyan.
So after T'ang foolery and Tancred
(the Black Pope of Umbanda)
I've lived my life in sevens
not imagining that God could holler,
"Bring me my millennium!"
The sevens are married to each other
by what dogs I owned at the time,
where I fished and hunted,
appealing storms, solstice dinners,
loves and deaths, all the events
that are the marrow of the gods.

SAINT MALTHUS

The spot I spat from time and time
again, year upon numbered years,
midpoint across Fall Creek's
suspension bridge, was the same spot
my student berserk on acid leapt
from one gusty winter night
and since his parents, gone crazy mean
with grief, were rich, though not rich
enough to level flat with nine trillion
cubic tons of fill the billion years
that grooved the gorge, they used a law
to erect these bars you must peer through
now to see the wide world caged
beyond the valley view, nor can you lean
now face to face with the abyss
as I once bent to watch several moons
of spittle vanish halfway down
into the backdrop moil of frothing spume.

Spanning all the years, I must have spat
one gallon full of spit yet never
did I compute, calculate or by any other name
otherwise count anti-dada called data:
numbers shot down from pythagorean flight
and mounted in the name of science, nor
did I doubt that beyond my seeing my spit
hit that stream you surely could not step
into twice in its spring run-off juggernaut
to reappear as a crescent seep of brown stain
across the inlet end of the flooded lake

whose blue placidity perplexed the viewer
suspended over a flood flying so fast
its hiss whispered even above a boom
of niagaran waterfall, shrieks of ice
gnashing upon ice, rifle shot cracks
of tree trunks snapping like tinder
and always at bottom a plutonic drumming
of boulders not standing alone
in the torrent's midst but tumbling
with drowned mutters over some exact spot
where on some precise date Charles Lyell
paused to jut his beard aloft and count
the layered eons, his shale-gazing squint
sweeping down the glacial fairway
of slate-grim sky and surely glancing
through that cubic square of empty air
from which I would spit so many timeless
times, but from where again and again
no one ever leapt but once.

On some exact date and time that spring
his bloating corpse glimmered wraithlike up
through black waters off the old salt mine
halfway down the swollen lake, balloon limbs
star-spread as a human mandala, a totem
found crypted in some forgotten cavern,
or featureless artifice of eternity
rocketed aloft into endless space to show
the universe ourselves as everyone
in a cryptogram of no one, hairless
and sexless as a great black and blue baby
swaddled in gritty soapfoam, cradled

in a gently rocking carpet of driftwood
and plastic jetsam, gazing face to face
with the wall-eyed, blue-lipped everyman
in the nacreous moon we keep thinking
winks at us alone as it appears to ghost out
of black clouds to stand stolidly alone
in the midst of blackness up where
the way up and the way down indeed
are one, where a speck of spittle
and the meat of a man, together or apart,
neither fall nor rise, but float
in timeless, weightless suspension now
and forever out of sight, outside our bubble
of gravity, beyond arithmetical counting
up or down of all begotten and to be got,
out into limitless geometry.

The putrid flotsam only known to be him
by coded metal in its teeth would have sunk
again had it not been gaffed from muddy shallows
at some certain point of shore invisible
from my spitting spot suspended in mid-gorge
and though I was not there to see my townsmen
bending to that work, in the hearing
I could see their yellow slickers glimmering
through rising lake mist, even as I hear
below the uproar of the living
hissing whispers of the outnumbered dead.

MICHAEL HELLER

THE CHRONICLE POET

From the razed word-hoards of the century,
one tries pulling syllables clean, like freeing
old nails from plaster. Undoing the dismantling of
human gantries by listening, as though one had an empty
water glass to the ear, wondering about the other side,
shushing wife, child, visitor, the gnawing of the rat,
to catch sounds between our histories and our apartments.

What is overheard is mere scratching, someone perhaps
short of air, desperate, a man eating dictionaries
quickly, avidly, hopelessly. *Useless, useless!* Nothing
impedes thought's passage more than an unuttered word, one
desperately cut short or untimely enough to have become stuck
where it makes only a shameful noise, a beetle's endless
clicking in the throat of a corpse. A noise seeking to reach
its fundament, trying, out of pure sound, to form itself
as honest language, and by that failure, painfully embarrassing.

FAREWELL TO THE TWENTIETH CENTURY

Seems to me the Twentieth Century has been more wasteful, cultur-ally, of its gifts than any other except the ninth (out of the last score or so centuries). It will have to work hard to redeem itself as anything other than a time of pretentious repression at its end. It started out well enough, providing new visions and models. But the time of pros-perity in the mid-years, while fairly productive, was marked primarily by a seizure of all funding means by ultra-conservatives who called themselves "Post-moderns," and whose attempt was eclectically to revive forms from previous centuries, forms which were not suited to the needs of our time. Seeing this they argued that a new technology would make these more suitable in some mysterious way, and they then attempted an arcane and scholastic theory or language to explain why this would happen, called, depending on which dialect one spoke, "Structuralism," "Post-Structuralism," "Deconstructionism," "Post-Deconstructionism," etc. By focusing on this material they attempted to keep the attention away from what actual works and innovations were still being made, this last usually by more or less starving artists who had no access to such funding support as was still available (grants, academia, etc.) but whose integrity and identity depended upon their doing their work.

Such being the cultural history of the past few decades, what can one say about the year 2000? Only that, as said at the outset, hopefully the next seven years will be one of rapid improvement in the cultural environment. This is doubtful, since the infrastructure does not exist yet to rebuild it. With nearly two hundred thousand people applying for Guggenheims, how many of the applications can be given serious attention? And that is money which might be spent better on support-ing the most deserving fellowships. The same is true for Berlin DAAD fellowships, and even for NEA ones. The worst served by the system are those whose work falls into several categories, because people who sit on panels do not take responsibility for them. Music people support music, theater people support theater, but musicotheater, while honored in the breach, goes unsupported. Having developed the concept of intermedia in the sixties, I would now advise any artist who is drawn to the possibilities of intermedial areas, "keep it a secret, if you want to survive—pretend to do something else, and hide your real art." But if anyone follows my advice, and many will do so whether they read these words or not, what we will have in the year 2000 is the same three kinds of literary, musical, visual, performance and intermedial art that we had four decades ago—public (one hesitates to call such commercial stuff "popular"), academic and actual, this last about as secret as the repressed art of Eastern Europe twenty years ago, though for different reasons. One hopes that in the next millennium the hidden door will be opened and this hidden, actual art will be discovered, waiting to provide a new send-off into something beyond a small circle. But that will take people and an infrastructure which, as yet, shows no signs of being developed, either in the Europe or Asia or, especially, in the USA.

WEST IS LEFT ON THE MAP

> *?*
> *trace my life on the map*
> *a new geographical treatise*
> *every day*
>
> *check the table of contents*
> *let's see*
> *where will I be tomorrow*
>   Mihail Cosma
>
> *Worstward Ho*
>   Samuel Beckett

wee terrible human race
soon to go down   or else into space

let it go let it bleed
into stellar fuzz   the light of another sun

whatever it ever was
fights among capos

a puff of dust where the lampshade bloom'd

Marlene forever young

like Marx or Helen's ankles
at the gates of dusk

or a recital

of Etruscan tunes   what a treat

    "poems in 2091
    objects of monkish interest"
    sez Vidal
    Gore, not Peire

    like poor but civilized urban existence
    another thing of the past

    *Petrus Kalm (1716-1779), a native of Finland, went west & later
    wrote in his "Travels in North America":*

"once this old white man went to the woods with one of the savages
& they came upon
                a speckled red snake
the old man reached for a stick but the savage begged him
in the name of all that was sacred
                            not to hurt this snake
saying it was
              one of his gods
so the old man picked up a sturdy branch & killed the snake
& told the savage:
'when you said to me
                that this creature
                       was your god
you left me no choice but to kill it'"

& if that old man had not been so old

he would have killed that savage too
                            no doubt

yes   that's what's wrong with them:
                    n o
                    d o u b t

watch out

            for the wailing Fundees
            & *their* "god"

their god grows out of the muzzle of a gun

Odyss   on the old plate
looked so comfortable in his body   old enough
to fit a few words together

bare twigs
        cracks in the sky
long lines short lines no lines

let us sit down & enjoy a really empty experience

            write what?   to a tree?

"dear chords of night: one is not rhymes
but civil fur   come to bliss late"

this creature called god
    left one no ma

boat sails into sun

west
    is left on the map

an endless warble of dreams

Was there a time when thou, too, wert an optimist,
Falling about in fits of pseudo-mystical glee?
Sho' nuff—when Goddess Utopia roared in mine head
& I refused to be of time & place . . . Well, I still do,
Still wince at epithets that smack of Church or Nation
& would prefer to be, not just *El Hombre*, but *El Animal
Invisible*—one of those invisible beasties of the Lapps . . .
A follower of Lingo Rapture: she is never opaque,
Turn as she may—Mother Discourse, ever transparent
Even when terrorized by vagaries of head & heart.
Sad, dignified as the winds on the moon
—minimalist intensity! Ah, well, the fire went west
& whims and winds took hat & head. Without
A head, no cigarette. Without a heart, big trouble.

remember Bear's Head who saw
         between midnight & dawn   1833
    ten thousand meteors
        cascade across the heavens
    from the constellation we call The Lion

remember Bear's Head who saw
    a comet in the sky
        between midnight & dawn   1858

remember Bear's Head who that same winter
    in dreamtime
        between midnight & dawn
saw canyon waters rise
        & flood the land
        & wash away his people   Arapaho
saw
    when the flood subsided
        only the white men remain

    remember him
who saw these things between midnight & dawn
    in this place   Boulder
        on this planet   Earth

all hail
    to Mother Mail

    3:30 p.m. the view is

Flatirons above trees &
neighbors across the street
in the window a rear end
of squirrel for half a nervous second
of its life (my life, your life) & that
does of course include
the front end too, my front end
is waiting for the mail
Great Mother Mistress MAIL
be praised: you bring the best, you bring
the worst, but "Lots of mail! I feel pretty
good!" said Ted in a poem, "I open
a beautiful letter from you. When
we are both dead, that letter will be
Part Two of this poem." Give us
our mail fix today & every day
oh I can remember when it came
twice a day, a dear old man
bending to pick it up off the mat
    after it shot
    through the slot
    in our apartment door
    in Helsinki, Finland
    in the early years
    of the millennium

"so what's the diff
between a hopeful sort who believes he'll go to 'Heaven'
& a hopeful sort who believes his descendants

will colonize the universe?"

    asked Tattered Old Bird
    minor warlock
    invisible when at the top of his form

& the tribes unfurl the old demon banners:
oh let the dark ages begin again   so we can join
our dimwit ancestors in gore & glory

    most of the populace blank
    resigned to the neo-feudal

Geronimo stern: "YOU FOOLS"

    God is a speckled snake

    cat turns mouse into mouse dust

"have a nice day"
        said Tattered Old Bird
"have a nice dog have a whole bunch of fine gods dogs & days
in view of the indignities that await us
that doesn't seem too much to wish for
on the way to the old *pulvis et umbra*   *il faut s'amuser, non?*"

    & the shades they are a-massing
    at the gates of ghostly Troy

ANSELM HOLLO

trying not to be
                pissed off because
                                the truck won't start
        (too cold)

I pick up a book
                peed upon
                        by long-dead cat
        in distant other life

        & see the stain's
                        still there—
        of the cat
                not a whiff

but find the poems
                of the late urban ironists
        still pungent & deeply
                        amusing
        so let the truck rust
        the book
                take me back
                                to streets once walked
        nights
                talked
        dusk to dawn
                        in the Eolian cities—

"borne
        deposited
                produced
                        eroded
                                by the wind"

think "son"   *walking through a geometry*
night's sleep gone   *in a gold & green light*
                                reading a sculptor's notes:

"we know you're in there"
locked inside   *to create latent motion*
crowded hippocampus world   *you set up something*
                                one would expect to move

of drums & demons   *but it doesn't*
distance   absence   *it remains*
                                in the same place & position

haunted years   *& it keeps doing that*
of wish & rage

                                as eye & mind
in mislaid brain   *repeat the event that does not occur*
& slaughtered time   *again & again*

so the ghoul weeps   *you might call it a raging balance*
he the ghoul
weeps so   *space*
for his son   *is mostly*
                                light

come out please come out
arise   *what's tactile*
take up they bed   rejoin   *reaches out   grabs*
whatever we might be   *the 8 corners*
outside this maze   *of the room   (Ivan Liljander)*

ANSELM HOLLO

in Heaven which was the darkest corner
of the tavern right next to Diogenes
we hung out over cappuccinos
& munched on tasty raw veggies

I told The Old Dog
people on earth had finally managed
to kick the nasty expensive habit
of raising & eating cows

Diog' said Pythagoras
would have liked to hear that
personally he said
being the first citizen of the world
I've never been one to proscribe anyone's habits

then we leaned back to listen to Gerry
Mulligan play "Waltzing Matilda"

& as delighted as I surely was
to hang out with my favorite Cynic
I was homesick for Earth
& wished you were there with us

(not worried at all
you wouldn't know how to deal
with The Old Dog
who wasn't really a misanthrope
merely defined
anthropos
very strictly)

then opened my eyes
to the light & your eyebrows
& the golden light of your eyes

for him her face
goes out of focus
before his does for her

so that when she's
in focus for him
quite adorably he

seems sadly distant
to her but they refuse
to be terrorized

by that or any
other contradiction

though but a weave of dust and shade
caught in the chandelle of our days

who writing shovels grief's doubloons
I can say this: hello! dear woman I name Dream

dear called *Because*
with you, a thousand years would not be long enough

Notes

Mihail Cosma—author of the poem titled *?* (1927): Romanian poet, b. 1902 in Tirgu-Onca, d. 1968 in Paris. Contributor to the avantgarde journals *75 HP, Punct, Discontinuité,* and others. From 1928 on, Cosma wrote and published his poetry in French, and also translated Tristan Tzara's Romanian *Primele Poeme* into French. These biographical details, and the poem, gleaned from Manfred Peter Hein's remarkable anthology *Auf der Karte Europas ein Fleck* (A Spot on the Map of Europe; Ammann Verlag, Zurich 1991), a treasury of poems written by members of the East European avantgarde between 1910 and 1930.

Worstward Ho—Samuel Beckett's prose poem (Grove Press, New York 1983). Should be recited at every presidential inauguration from now on.

"fights among capos"—capo: (Cosa Nostra) boss.

"Gore, not Peire"—"if novels and poems fail to interest the Agora today, by the year 2091 such artifacts will not exist at all except as objects of monkish interest. This is neither a good nor a bad thing. It is simply not a famous thing." (Gore Vidal, in *Screening History*, The New York Times Book Review 30 August 1992.) For Peire, see Paul Blackburn's wonderful *Proensa: An Anthology of Troubadour Poetry*, University of California Press 1978.

"Odyss   on the old plate"—in my late sister's copy of Gustav Schwab's *Die schönsten Sagen des klassischen Altertums* (The Most Beautiful Tales of Classical Antiquity), 1925 edition.

"watch out / for the wailing Fundees"—an ideological mega-gang that seems to be multiplying all over the globe. Its members are particularly fond of killing the *already born*, when and wherever they have reason to suspect that these are championing the cause of rational existence governed by the Golden Rule.

"one of those invisible beasties"—in the first novel written and published in the Saame (Lapp) language, author Johan Turi mentions the "invisible animals of Saameland."

"remember Bear's Head"—Bear's (or Bear) Head was a Southern Arapaho of the mid-19th century; see pp. 63-66 in: *Chief Left Hand, Southern Arapaho* by Margaret Coel, University of Oklahoma Press 1981.

"pulvis et umbra"—dust and shade (we are); "il faut s'amuser, non"—one must amuse oneself, no?

"said Ted in a poem"—*Today in Ann Arbor (for Jayne Nodland*, in *So Going Around Cities*, Blue Wind Press, Berkeley 1980).

"think 'son' / *walking through a geometry*"—the lines on the right, which may be read as more or less aleatory "*marginalia*" *or* heard and seen to resonate with the lines West, come from a page of aphorisms by the Swedish sculptor Ivan Liljander that I picked up in 1992 at a posthumous exhibition of his quietly radiant three-dimensional abstractions at the Thielska Galleriet in Stockholm.

"in Heaven which was the darkest corner"—see *Herakleitos and Diogenes* translated from the Greek by Guy Davenport, Grey Fox Press 1979.

"Gerry Mulligan's rendition of 'Waltzing Matilda'"—on *I Giganti del Jazz #49*, 1976.

"caught in the chandelle of our days"—chandelle: abrupt steep climb of airplane propelled by the plane's momentum.

BOB HOLMAN

THE COLLECT CALL OF THE WILD

Here it is, just where you said
It would be. Your mind is quiet
And your shows seem to be going
Somewhere. The road, the road, as was once
Said, or twice, is where we go on. Where

Everything is acceptable, the blame more
Than most. Gray hair, cigarettes, tightening
Pants. To be gored by age is not exactly sexy,
But it's not to be denied. Not anymore.
Not any less, either, as the sun earnestly plies

The window dressing. A vocabulary, not the secret
Of life, that's all. If it taxes your spirit,
Some kind of government must be flowering. Blood
Is one example, the example of constancy, readiness
and effulgence. Another is lit up like Reno, popped

Champagne and caviar on a paper plate. What does
Doesn't last, and what is lost will probably
Transform even if it's found. That's the problem,
That the idea of the thing won't stand still,
A doggie finding its spot. Which name *is* Spot!

Of course the pay phone rings in the crowded lunch
With no one caring the slightest for its emergency.
Too many crackers in the soup, the glass is greasy,
Yet we rest easy. It's the company, I'd guess. That we
Finally have accepted knowing each other this way, and that's
The way we find ourselves, little by little, by and large.

AS QUIETLY AS DISTANT

Under the century, under the text,
blood and shape outside a certain bar
where a casual cop discovers (urging from himself)
the singing beauty puzzle.
An actual town. The salty smell of a cry.
We smile at the century painted.
Desire in movement's place.

Memory shines on the face of the reader
heading down the chutes of disaster.
Memory lies in the margins of gardens,
outside its rhythm as language.

The monotone speech of disaster.
The rainy taste of the window
where memory falls to water.
In musty rooms, desire is a success.
The sun of heaven
deepens like a glacier.

The flexed muscle, the world,
the deepening rain transparent.
At the margin of disaster, she lives
in the movements of gardens but not in blood and place.
In the mother sense, memory yields
the hazards of a nightdress.

The nightdress is the said,
as if to suggest a similar world
where light bends over water.
At her least hesitation,
the memory of nameless gardens

where two boys play with a white mouse,
holding it like an egg.
Gulls sweep past what changes.

At the level of a cry,
the shining train desire.
Flesh is in the text,
the deepening rain transparent.
In blood and even this window,
desire is a telescope
where the reader of poems can be constructed,
field by field, like a painting.

Let it run in the margin of gardens.
She places her head in heaven.
The blunted hours. Memory's indifference.

Her painted shadows offer compensation
for the hazards of these ruins:
the moving landscape and waiting trains
at the far end of those gardens.
A fine rain falls beyond the beauty puzzle.

The memory has falls,
hazards within the fragments.
Urgent lovely strange,
but not the only whole.
At the far end of the new sense,
memory has its gardens
where, unlike light,
the history of her impressions
shines on the century painting.

SIGNS FOR THE 21ST CENTURY

THE PRESENT
STATE OF
THE WORLD
IS PERFECT

PLASTER
SIMULACRA'S
AUTHENTIC
GAZE.

THE CHILIAST

It looks as if I have survived. I now stand poolside. The steam is never clearer than at night. Every inch tamed. Ducks make a splash at 4 a.m., then punch their quacks in at the bill. Roots are squared in the room, lets no circulars in. Fleet lightning off the screen. There is a brown man in the garden dignifying paperish flowers with clippers; he is closed in his gloves.

White boys career and brutalize the outer atmosphere. I hear them and know who they are even when I can't see them. Their violence is a form of optimism. Nothing smells. The divine is the nothing that is something. Fringe fires in the electric-like lines. So as to be homeless and near to outer space, I left the city of my childhood for this desert institution. It's normal to want to be safe, but that wasn't why. Passed away, more, from that battlefield.

I like to tell men who beat up women and who shout at their children that even so, their victims are free. I know this is so because the line between the genitals and rage is always open, and always free. I saw some Muslim men rolled up in paper on the screen while their mothers cried, Such beautiful children! And here, a notice: Mr. Thigpen will serve you lunch today.

The plutonium is under the sink. Post-human actions approach the millennium with the extravagant stupidity of neo-animals. Then to sit holed up in a hotel that's called a Cathedral Without Wheels, is hell? Clip away at the telephone bill, I have no one to call. Don't talk fat in front of fat people, but diet tactfully in secret, I was told. Slab the ice-o-cados.

To cut through all the pain you have to have a beam from alcohol, or somesuch. Now there's something dull out there like the cost of concrete. I hear the thud for hours and can't manage a scream. I think tangerine: concept of veins, juice, and compartments inside dry skin. The narrative of fruit is libertarian. Food is free even when it has a price on it.

Who to kill? Who not to kill? These are the two questions that interest me, besides which way to rotate the children. Is this the world? Someone keeps talking about drywall, and all I can think of is the single word COUNT, as if to say that money won the war between numbers and words. Margins remain abundant, of course, like a hibiscus bush outside a sliding glass door.

Now I know something about purgatory. It's a cleansing through counting. Get those numbers off of me. Better to be the dancing people, the ones who drew neither numbers nor words. When I think of a person like a little midge out there in the atmosphere, well, I want to speak pidgin english and wander around with a spyglass and fan. Guess why. I lost a person, the person lost me, we missed each other, we never met again, it is the end of the century, and thirty years have passed. I have to give up, give in to the absolute NO. The pleasure of relativity is the way it speaks YES.

Why is the uncanny so much like sex? Why is sex so much like a scary story by a fire at night? From fear to genitals and back again is an open line. Top of form. Third day in a row I ran out of gin and magic. Magic? Medics. It's time to think the way the majority thinks. Be ambitious; it's nationalistic. I want to tell you why. My sex drive is like second person, the way a pile of fat can be to someone overweight. You know. Company. As a result I never really liked to let myself out of the house. It's time to change though. Look, I've had an incredibly good life. They didn't skimp, were generous with the details. My gratitude is what's obese here. And I have to inquire: is everybody here? more people alive than under the ground ever? are we all together now? is this the end?

ROGER KAMENETZ

SLEEPING IN AN EGG

The legend was like a tiny cup
it held one drop of precious liquor
sipped or evaporated, like a tear
that knew an eye and then was gone.

That tear was a river once, a cloud
even a spark. It was gas floating
in the bowels of a sun, light
murdered in a tree. A tear was shit once,
many times. Let's not speak of chemistry
or physics, or even the math of sorrow.
We heard these dull lessons long ago
sleeping in an egg in thunder
the blood rushing around with strands
from thigh to ovary to womb.

We heard the music the angels taught
and knew our privilege was round
and when we dropped, shaped
perfectly like a tear.

Egg in a cup, eye in a socket
the shape the mouth makes in slumber
when we have exhausted hope and fear:
oval, oval, oval, time will not be over
until all tears rise into one perfect egg.

GOODBYE

You ask me to say goodbye to the 20th
century, o k, goodbye, but
I want to say goodbye to the second millennium
even more, I want to say goodbye to Pope Innocent III
goodbye to Philip called (falsely) the Fair
goodbye to the Fugger Newsletter and the Belgian Congo
goodbye to Col. Younghusband and the Foreign Office
goodbye to Kant and goodbye to Calvin and Cromwell,

goodbye Doctor Morton thank you for anesthesia
goodbye Wagner thank you for Parsifal
goodbye good bye mein lieber Schwan
notre petite table Couple adieu
je vais voir l'ombre que tu deviens
goodbye Marie Antoinette I kiss the sweet nape of your poor neck
goodbye Citizen Bonaparte the mildew of St. Helena's gets into my
    eyes
goodbye Sadi-Carnot Kennedy Nasser the three Gandhis gunned
    down
goodbye John Borgia goodbye Freddie Fitzsimmons
goodbye Dorothy Sayers good bye Mary Butts with your sassy nose
    and scarlet hair
goodbye Quirinus Kühlmann whom the Russians burned at the stake
goodbye John Wilmot I believe your deathbed confession
goodbye Wilhelm Furtwängler goodbye Jussi Bjoerling
Christ I am tired of saying goodbye

let me say hello for a change

Hello hello Peter Samothrace:
you will rediscover Atlantis while rescuing sea-fowl from oil spills
hello Millicent Wonderby from South Island (NZ) who will revive
      all Bellini's heroines as good as Callas in stereo
hello Arno Gleb who will come to the throne of Mingrelia and
      restore the Mirsuvian culture of our common parents
hello Tiffany Shapiro who will create a mathematics without number
      based on pure linear relationships of shape alone
hello Istvan Adar who will decode the language of shadows
—all these beloveds are coming hello hello they're on their way
hello Boffo first cat who can speak Finnish
first of the new kind of animals who after watching our lips move for
      (in the case of cats) only a few thousand years have at length
      mastered human language
though like poets they're not sure of the meanings of what they
      pronounce

hello new sports of the third millennium
like listening out loud
and running your fingers over hologram projections till you blow the
      fuses
new sports like wave knitting (surfing on your fingers alone, the
      Kiribati islanders will teach us)
like Hoopsic, a combination of basketball and the string quartet (one
      player is silent and may never touch the ground)
like finishing operas left incomplete when the composer passed into
      Elysium

like competitions to see which team can milk the most stars
and the winning team gets to keep dawn in its city hall all year

hello the Swiss Revolution hello the return of the Ottoman Empire
    this time run as a department of Juilliard
hello the Two Sicilies and the Three Italies
(north, south, and Leopardi-in-Exile)

hello new money new fruit from tropic isles, hello new diseases and
    preposterous unfathomable therapies
that work no better than what we have now

now I'm tired of saying hello.

AN AGENDA FOR RENEWAL

I.

A failure of nerve cannot be tolerated, said the Commissar, we have suffered and we have no right to do so. There is a lack of earnestness, a lack of belief, *we* have to rise to the challenge, for whom else can you trust to bring about change?

As we know, any problem can be solved in four steps. First, we must ask: what is the problem? The situation is obvious; our confidence must be restored, we need a vision, we have to choose one, multilaterally and holistically. Second, we must ask: what are the causes of the problem? The question is not of causes, we must respond proactively, move beyond these steps to the real issue: that of trust, in a caring society, while waiting for the horrible end ahead, we are talking about change. Third, we must ask: what are the possible solutions? This we must bring to the table, we must discuss, for the century is almost ripe, we have lost our talent for sleepwalking, our agenda is clear, let us not lose sight of it, we have no doubts and we would be lost without them.

Fourth, we must ask: what is the best solution? The solution is evident: education, for we understand too little, and thus we must stop listening.

2.

A new attitude is required, said the Commissar, this is a new era, to be approached with penitence and sincerity; only then can we understand the objective reality around us, and only then can there be learning.

For a good education is about questions, not answers—and all questions can be discarded when doubts are removed and gravity is restored, thus completing our task.

3.

She was taught, with the best of materials and intentions. We sacrificed all that we had to improve her understanding of our vision, and there was no change.

Why did we fail?

We have reason to believe that she did not understand her role, that of a *customer*. Her failure was the failure of the system; no requirements had been generated, no product manufactured.

Was our suffering not enough?

A judgement is due, an accounting; the budget no longer balances and the ledgers are blind.

JUSTIN'S CAT

First of all, the voice is always better in the bathroom, and I'm awake, blaming the railroad like prayer: *Give us this day your daily genitals.* The worms eating me crawl down from dear dad's legs to do it, each word a pin of paper tied to it. "Makes me want to shit in my underwear here in the bellies and throats of the cannibals don't even know God's English; need the death penalty; where's the crematoria, the bomb, when you need them most?" Off killing ducks and school children, practicing their bullets: "You'll be a father soon and have the Divine Right to invent new uses for box cars. There's nothing more satisfying than watching something you've killed, die." "Human sewer, sly and lazy, they'll eat their mother's brains right out of her head; there she is, squatting down to take her yearly crap on her youngest, born dog-like into what used to be a pretty decent alley; worth millions; investors coming from their heartburn to bid on it."

Sixteenth Street, walking down from the comic book store, the old guys talking Pound, okay to be a Nazi if you're a genius; afterall, it ruined his career; and Céline, grousing in his vegetables; Guerrero, cops with flashlights walking down both sides of the street, looking for a baseball bat, four hispanic youths on their knees, cuffed, facing a garage door: "Random; just beat the guy in the head":

nothing to do with the neo-Nazi snake handlers wake up one morning they're Chinese, Turk, Black, their girlfriends unbutton their twats, take them off the menu.

God is a dimwit, the youngest of four stillborn births before him. It's in the papers everyday for the last thousand years, and before that, you ride the tractor back far enough, catch yourself a louse-eating beggar been shaped to his calling by his mom and dad: "It was good for business twist his legs up like that, chop off that arm; what's he need two

for, anyway? Put him on the unemployment is all; this way, he's got a
profession"; both pickled in the stomachs of what ate them, their ever-
lasting in a meadow, throwing his seed up a sheep's ass; same story,
same prayer: *God the pisspot, the hemorrhoid, the cancer for brains:*

There had been a boat, but it caught fire as well as the tree it was
tethered to, all burned to kingdom come, all dead and gone, the
mullioned windows, the vertical spars, the weeds and grime that had
snugged it, had nursed from it, plants, its wood having sunk so
deeply into the ground it had sprouted, leaved, flowered, and vines,
and creeping things, and birds, and rats that leaped straight up into
the air, or tunnelled, fitting into holes smaller than themselves
because their chest bones closed together into one small cage, so
hard to catch, but caught, scalded the hands that tore them, and bit
the sticks that beat them, their innards steamy in caps, all savory; it
was the Lord's blessing afterall; it was fleas, beetles, the creatures
alive in the wood that crackled and spit and put out an eye or two,
the wood softened only while burning; good riddance, the boat was a
distraction and had only earned everyone near it misery; where was
the sea it sailed? and how many, standing in the dirt near it, pissing at
it until their bladders flattened, could make it float? It was Noah's
boat and good for nothing, the pilgrims who came, beat and robbed
those who lived near it, and stole their rags, sleeve by sleeve, and
their hair and teeth, and kicked and punished them until their bums
bled and their voices gagged, and every hen and pig was given back
to them as dung. That it burned at first frightened them, the fire
leaping everywhere, and their faces blackened, and the soles of their
feet welted so badly they had to crawl because they could not stand
or walk, and none of them had enough spit to heal the wounds that
covered their bodies; they believed it was judgment, and they were
lost forever, and wept, and cried for mercy. Ashes fell; it was night; it
was day; good riddance.

Except for the dimwit because the boat is where he had taken his sex, the photographs of clothes and mouths and adolescence he sequenced, lying each separately and slowly against his nipples, then his knees and throat, before lining them out on the boat's curled wooden planking, parts of the photographs thrust up, parts cast down in shadow. Slowly, each photograph taken from the grip of the cheeks of his ass where he hid them although there had been threats of invasion from his aunt and those she called her kinsmen, contentious beggars who travelled with dwarfs they kept roped together and displayed for money, at fairs, at public executions, sometimes at crossroads, bullying the dwarfs into the ditch below the gallow's tree, then mounting it and driving off the crows and other carrion birds, and calling to the travellers and everyone who could hear their voices, to come close and see what death birthed, what size flesh the soul wore when it crawled back to life from the horror of its terrible voyage. Sometimes they draped rag walls down from the gallow's tree and pegged them out in the shape of a tented room, and stripped the dwarfs, and mated them, that audience paying more than the first, the males' genitals causing each observer, surreptitiously, to reach down inside his clothes to finger what was skimpy and shrivelled by comparison. No offspring happened and the kinsmen, if they were not robbed and beaten first, sold the dwarfs as pets to the rulers of the various kingdoms they travelled through, listening always for gossip of new births; the village, hamlet, hut; and heighing there:

for it was God's cursed long black fingernails, first killing the shade trees, then breaking through the roof beams to pierce the hearts and crotches of his tiny self-portraits, making visible to all the condition of their souls in the afflicted shape of their offspring. When dwarfs were declared merely secular and found jobs in aircraft factories, crawling through the narrow places in wing structures, the kinsmen discovered the earth was round, there were new worlds, and they hacked and mutilated their way through them until where they stood was poverty, violence; in technicolor; familiar, and harmonious.

The flat earth lies like a flake of skin on the surface of heaven's vast sea, and god, at whim, can lift it up to His eye or nose, or crawl above it on all fours, His face inches from its dirt, moving His head, His shoulder, watching the shadow move, change shape as He moves. He tries to claw it up off the ground, sometimes digging holes around it or into it, imagining the rest of it, its bulk and roundness, is in the dirt and can move through that material as He moves through the air. His aunt, her foot clubbed from spinning, kicks Him. It tires her; she is permanently injured from doing it, her knee bent so that she walks awkwardly, her hips and shoulders severly canted.

Her penis, which he has watched bristle straight up from her groin to her chin, and waver in the air until she puts both hands on it, thrusting it through rag shelters, thatched or timbered or mud-made walls, lifting squealing, fleeing men, women, children up, impaling them, bloodied and torn clothing falling around her, fascinates him, squatted like a bunion, no part of him moving, until she has dislocated the penis, a bronze noose around its head tied to a braided leather thong and held by her hand so that it hangs down her back like a long red sausage. He imagines eating it, his legs and arms growing as long and dangerous as it is, and ever after, anything he chases, he catches, his belly contented and solid as a hill.

His aunt is lycanthropic and, when she isn't menacing doorways as the chalk-white eyelid of bacterial death, she is out in some part of the landscape tearing the throats out of swans and stags and he-goats with her sharp wolf teeth. The penis is as long as a prophet's staff, longer, in fact, than his spine, and he carries it down his pant leg and up under his arm, tight against his side, trembling at the thought of what his aunt will do to him when she catches him. His teeth can't break the flesh of the head or shaft and he walks stiff-legged, looking for a sharp stick to cut it with or a fat stick to flatten and soften it enough he can bite into it.

His shadow lies on the ground ahead of him, lengthening, and by some miracle of cloud and wind he remembers who He is, and in a redundant act, falls to the ground, breaks his chest open, and molds the penis to the bone cage from which it has been wrongly said he pulled the first woman:

"No," he corrects, pillowed in the dirt, his chest swollen straight up like a wall in front of his eyes, "it was not her that day; it was instead a small propane cook stove and a nice fat hen for Adam and at the time seemed appropriate that two things so useful to him should come from him. The woman was made earlier, and was meant to be a friend and companion for the angels. But they bored her and she catharted her ensuing depression into an eating disorder and ate the palm trees near the backyard fence, and standing on her toes, began eating the thatch from the house I'd made for the sooty fat spiders that jump down my arm whenever I scratch my head. It was out of fear she'd eat them too that I shit the clay I molded Adam from. They were both mistakes and I had to change the locks, invent the calendar, and send them both off toward the creation of history."

Which is the photocopied, handwritten pages the homeless man leaves in stacks on the counters of businesses in the Mission. He is an old testament prophet in denim and rags, the first letter monks illuminated into their manuscript pages, working in trance, having first flagellated themselves until they bled into the leather pots hooked by barbs to their skins, catching the blood, later, carefully, emptying it into tiny silver thimbles, each incised with the names of all God's angels. The beeswax has come unsealed and the man with surgical gauze wrapped around each of his hands is Mary's menses wrung from cloth to holy those touching it exploded into fiery pins of light that were immediately sucked from the air into the bellies of insects where they are now and will be forever.

Through the translucent, moth frail skin raised up before his face, the dimwit saw his aunt crouched on the limb of a tree, eating sweet potatoes. He howled and kicked his heels into the dirt under his feet and moved himself around and around in a circle, like a pinwheel, boaring a hole straight up the cannibal ass of the sentient corporate structure. His aunt pushed the branches in front of her aside and knew she would have to tear her nephew into pieces the size of small green frogs to shut him up, and leaped down from the tree through the mosquito netting time on to the roof of a Ford Fairlane in the China Basin. There were saints and holy men everywhere, and some of them had strong white teeth, and some of them masturbated openly while calling on Jesus to kiss them. Their irradiated blood glowed in the veins in their faces.

The aunt's lungs were in threads and she ate candy wrappers, road soot, and copper wire she pulled from the housings at the base of traffic lights. Her body was filled with memory; it guttered and sloshed and had my full attention.

FIN DE SIECLE BLUES

I.
At seventeen I'm forced to write a paper
on "My Philosophy": unconscious Emersonian
clone, courtesy of my Father,
"There is no evil," that's what I say,
"merely the absence of good." I read the papers.
Where was my head? (In the clouds, like Father
and the senior William James.) I must have known
some of the bad news. No evil, eh?
Ho, Ho, Ho, Holocaust! Tell it to the Jews.

I had a great interest in architecture
in my late teens. Still do.
I wrote another paper, worrying
About the fate of historic monuments,
Art, not people, during World War II.
Give me that tired query from Ethics 101
concerning the old lady and a Rembrandt etching
in a sinking row-boat; which one would I save?
Now that I *am* one, still I have serious doubts
about saving the old lady.
Rembrandt would have won.
And if they could have been crammed into the row-boat
so would the French cathedrals and the Parthenon.
(There was some kind of screaming aesthete
Naked within my transparent ethical over-coat.)

But now, take Sarajevo: Old ladies, buildings,
children, art all perish together
along with honor and philosophy;

the hypothetical row-boat long since sunk
in the polluted Mediterranean sea.
The century suffers entropy—and so do I.

2.
Well, it's been one hell of a century:
Endless list of victims, Armenians, Jews,
Gypsies, Russians, Vietnamese,
the Bosnians, the Somalians,
torture and rape of dissidents all over
the map; and as Time winds down
the music slows,
grows scratchier, plays off-key,
America chimes in with its own obbligatos:
what we did to the Nicaraguans, the Salvadorians,
diminuendos with Granadans, Panamanians—
and we're still hassling poor old Castro.

Whole continents go on living under tyrannies
till tyrannies give way
to chaos and criminality.
Is it the horror, or that we know
about the horror?—this evening's blood
on the screen.
Yugoslavia, before our eyes, is Balkanized
to death; but today, brave us,
today we recognized Macedonia.
(Vasco is dead, thank God,
and how are you faring, dear Bogomil?)

And we have AIDS...

(Maurice, Tom, Tony, Gordon, Jim,
bitterly I mourn you
and wait for the next beloved name.)
The redneck Senators who would starve the arts
are a less efficient scourge.
We who are merely witnesses
to all this grief
also pay a price.
NOT AN ORIGINAL THOUGHT
(that's part of the price).

Horror numbs.
Violence, whether fictional or true,
is socially addictive.
NOT AN ORIGINAL THOUGHT.
Serious satire undermined
by sexual and political
grotesquerie.
NOT AN ORIGINAL THOUGHT.
So why go on? I'm blue. Boo-hoo.
Got those End-of the-Century Blues.

3.
Now to personalize and trivialize the topic,
As writers, what are we to do?
We gag on scandal, our lives are gossip-fodder.
In our marginal way, we are becoming stars.
Never mind the work. Who cares for that?
Did the man who re-invented the sonnet
urinate in his bed one night, when drunk?
Did our great fat nature poet

throw up in his hat?
Forget the revolution they created
with their raw confessional poetry;
it's the suicides of two women
which fascinate,
not their way of working
but their way of death.

O you serious men and women
who wrote your poems, met your classes,
counseled your students, kept your friends
and sent magic letters home,
your lives are pillaged and re-arranged
by avid biographers who boast that they tell all,
so it seems you always reeled in a mad whirl
of alcohol, abandonment and sexual betrayal.
(I sorrow for the stain on your memory,
Anne, Randall, Ted, Elizabeth,
Delmore, John and Cal.)

As living writers, what are we to do?
Our roles as witnesses ignored,
our fine antennae blunted
by horror piled on horror,
our private matters open
to the scrutiny of voyeurs.
If we have wit and learning
it's met with the apathy
of the ever-more-ignorant young.
How do we hope to carry on
in the last gasp of this millennium?

Much as we always have: writing for one another,
for the friends we tried to impress in school
(like Tonio Krüger), for the dead father or mother,
for our first mentor, compassionate and cool,
for the dead authors who watch over us.
We'll write when bored in strange hotel rooms,
we'll write when the conscience pricks,
we'll write from passion, present or reviving,
making copy of our pains or perverse kicks.
We'll write if a cookie dipped in tea
transports us to the fields of memory.

But first of all we'll do it for ourselves,
selfish and narcissistic and obsessed as ever,
invading the privacy of those who care for us,
spilling sad secrets confided by a lover.
We take note of the café where Valéry took notes,
Van Gogh's yellow chair, the monastery
where Murasaki wrote, as Petrarch did,
in a room eight feet by three;
Name-and-place dropping, grooming our fur,
Fanning and shaking our peacock tails
(dry sticks rattling in the wind),
always, always ourselves our own mirrors.

The burden of our song: good luck to the young!
Let's drink (for we drink) to a better world
for them, if they should live so long.
As my Father, the optimist, liked to say,
"It's the unexpected that happens."
There is little point in being fatalistic.
Whatever occurs will be different

from what we anticipate,
which—to be frank—is universal doom.

Everyone who reads this is older than Mozart,
than Masaccio, than Keats, much older than Chatterton.
We're taller, handsomer, healthier than they.
So let's just count these years we've lived as velvet
as Carver said at the end—sweet Ray.
I'm blessed by parents, children, husband, friends
for now. . . Nothing can take that away.
NOT AN ORIGINAL THOUGHT:
Call up Voltaire. Tend the garden.
Seize the day.

STILL LIFE

For an hour he's been pacing back & forth
between the double-latched front door
& living room,
insisting that he has to leave,
that Gertie's waiting downstairs
with the car.
Patiently, my mother tries to coax him
back into his chair—then suddenly
explodes: *Mickey, please!*
You're driving me insane!
take your jacket off & just sit down!
Your sister has been dead for thirty years—
& then starts sobbing
uncontrollably.
Contrite, all that belligerence
knocked out of him,
he sits down on the couch to comfort her.
All right, he says, I won't go anywhere.
So there they sit—together,
holding hands. It's night.
Beyond the spathiphyllum at the window,
with its single flower,
downtown Philly's skyline, etched in light,
somewhere near the end of the millennium.

REHEARSING FOR THE FINAL RECKONING IN BOSTON

During the Berlioz *Requiem* in Symphony Hall
which takes even longer than extra innings
in big league baseball, this restless Jewish agnostic
waits to be pounced on, jarred by the massed fanfare
of trombones and trumpets assembling now in the second
balcony, left side, right side, and at the rear.

Behind them, pagan gods in their niches
acoustically oversee this most Christian
of orchestrations: the resting Satyr
of Praxiteles, faun with infant Bacchus,
Apollo Belvedere, Athena, Diana
of Versailles with early greyhound.

When the wild mélange cries out
Dies irae, all of our bared hearts pulse
under Ozawa's baton. He is lithe as a cat
nimble as Nureyev, another expatriate.
But even Ozawa dressed in white sweats
cannot save us up here in peanut heaven, or save

patrons downstairs in the best seats canted back
for the view, who wear the rapt faces of the fifties
tilted to absorb the movie on the 3-D screen.
Naught shall remain unavenged, sings the chorus.
*What trembling there shall be when we rise again
to answer at the throne.* That's all of us

since Adam, standing on one another's shoulders

three or four deep, I should imagine,
acrobats of the final reckoning.
And what terror awaits those among us
whose moral priorities are unattached
to Yahweh, Allah, Buddha, Christ:

forgiving without praying for forgiveness,
the doing unto others, scrubbing toilets,
curbing lust, not taking luck for granted?
Are the doubters reckoned up or just passed over?
Hector was almost passed over, his *Requiem*
unplayed, save for a general killed in battle . . .

How should one dress for the Day of Judgement?
At a working rehearsal the chorus is motley,
a newborn *fin de siècle* in t-shirts and jeans.
But what will they wear when the statues have crumbled
in 2094? Brasses and massive tympani close
the *Lacrymosa*. Metallic spittle is hot in my throat.

Now we enter the key of G major, the Lamb
of God key of catharsis and resolution.
Like a Janus head looking backward and forward
pockmarked by doubt I slip between cymbals
to the other side of the century where our children's
children's children ride out on the ranting brasses.

AFTER THE POETRY READING
for Marie Howe

If Emily Dickinson lived in the 1990's
and let herself have sex appeal
she'd grow her hair wild and electric
down to her buttocks, you said. She'd wear
magenta tights, black ankle socks
and tiny pointed paddock boots.

Intrigued, I saw how Emily'd
master Microsoft, how she'd
fax the versicles that Higginson
advised her not to print to MS.
APR and Thirteenth Moon.

She'd read aloud at benefits
address the weavers' guild
the garden club, the anarchists
Catholics for free choice
welfare moms, the Wouldbegoods
and the Temple Sinai sisterhood.

Thinking the same thing, silent
we see Emily flamboyant.
Her words for the century to come
are pithy, oxymoronic.
Her fly buzzes me all the way home.

ALEX KUO

CHANGING LEADS

> *What is lost is lost.*
>   Ignacy Paderewski

I.

It's strange when I stop and think about it
How it all started on a Steinway
When I was seven and you
You probably weren't yet born

How I didn't wish it, but flopped my hair down
Two hours daily, Sundays and summer
Accelerating the red-and-white Thompsons
Until I could play the originals
Like that older girl up the street in #5

It was not a question of a virtuoso's hand
Not even the music, but the regimentation
Drills, exercises, preparations, value control
The squall of the Immaculate Conception
Sister's metronome and ruler while I sucked

Back the bile and shakes. Some firsts
In easy school competitions, like all children
At that age whose parents kept proud silence

It was probably the only Steinway console in Asia
Before you were born, destined
For Madame Chiang, but displaced over the Hump
You know what must have happened next

Just as I did, perhaps too much later
Such early tidiness, such obsession
For all the correct notes
As if someone was always listening outside
The apartment door for that slipped quaver
Dropped note or cheated third

2.

When I went away to school I stopped
Playing, and for 27 years
Stayed away from any keyboard
And paid no particular attention to any music

Though I knew by this time you were born
And had your own troubles to negotiate
There was Sandy Bull, Richie Havens
Peggy Lee always there, but
Somewhere for each of us
There was something displaced that language
Could not represent or interpret

So 27 years later I took lessons again
First it was Bach's *Toccata and Fugue in* C
Which I played at my son's wedding
After that disaster, it was the *Goldberg Variations*
Insisting on playing every one of its 30 masks
To a jury less than half my age

And now it's Beethoven's Opus 111, his last
Without a teacher, free at last
To bear knowing what I don't know

Maybe a last chance to risk it

3.
As if you did not know too when you heard it

What did you want from me anyway?

We are beginning to tell each other
What we already know, damn it

Is it the silence that we keep
Locked away as weapons
From our children? Like

Our parents, are we maiming each other
With our own language that we use
To say so very little to our children?

What is it that we want from each other?
What was it? What was it?
How much longer can we keep on
Saying, *Goodbye*, *Goodbye*?

SUDDENLY!

The same   Moon   in the next century!

ART LANGE

SEVEN HAIKUS
IN ADVANCE OF THE NEW CENTURY

Cold Chicago white
covering all sound prompts dream
notion, slow motion

ghosts drift through those now
distant events word-frozen
as history or

hidden by horror
the mask of pain survivors
wear, will not, cannot

face as truth, simple
sins of intolerance, greed,
too late to escape,

seek absolution
for a century's debris
of hubris; Dante,

Donne, Bunting, others
warned of civilization
as a single soul,

burning, worse, turning
from a future of light to
footprints in pure snow.

BLUES FOR THE EVIL EMPIRE
(with a line by Unamuno)

Consider the late *Eurasian entity*, how it lumbered
into the groggy arms of history where it was

buried. Which is more than you can say
for Lenin's body, chilly like a mammoth in an ice

floe, if less hairy. An old man in the square
asks "Who is laughing at us?" then drifts unevenly

away. The czar's nephew comes alive
in Finland like some cyborg, sent into the future

with a mission to annoy; there are the plagues:
evangelists, economists, and experts

of all kinds, Americans who read the future
in a glass of tea, and analyze "the Slavic mind."

At home, cold warriors, like dying jellyfish,
grow dim. Why no joy in Washington, no dancing

in the streets—we "won"; but sleep uneasy
in our victory. The evil empire, vanquished, seeks

a plusher berth within—a red and rising sun?
A few blocks from the White House, my city twists

and keens, and someone's child is bought and sold.
—We do not die of darkness, but of the cold.

AMERICAN POETS SAY GOODBYE
TO THE TWENTIETH CENTURY

I.

And the Vatican embraced the robins' corrosive contingent
imprecations.

Cyclical mystery pinup-honeys people lost
whet fastenings.

The frogs' singularly thoughtless little girl had a lovely
sable cloak.

Boys' gravity fields,
too glowworm-academic,
coal-barge-
paralyzed
discovery.

Tappan Zee Local.

The accidental tourist through feelies models the Balkan state,
switches the aurora borealis,
akin to thirty chanters,
immediately out to sea.

McNuggets on the right kind of causes tense tones'
mortuary encrustations.

Nectar some way off,

alarmists imitate the others,
either
crepuscular robber barons
where they claim knowledge of what it's about
or
mystics with clerical data and borax sonar-tangent
planning gats.

Corresponding to the least distant years' executions,
satellites labor with remainders of
your manly conduct.

Glowworms do not let that cross sort o' collie . . .

Feeder phlebitis energy flux fortune the Soviet Union toads:
tortillas ghost clerical data too.

Swept clean,
ocean surfaces' feints invite observers' scholia.

Galante.

The beautiful.

Neither the wherewithal nor the subdominant colon:
ceasefire.

A senator's laptop hiatus,
temporary and very clever,
improves tree-putters:
everyone's fascination.

2.

Affiliate with the improved tree-putter:
everyone waves it around.

I don't care a straw about orchidaceous wall-clinic photography.

No taking gleefully writing autobiography
or crab scraps!

Stygian sapient hey giblet!

Solomon chortles.

Feeder seep-beeper guilty gangster telepathy.

Colossus the chortle the aurora borealis tailor-made swirl,
feelie-model thinking makes it so,
admit it—
—leave it here.

Tipsiness:
sacerdotal philosophers' stony allotment:
carousal's tentpole:
dunces' tactical inclusion.

Matterhorn whiskey priest.

Actaeon employ yourself in embroidering.

Cheerios quarks passion flowers.

Regency.

Nice place to go to.

State Senate Primary.

The Palisades' local gleaming quarrels beat focusing
on sumps' hanky-panky or
anything else—
—glee-club monotony,
cross sorts o' collies,
CANDEGO bran bread,
plenty o' notable teeming—
—how it surfaces!

Take chloroform.

Openly ambition tocks twelve-knit.

The accidental gesture plenty agin the Self,
that greening
whiffletree.

Contempt's plant-pathology critiques
support currency.

Sun feathers speculate and borax fantasizes.

Anna.

Amagansett.

3.

A long way off:
ammonia;
—everyone correctly fissions mosaic sappy-paper.

Nervousness,
pinup-honey movement,
the continuous technique,
banister appendectomies,
seacode magic.

Stygian gist songs ferry about the fireworks.

Rhode Island metabolizes the Crystal Palace in the sea hare
two feet long.

Poll tax token-oppository.

The beautiful,
the great clock too,
two feet long,
prefer,
when you get to robots,
ambitious texture.

Forestation armed with catalpa,
mescalinear pinup honeys out to sea,
fortune's duller,
raunchy,
and very clever.

Employ yourself in embroidering the Balkan states
and,
religious to click,
stockcroakers' sappy papers.

I cried on Peachtree Street—

corrosive the vibrations of
pasture rapeseed!

Sheila's rattletrap:
anything'll come,
galactic journalist.

Rhode Island the disintegral.

Itsy-itsy plenty returned to look after her
through bowls,
tone rows,
the Alaska salmon—
there is no other way to go.

Oh twice twenty-five kisses to the Budapest Quartet!

Planning gats
—whittle-leaf-tenacious the race—
kiss a potentate.

Telegraphy . . .
came out on the development trail,
beneficial,
fastened in your eyes
dapper ashtrays!

All
—immediately—
Cheerios characters.

Gallipoli's tactical penoplain-reaction polemic,

                                        a one-billion-
                                           year-old
                                           stain,
whets laptop-calisthenic salamanders' paratactic phylogeny,
      graphemic distortions' local scoop.

4.
Alamo-immense events,
                  ovarian enclitic particles,
               regional mountains' phytoplastic mosques.

      Openly ambitious texture.

                              Palisades search for calisthenics.

            Boy,
      go to the marsh the dormant flowers render durable.

      He doesn't only imitate the others either!
                              Daphne escalation.

            Trianon cove to click a chimney.

The Budapest Quartet trashed a vasty swirl the chintzy events,
                  matching,
            challenged.

                        Sweetmeat:
                              —the great clock.

            Neither the wherewithal nor the subdominant

claimant's neater.

Venus whither fixture the northern lights.

I am only grateful,
armed with imprecations the robins' quirt-territory embraces.

Rorschach children,
                    paternity costal:
                the least bottoms.

                                        What's living?

            Straw hats,
                    maculate,
            if you give glass motors,
                    humming.

                                He only imitates the other,
                the disintegration of Chilblains.

                                    Guilty in your eyes,
            they are a cowardly folk Lorca ticketed.

Chrism energy flux.

            Timorese awoke.
                    Frenchify,
                kin to roisterers,
            ambition more electrically charged than a whiffletree.

        Rorschach challenged necessarily punctured balloons,
                ashtrays,

and the influx of a key strategist and very clever affiliate,
who imitated the others and everything else—
in whirligig
fascination.

The arctic region's rotogravure reaction—
ptomaine!—
rocks freedom of expression as spittle focuses sappy papers
matching challenge grants
—hey,
giblet?

Solomon's shoes laced laudatory itsy-bitsy whinny
allowances
out to sea.

Tepid your fate is sealed:
texture thirty chanters.

5.

The Alamo smiles.

Ezekiel courts clerical enforcement immediately.

A Volscian.

Palladian complex crustal models,
freedom of expression past their tails,
crimsoning senators' false forms of morality,
phylogeny,
graphemic distortionment,

honesty . . .

A frog's road narrows.

Azerbaijan is likely to seep as beepers tree putters.

To José,
head-on smashes cheapen the shape of everything.

This territory swirls with clerical data?

Openly ambition admits it leaves her the wherewithal:
northern lights.

Machines focus assignation.

Neither the wherewithal northern lights comb,
Mesopotamian tinctures certain to know Peanuts,
the aurora borealis
(largely autocracy's amateur emergencies),
alarm clocks' mystic alarm-clock clamor,
nor attar anachronisms
peck a clementine.

Forestation's cheap
fornicator thithers.

That's the age to . . .

Sapodilla salamander.

Hey,

gleaming quarrels:
colostomy!

Sforzando pond opals:
bran-bread dog days.

Risible Trianon.

Rosamund was two feet long,
the keel thirty.

Twelve chanters knit the map.

Munster's nemesis tailored its stance.

Is no McNugget
noteworthy?

Charlie Parker's republic tensed fixtures
(Hot Peanuts).

The North Pole's gravity fields atonic emissaries,
when Tampa's vibrant
(an alien emotion).

Particles' bitter appendectomies.

Phylogeny posthaste!

More electrically charged,
the U.S.
lists
schismatics:

San Antonio,
Capistrano,
amylation,
generation . . .

José chortles as academicism scumbles beauty
risible.

Trianon moguls provide.

They hold fornication cheap.

The map switches.

Speculate on magnetism's ghostie,
Rachlin.

The State Senate Primary's inessential,
philosophical
cokehead!

Self-alienation candegoes newts if you give them bran bread.

A raunchy anachronism,
His Eminence is a cheap fornicator.

In emergencies
clerical data click to telegraphic sanctions.

A poor set of fellows,
—more assertive than they were supposed to be.

The Budapest Quartet's fifteen-pound snail,
space,
some sorts of sapodilla,
a talisman,
or anything else.

Gallipoli.

A poor set of fellows photocopies
Rhodesia's mutability,
grassy as a . . .

Whistle-stop transactions toast tortillas' rhapsodic freedom of
expression.

To head-on smashes two feet long
we prefer
raunchy Ascot adoptions.

Seeping beeper-escapists
didn't bother to plan for
canned Alaskan fishermen.

I fear the sanctions of fortune
(Jessup's murmuration).

Derived from "Forties 20 - 30," eleven "intuitive" 40-line poems by JML (7/8/91–10/10/91), with the intermediate aid of three programs, GEN (John Unger), TRAVESTY (Hugh Kenner and Joseph O'Rourke), and DIASTEX4 (Charles O. Hartman's automation of one of JML's diastic text-selection procedures developed in 1963), using as seed string "American Poets Say Goodbye to the Twentieth Century," and by extensive editing of the latter's output.

THE FOAM

IT IS BRAVE TO BE THE FOAM
and sing the foam

IT IS BRAVE TO BE THE FOAM,

not really!

Inside is no place but an infinitude
of places
—positions
becoming everything
in there.
THIS
is
THE FOAM!

LIFE-LIKE STARS,
they too are the foam.

The deer antler fallen on the grass within the yard
is foam
as is the dew that mottles it.

Thousand foot deep clouds of one-celled beings
with shells of silicon and waving pseudopods
in oceans in another time and place
are foam
as are the uplifted peaks of shale they leave behind.
The visions of William Blake in future caves of thought
that are meat and plastic-steel are foam,
—as are Whitehead's luminous dreams
—all foam!

MICHAEL McCLURE

Matter, antimatter, Forces, particles, clods of mud,
    the wind that blows in cypress trees, pools of oil
        on desert floors

    THE BOY'S EYES NO LONGER SQUINT, LOOK DOWN,
                                      (photo)
        and there is nothing in his hand
          nothing in his hand that's everything

      and he stares through squeezed caves
          of blackness
                at a man's eyes
    that shape a photograph of him
        upon the fields of war and of appetite

for iridescent foam of nacre-red and green and

      MORTAR
      THUD

    on beaches on a wave-lapped shore

   WHERE HIS MOTHER/FATHER SCREAM AND SHOUT
   and throw each other on the floor

     and

     HE

     HAS
    ! ARISEN !

    ebullient
    from this exuberance

and wears this red Y upon his woolen chest
          for it is his
            —as is the future state.

         THIS IS NOT METAPHOR
              but fact:
the green fir forest just beyond the sleek
and glossy plastic edge; shrews, in their hunt
for crickets, hiding in moon shadows
underneath a rusting ford. Blue-black waves
     beat on hulls of ferries. Light moves
       from one place, or condition, to another!

HE'S THERE NOW AND EVERYWHERE

_____

HE'S THERE NOW AND EVERYWHERE

       as are the covers of detective magazines
          with evil scientists who scalpel-out
          the hearts of large-bosomed virgins
            strapped to beds, then implant
          the pump of chrome that sits upon
            the operating table;
       as is the broken toothpick lying
          in the rain; as are the

       HUGE

       HUGE

HUGE

PASSIONS THAT HE FEELS

(shaking in his boy's legs and cock)

    —And those are the stuff of stars
   that are the flesh of passions that he spins
   into this rush of neurons and of popping foam.

   These make immortal perfect shapes of the moments
    that hold copper-colored leaves or twigs within their hands,
with each foot upon a war and each arm
and every thought in one.

AN ANIMAL IS A MIND!

—A MIND—AND DOES NOT KNOW WHERE IT STOPS!

—Knows little of bounds or limits or edges.

—Goes on into all times and directions and dimensions.

—KNOWING ONLY THROUGH LIMITS THAT CAN NOT BE KNOWN!

—IS A BEING OF SHEER SPIRIT!

—IS A BEING OF SHEER SPIRIT!

—IS A BEING OF BOUNDLESS MEAT!

—IS EVERYTHING IN ONE DOT OF THE CONFLAGRATION

IS EVERYTHING IN ONE BARE DOT

EVERYTHING IN ONE BARE DOT OF THE CONFLAGRATION!!

This is war that he is, and melts in

AND
IT

IS
NOT

FOAM.

HE

IS

A

BE-
ING

AND IT IS NOT WAR,
HE IS A MAN
!   !

HE IS AN ANIMAL BEING
A
MIND

HE IS AN ANIMAL BEING
A
MIND

through the windows of his
    fingers and his eyes

THREE POEMS CELEBRATING THE
END OF THE TWENTIETH CENTURY
(form>content>text>entrance>reader>critic)

Poem #1

Poem #2

Poem #3

HORSE SAYS GOOD-BYE (AND GOOD RIDDANCE)
TO THE TWENTIETH CENTURY

Forewarning:

Horse will not miss the Twentieth Century.
Horse is action.
Horse is captured spirit.

Horse speaks:
It is essential to get a few things straight:
Horse, politically speaking,
looks forward to the passing of this age.
When pushed Horse kicks up a blue storm.
Horse does not ride skateboard.
Horse does not play rock and roll.
Horse does not sail on sailboat.
Horse does not eat processed food.
Horse does not believe in perfume.

1.
Upon Horse's sixty-millionth birthday,
Horse is more than ready to say good-bye.
From the beginning Horse voiced complaints—
like Whitman's great redwood talking
to the wood-choppers whacking away at them.

2.
And why does Horse complain?
Horse: used, neglected, mistreated,

misused, abused, refused.

Horse explains:
Since you first climbed upon Horse's back,
thousands of years ago, Horse's back has ached.
Your ass is heavy.

You make Horse ache all in his fat.
Horse aches in his forelocks and fetlocks.
Horse's jugular, shoulders, and grooves ache.
Horse's pastern, his gaskin, his docks, his hocks,
     his breast-muscles, his thighs:
all ache from the weight of your three-hundred pound ass.
Horse's knees ache from the galloping you force on him.

Poor Horse, poor Polish pony.
Horse son, Horse Polish Arab father shot after snakebite.
No light left in eye.
And you ask why does Horse complain?

3.
Horse complains because:
Horse is poor Turkoman, walking chest out.
Horse is poor little Falabella with bleeding coronet.
Horse is poor Justin Morgan with broken cannon bones.
Horse is Paso Fino with gaping abdomen.
Horse is Chinese with axed-open chin groove.
Horse is poor Persian, walking, sheath hanging.
Horse is poor Arab, walking, saddled to death.
Horse is Got on a bridge—Horse *is* bridge.
Horse is Sumba with a bullet hole in his geometric head.

Is Horse's kinship lost for good?
Horse has only Equus memory in his energy,
only Miohippus in his motion.
Horse has ancestry dreams of grazing and sunning,
cold-blooded and hot-blooded dreams,
dreams cluttered with fear and running.

Horse gazes, batting his eyelids
at a horsefly big as Mongolia.

4.
Horse is this horse and that horse:
Horse is Cayuse: small, hopeful horse.
Horse Kentucky saddle horse,
anchored to fence by unlettered, at least
Horse treated better than black slave
(and where is the rope?)
in the sun burned senseless,
lacking light, water, hope.
Treated better than gold-boom mistress
in drawing room with delicate sense of narrowness.

Horse big Tennessee Walking Horse, yet
Horse sings because Horse is Horse.
Horse sings his complaint because Horse hates the fox hunt.
Horse complains because Horse has to wear shoes.
Yet Horse sings,
Horse truly sings from the hollow of his heels.

5.
Horse sings from the pain deep in his haunches.
Horse sings from the pain deep in his foretoes.
Pain spreads throughout Horse's loins, yet he sings.
Pain gallops throughout Horse's flanks, and he sings.
This unrelenting pain eats its way from Horse's long stomach
up through his long throat. And he sings about it.
Bursting with song, Horse aches in his axis.
Exploding with song, Horse aches in his atlas.
Wet with the sweat of song, Horse aches in his withers.
Even when Horse is a horse blind with a pain,
without direction,
Horse sings his way along aching from deep within
his very being.

And though you rode him with your face facing forward,
you rode on and on into the sunset
without knowing the Horse on which you sat.

6.
Horse, all horses—
Polish, Got, Turko, Anglo, Warm-Blood, Cutting, Cold-Blood,
    Justin
Morgan, Quarter, Americas, Paso Fino, Caspian, Arab, Wild,
Sumba, Chinese, Pinto, Don, Teke, Zebra, Andalusian, Busato,
Lusitano, Flanero, and little Flabella and the others too—
fare captured spirits, dreaming.

7.
Horse is a captured spirit dreaming of release.

Horse is action dreaming of its own motion.
Horse is something truly in motion.
Horse is motion.

Horse is something caught static, too,
as in paint or stone,
something with fleshy thighs,
hooves, all, in a watery field, shimmering
and
each time you look,
Horse has changed.

Horse likes you when you slow down
and read the Hyracotherium inscription
on the simple gesture of Horse's presence.

8.
No tears.
No, Horse will not miss the Twentieth Century:
Horse was treated badly for forty-million years.
Horse was treated like dirt in the Nineteenth Century.
Treated slightly better in the Twentieth Century.

Now, before entering the Twenty-First Century,
Horse would get rid of these things:
spurs of any type,
horseflies and all related insects,
bridles and snaffle bits,
bit-less bridles and hackamores,
any person even thinking kindly of spurs,
short cheek Pelhams and bits,

throat-lashes and reins,
girth flaps and stirrups,
crown pieces and brow bands,
nosebands and eyeflaps,
horseblankets and horse trailers,
horse diseases and shallow rivers to cross
horse shoes and heavy wagons,
circuses and flaming rings,
race tracks and horse traders,
parades and paraders,
show jumping events,
horseback polo and polo players,
Central Park and Central Park police,
London and Sydney horseback police,
horse-carts and police even thinking about horses,
fox hunters and foxes,
herding cows and herding sheep,
herding buffalo and being a warhorse,
photographers with cameras,
photographers without cameras,
having to kick somebody for standing in the wrong place,
cold weather and mean people who beat horses,
snakes and mountain lions,
racing saddles and western saddles,
harnesses and riding whips,
and all the other things you thought
Horse needed to be happy.

THE MANUAL FOR TWENTIETH-CENTURY MAN (AND WOMAN)

This is the manual for twentieth-century man—and woman.

That field of flowering mustard, so brilliantly yellow against the darker green, is not what it seems. Atomic waste, buried miles beneath, provides it with that iridescent sheen.

If the sky is blue, it's raining two states over. If you love your wife (or husband), you must hate your mother (or father).

The woman with long blonde hair driving the car in front of yours is probably a boy on his way to a baseball game.

To be late for a lunch with friends is to miss the auto wreck that would have smashed you to steaks and chops. Or is it the other way around? You'll never know, unless you were on time for the auto wreck, in which case you missed a good lunch.

If you rise one morning with a sense of wonder and joy pulsing through your body all the way to your nerve ends, it could be a signal that a cancer has erupted in your colon or a black wen is budding on one of your lungs.

Something is always happening that you can't see. The worms are digesting the field. Mosquitos are hanging like tiny hams from the spider's tremulous rafters, while a squadron of bees, in Africa or Brazil, has begun the flight which will result in the end of the human race.

As you fold the laundry, finish your coffee, or read these words, keep in mind that hundreds of light years out in space, an asteroid, which will crash into our planet two thousand years from now, is about to be deflected from its original course by the last ripples of a starburst that occurred three billion years before our solar system was born . . .

O this is the manual for twentieth-century man, tra-la, twentieth-century man, tra-la. O this is the manual for twentieth-century man, tra-la, and the womanual for twentieth-century woman.

WING AND PRAYER

Dear fellow infidel, let's pray
   That this poisoned rain daily pouring
Torrents of contaminant crude
   Does not become the norm from now on,

Or the nightmare dreamed I know now for sure
   Will be delivered. Earth's not cherry anymore. O-
Zone's broken hymen, eroded topsoil, rising waters, and forests
   Burnt faster than fired brain-cells, quicker

Than you can say "The self's cry
   In roasting meat tastes but cannot
Touch the source it eats," fire's
   The future. Prophets had foretold it, though

Prophets and the news they carry are always
   Too late. While the plane of fire more swiftly
Plays out what on the plane of earth takes
   Time, things have never been so

Hot as we are going to make them. Circling the center
   Close to all the extremities, there's something
Nuclear going on. With the compliments of
   What corporate birds of prey, casually polluting

Slaughterers, have the time-released, barely traceable air-
   Borne gas chambers been set
In motion? Who'll make a living
   Text out of the toxins? God must

Be real
    Pissed. Torched garden, infected fruit, dwindling
Herds running for their lives; sex never more
    Iffy, and loose

Sex definitely
    Out. In less than a lifetime, to see
Birth, and death, and the imminent unimaginable
    Death of birth, O endangered

Unborn
    Lovers of the golden-headed
Tamarin, wild mustang, Bengal tiger, snow leopard, bald eagle,
    Even the pea-brained dinosaurs lorded it

Over the mammals for 60 million years
    Until a hail of comets fused
Their molecules into fossil fuel, opening
    The way for us. Thank our lucky stars, indeed!

In a world where silk is
    Thread, web, and spider, too,
A door swings open
    On a life when the limbs in question feel

Underfoot the richness of
    Generations gone
As you pass them tumbling
    Down all the way, and light

From no solid source, illuminating no solid
    Body, presses for a little while the

Figure out of shape. It needs, like us,
    A wave

Of enchantment welling up from the lower levels
    To draw it out. Inexhaustible,
The combination of enchantments possible
    In the combination of one person

With another, offering looks that awaken, looks
    That can touch
You back. It takes
    Two to have one's

Heart
    Broken. Not I, but
Erik Satie has spoken
    Through the notes, echoing oceans

Apart between the hearts left
    Unbroken. And that's only the tip
Of the hunger there must be in paradise
    For its children to leap into hard,

Hard rest. They walk, bickering, out
    Of the past into the distant
Present, on the street before the wind
    Leaves for the other street

Corners of the world, undoing
    What's been done by doing
What needs to be but won't be
      Had. Now a lunging

Greyhound on the beach goes running down
   Perfectly synchronized flocks of birds swooping
Offshore, that tremendous outstretched underbelly, outflung
   Paws defying gravity, coming

As close to flying as we'll

      get to heaven

THEY

They have seen the famous through eyes baked
in the hot wombs of lost mothers

They have used the latest telecommunication devices
to call premier X and actress WHY
to attend a major event
in honor of an idea
that would persuade rational animals
to embrace irrational impulses
when the sky appears to a woman with tangerine breasts
to be something more than a blue vegetable
in a pot half filled with liquid philosophers

They have nothing better to do

They have tired of pushing metal carts
filled with root beer cans and discarded feather pillows
down main streets
under the watchful gaze of affluent bodies
pumping gas into sad cars
with nowhere to go

They have memorized the sidewalk rhetoric
repeat without hesitation
the exact syllable the moon whispers
to shapes that linger
by rivers flowing
through silk towns

RICHARD MARTIN

They are here with us
whether we like it or not

They record what we think
when we think
the world is a porcelain gift
left on our doorstep
without consequences

from *White Man Appears on Southern California Beach*

derangement, on beauty, course of the sound
a wind blew the little man away you might think
of someone in particular but it was no one
always the courses and flights of new forms

try and stand up in the midst of a 17th century sentence
so that dost thou or dost thou not configured as it was
become this other you tried to construe by learning

what the fuck man you blew it & there is no fuckin way
to construe it till way past when hell freezes over
for the gals & guys of our times

darling I think of you often specially when I'm writing
which is to you you bespoken like a bird's-foot violet to me
future tragedy like a box at the opera like all
there is hardly nothing

sweetheart I don't know I am fuckin fucked up & you're
deranging my heart which is a real heart prone
to heart attacks much less the fact I've got
bad habits as well

oh my tea my little drugs I adore you quite as well
as any thee so what the hell is the matter
with me, I know we haveta be sharp these days,
what should I say?

mention the movies? mention some things?
the place I eat in, the stories I overhear
like the one John told me: two guys walking down the street:
one says to the other, you're so fuckin smart you must think
you're Richard Einstein!

Well if you think you're that fuckin smart in our love
you've got another guess comin & besides that I think
we could be alot more sublime than all this all a time

not to mention the landlord oh now it's time to mention
the landlord, you cannot even attend a party lately without
getting involved in a discussion of how to generate an effective
     rent strike
much less how to simply deal with the man

we aren't starving & still we have some shelter
though we have to fight for it
inertially maybe the way Sophia fights with Max
that is it's inevitable but I don't believe that
nor do I believe my little poetry compunction
has to turn into this recounting of wrongs done

My love I'd rather sing about this love that would be able
if it were not here & there, don't you think so?
I'd rather easily glorify the outdone love I feel
than not remember so fast the meaning of each word I use
& have to look it up in usually so complementary a dictionary

though love is ill & that means it is not well
startling things look, appear & be & also be well

though you may look for omens to reflect how you feel
pretty much you'll find nothing or none
except a wind learned like today that blew ill what?

& if the world's ill, I'm sick of it
& will be & with my love, sorry, forever

Greg stood there, & Max & John & Lewis
& then Julie & Rochelle & Marie
altogether with me observing this wind coming up

Julie encouraged it, Rochelle denied it
Marie knew it already but it was only me
my own self as Max would say that wound up getting rained on
by the hideous condensation of the startling anonymous mist
that seemed to place itself in the air
& then fall down which was not rain
or even close to snow this 12th of November
parody without beauty of Indian summer
this warm day without power
crazy day of fear

& can you stand to live at all? No,
I can't say that & I can't say that
many are gone from the moment & plus unfairly
amazingly you & I continue on in the deal that's struck for the
        moment

still falling down like apostrophes or the rain
still being falling the way thoughts are just like rain
even if you don't say anything, if you never speak

Love alone is not the cynicism of Julie
or the wanton mistrust of Rochelle it is actually closer
to the meeting though it's much more nothing of all on the porch
or close to it & at random this day wind blowing something
in the bad bad air of our times, listen

sweet darling sweetheart my tea my movie my heart
if you can't love me & I can't love you then no wonder
there is gonna be a war or else the war is making me not love you
so therefore war father mother let me be & leave me
I know how to propagate the race for slightly peace that is
to only give birth to women: or to sweet loving boys who have in
    their builds
no desire to make us war or crazier

Nor do I or does anyone blame the whole thing on the men
but it sure is easy to hate the stern unwholesome father
easy as it is to hate the absolutely feeding mother

Poetry reminds me I'm an idiot for saying this & now it pours
real rain finally though in new york you don't feel a drought
though stark & fucking unremitting might be the dryness
you can't say that & there are many things you can't say

speak horribly then to me my friend as well as you can
& admit to the idiocy of our beginning love otherwise
nobody will & beg me to permit you to let both of us speak
& say all we can in that clarity beyond sirens & the going off of
car burglary alarms in the street, luckily our love
is more enduring than that though those seem to last forever

Everybody's got their plants & then there are those who

don't have any plants, well it don't make sense either way
I'm either gonna write my reminiscences or try & change the world
or both! Nevertheless

Nevertheless I love you I do love you I love you more than
anyone & than anyone has ever loved anyone & though it's
difficult to say so I thank you for loving me also because otherwise
I don't think I could quite ever have survived thus far without your
love,
            thanks a million!

METEOR

It's been twenty-seven years
since our toolshed was hit by a meteor
About four or five in the morning
a few days after New Year's
It sounded like a heavy door had been slammed
but none of our doors was heavy
I knew not to look at the sky
for the mushroom
the flash of white that would surely come
(My eyeballs would turn to goo
and run down my cheeks)
There was a smell of hot cement
scorched sand and grass
The dogs began to bark
our collie Spanky
Davy Frank's cockerspaniel, Mr Murphy's poodle
The Lemmons' aged dachshund
We lived close together then
our houses all looked the same
the sidewalks were level, the trees were saplings

We picked our way across the lawn
my Dad had a flashlight
my mother kept her hand on my shoulder
like a vise
For the love of Lucy said Mr Frank
He had on his workshoes
but no socks
Mr Murphy wore a flannel bathrobe just like my Dad's
Well Walter he said
You won't need to dig a shelter now

I knew I would be famous
my photograph in the book
that told about an old man who spontaneously combusted
that showed a pumpkin the size of a Volkswagen
a girl with an extra foot growing out of her knee
But the next day
my Dad brought in a truckload of dirt
Mrs Lemmon said she heard something about our meteor on the
    radio
But she wasn't sure because she was in the shower at the time

Not long after
Apollo went to the moon
Davy Frank went to Vietnam
We moved to Dallas
The Lemmons rented an apartment by the freeway
Mr Murphy retired to somewhere near Phoenix
last I heard
I'm sure he's dead now
Then I was transferred to Atlanta but here I am again
in a rented car
(not famous, yet)
The tree trunks are thick and craggy
the pavements cracked and buckled
most of the houses have second storeys
The children riding their bikes
all look Mexican
If I were to knock on our door
on any of these doors

No one would believe me
No one would believe any of this

old reds to this kind in ace of knowing
old reds in blue prole denim workshirts
old reds following Robert's rules
old reds with thinning hair consuming huge bosoms
old reds met Friday night in a storefront
old reds in a row on metal folding chairs
old reds listen intently to ancient seer red
old red sage who'd been there and back and saw the impossible
old reds talking walking utopia with oldest red
Comrade Lenin in Brooklyn on a fund-raiser

old reds in gold lit memory reveries
old red fists clenched arms upraised
old reds arise against imbalancing power
old reds resist soul-gobbling machinery
old red hands coiled around sledgehammers
old reds skinny sinewy bony in rolled-up shirtsleeves
old red families picnic on worn park grass May Day fest
old red recalls Big Bill Haywood in Greenwich Village
old reds in a carnival tent hearing
Paul Robeson back from the Soviet Union
his silk black basso pops out speaker cones

old reds discuss endlessly Talmudic
old reds want Harlem back and the Depression
old reds want unions back
old reds want to know what to do next
verify demonstrate form a study group exalt
oldest red with piles in British Museum
rubbing frenzies with Rimbaud in the Reading Room

while outside Industry's soot ghosted roar
bombards promethean cathedrals day and night
gigantic blood-inked paper rolls
squash books into stacks tongued through gears
of night terrors seeding momentous activity
whose machines won't stop despite bodies stacking up
pulped by wheels remembered by ancients
in bookstores closing down
party offices now boiler-rooms run by phone wizards
pulling the plug out of the Good Life
for all you material rubes asleep at the spiel

DIANE MIDDLEBROOK

I turned fifty in 1989, and I hope to turn sixty in 1999. The good news was that I turned thirty in 1969, a fine year to be thirty, and female. No one trusted you—only those over fifty today will know what I mean—so you could do as you wished. Everybody I knew wished to indulge in the elaborate production of physical sensations. Probably fewer books were published then than now; people didn't read at the table, or in bed much, at least the people I was in bed with. As the millennium approaches, everybody seems to regard the body as a set of codes rather than a site for the cultivation of sensations. So I would like to plant a time capsule in the millennium with this prose poem to my body, a token of appreciation.

HAIR

She pulls away the sopping towel and blots the dripping briskly with a fresh one still warm from the airing cupboard, and begins combing the slick bunches into alignment. Then I feel her cool knuckles at my neck, parting the hair into hanks. She seizes one at the very back with her brush in one deft motion then lifts her wand of air and begins a slow, steady stroking at the back of my head. Noelle is her name: no (tug) elle (stroke), over and over. The dryer's hum makes a low wall like the boundary between terraces at the back of a London house: infrequently, our eyes meet in the mirror, but only for me to nod in affirmation: yes, part it on the same side as before. Today she is more abstract than usual, moving her practiced hands while her gaze drifts toward the window with a slight frown. My attention too is elsewhere. I close my eyes against the blowing hair and slowly tighten the muscles of my thighs, rocking my pelvis upward in response to the firm tug, brush-and-pull motion of the hairdressers hands at my head. The hair tethers us at a polite distance, but as she strokes her fingers

250

graze my scalp and the fine hair on my arms begins to rise in sympathy with the slow engorgement of the half-moons of flesh gripped between my thighs. Now she has reached the crown. The root of each hair nudges alive as she tugs and strokes, and a wheel of pleasure begins its halting spiral turn upward through my body. Tense, poised and silent, my face a smooth mask, I rock one knee against another, testing. And now it's here, the rising flood of sensation rippling along its plotted curve, drawing back, and again flooding the dark cave my subtly tightening legs widen and narrow for its passage, while her hands move in the same rhythm. One strong pulse, like the backwash of a wave, and the tide falls back. I have closed my eyes: now I open them and see two of my fingers lifted, as if in alarm. "Did I hurt you?" she asks, noticing. "No."

FRED MORAMARCO

SO LONG, TWENTIETH CENTURY

I'm going to miss the 20th century, aren't you?
It's the only century I've known, and I'm feeling some angst
about its passing because for sheer chutzpah
no century could ever surpass it.

I've tried to summarize its bizarre contradictions,
its surrealistic cast of characters, I've tried and failed.
I've composed long lists, tedious lists of its traumas & heroes,
scandals, inventions, movements and wars.
All those wars, two of them named after the entire world—
It's just too much.

What is there to say about a century whose memorable
political utterances run the gamut from "I Have a Dream"
to "I am not a crook"?

O, twentieth century, what a torrent of language you've spawned,
one of which is the language I speak and write. Words like
        "genocide"
"holocaust" and "chemotherapy"; "black holes," "double helix,"
        "toxic waste"—
What a list I could make!

And you left us unforgettable lines of poetry like "the woods are
        lovely dark and deep,
but I have promises to keep/ and miles to go before I sleep/ and
        miles to go before I sleep."

So long, twentieth century; you gave us the gift of Billy Holiday's
        voice, surely one of your

greatest treasures. And Frank O'Hara's wonderful lines about her:

"and I am sweating a lot by now and thinking of
leaning against the john door in the FIVE SPOT
while she whispered a song along the keyboard
to Mal Waldron and everyone and I stopped breathing."

Dear twentieth century, with both gratitude and rage, I tally your
     legacy:
You gave us condoms, communism, and compact discs; bikinis,
satellites, fast food and fascism; thalidomide babies, superbowls,
liposuction, and leather wallets full of plastic;
Should we thank you for the Manhattan Project,
periodontists and aeroplanes common as clouds?

It's time to bid you adieu, I hope you had a nice day.
You leave us with virtual reality, AIDS, rolodex and a darkening sky.

What can we say except goodbye, goodbye, goodbye, goodbye,
     goodbye.

FAITH IN THE TWENTIETH CENTURY

In my room overlooking Jerusalem,
I felt something like a leaf on my forehead
—I picked off a louse,
squashed it between the labyrinths
of my index finger and my thumb.
I have faith every louse in Jerusalem
has come through hair and feather:
Jew, Moslem, Christian
from wing to head to beard to crotch,
from cat's ear to rat's balls.

At the Jerusalem wall between heaven and hell
the unprepared are given skull-caps
—I refused a clean, grey paper cap
the kind given children in different colors
at birthday parties with other favors,
I picked dusty black rayon someone left behind,
despite my friend's warning, "You may get lice."
Whatever the time of day, a little before fear,
the sun hurt my eyes. I kissed the wall
but had nothing further to say to it.

My louse's cousins have spent time among hyena packs,
nestled in carrion, under pus, lip to lip with maggots.
Surely Christ who suffered crucifixion
felt the bite of a louse. My fingers are Roman soldiers,
if the louse I squashed had a trace of Christ's blood.
I have faith King David after all his adventures
had an itch in the groin, and a louse danced with him.
Once a winged horse with peacock's tail

and a woman's face, flew into this city from Arabia
with a prophet on its back.
We all can use a little sacred preening and combing.
I should be grateful for another louse.

MR. TWENTY

Everywhere I look
there's another bottle
of sparkling water
it's the new beer
new since 1978 or so.
Not so new.
Even the millennium is unspeakably silent
having been here so long
100 years of the naked emperor
is more than my eyes
can stand. His little penis
bobbing below his
big belly, his tiny toes
in small loafers.
Won't somebody stop
this man. The first thing we learned
was the world would end
in our time. Do you think
we give a shit by now
Lying at the bottom of the
toilet of the naked
emperor, every time
he flushes we're supposed
to applaud. We do not.
We yawn. That was a
really big turd the emperor
just made. Must be
for women we giggled.
Huh. I lifted my
glass to my lips

it's mostly silence now
the regular darkening
as he puts his fanny
down on the lid of the
century. It makes me just
want to do something great
for the world. If there's
another big race riot in
America I think I'll go
direct streetcar named
desire in the midst of
it. I'm sick of doing nothing
I want to help.
Naturally I'll play Stanley
an angry white lesbian
walking through the burning
streets yelling Stella
Yeah. I'm eager. I'm rubbing
my palms. No seriously
folks I was born
just a few years after the
Emperor put some big bombs
down. It was very
fertile ground. I remember
a screaming sound in the
sky but the world seemed silent
that day & then some
ashes fell, or maybe it
was a scrap of worn out
rubber from the side
of the road
somehow it fell from

the sky. It filled
with papers books
& clothes. Well how *do* I
feel about the end of
the world. He's become
beautiful to us. Look
at his color. Kind of
tawny pink. Little bits
of hair on his chest
streams of it pouring
down his legs & a
slight smile on his
thin lips. It's graceful the
way he just walks
around gazing at us
and you know why he has no
clothes. It's the ultimate
power stroke—to
show the world how you
start your morning
before they see
you, I am this
simply breast
and shoulders
forearms, slightly bulgy
waist thighs amply on
the chair, legs
crossed. Step out
& say I have no job
no interest really
in engaging, but must walk
and spin, an unclothed

lily, & you will greet
me with silence
my beforeness
my adamant
unbeginning to trample
all of you with my big ass
daily, to take that royal
ride on my own
for days and weeks till
the lie is the utter complicitude
of every living thing that
has seen me, the man,
the naked emperor
smiling at you fools. I'm
the beaming man on the motorcade
the eyes glisten
the man in the suit with
promises, my Dad,
to look into his eyes
and see myself
smiling.

The only wild thing
well we tried that for a while
some kind of truth
the only wild thing
is to complain & complain
about his nakedness
his ugly fucking naked body
marching up & down the world
making everyone pretend
to believe in him

EILEEN MYLES

it's more than I can
stand. I would
evacuate. But
he's everywhere.
Shitting on our heads &
our couches
children can't even see him
I mean that's a problem
Am I wrong?
It would be: in my time
there was nothing else
we gave up the fight
he was everywhere
the Sun

NO SAFETY

> *All that hate me whisper together against me,*
> *against me do they devise my hurt.*
> *Yea, my old familiar friend,*
> *in whom I trusted,*
> *who did eat my bread,*
> *has lifted up his heel against mine.*
>   Psalm 41

I.

I pick my friends according to whether they would hide me.
Once you're betrayed it's too late to choose better.

Jews like to argue
who was worst:
The French? in 1940, five million
wrote poison-pen letters
denouncing individual Jews.

No, the Austrians—Hitler, Eichmann, Waldheim. All Austrians.

No, no, the Romanians
who outraged even the Germans
when they failed to bury the bodies of those they murdered.

The war lost, some Nazis jumped into stripes and yellow star—
the Russians shot them all the same.

Some Jews survived death camps and went home
and the Poles shot them

their neighbors, the Poles
their neighbors shot them.

Why bother to shoot the dead?

II.
After Theresienstadt is it obscene to sing?
Unseemly to be alive
when such effort was made to stomp their bones?

"They"?
Say "we"
we Jews   still here.
My dear little father ran
rather than give over his bad (gold-filled) teeth.

The Jews are historians—remember,
in every generation some rose
against us but we were saved. Who
saved us? Who saves me?
What happens to one
happens to all. If my aunt is killed, where are her bones?

> Hopeful and over-obedient,
> they and we, the scared and the slow,
> neglected political and military science and so were
> twice-naked.

The voice of history
divides the flame of fire.
We don't conquer we merely persevere.

How long will—will the world look on?
Gnashing upon me with my teeth.
My babies, my children
it's so hard to raise the dead.

III.
I am a Jew.

I announce this
so I won't hear what I do hear when people don't guess
so I can't be a coward, so I can't deny anything.
No way out.
When I stay silent, my bones
wax old through my roaring
all the day long.

   . . . But my mother is English
doesn't that make me
half WASP shouldn't I be more
tactful? No one
wants to hear it why don't I
shut up? No one wants to hear it
and why should they
I wasn't there
they weren't there they
didn't do it.

The voice of history divides my flame from the fire.

The necromancers arouse themselves with the bones of the dead.
They warm the bones with their bodies

they insert the bones into their nostrils
they incite the bones to answer their questions
I shout at the bones until I am hoarse.

    "It would have done no good to protest
    they would only have turned on
    us
    this way at least we got
    a case of good wine out of it
    a country house
    when the old owners
    suddenly
    decided to leave the country."

The Jews have only their history.
We must remember—but why should we live
for the dead?
The irony of history divides the flames of fire.
I am cursed with memory. My life is spent with grief
and my years with sighing.
My bones are consumed.

No safety.
That's all I'm trying to say.
Next time take me first,
I already know as much as I need to.

IV.
Why should I have
resentments? Didn't
my friend's husband say

he couldn't believe
I am a Jew
and didn't he mean
he likes me and he doesn't like
Jews
and aren't I flattered
to be told I'm not like
them
aren't I flattered to be
my own person
not the product of a people half as old as time?

One must forgive one's enemies
but not before they have been hanged.
    —Freud, quoting Heine

V.
My friends think it strange
I carry three passports.
My money's in jewels, my bags are packed.
I pick the friends I pray
will hide me. Once you're betrayed
it's too late. I am cursed

with memory
the flames divide me from my past.

I am indebted to Susan Neiman & her book *Slow Fire: Jewish Notes from Berlin* for
material in this poem.

VOS BASTARDI RIDE

The electric chicken
and her electric egg
take the
senses
down
a peg.

"This is Cobra Pose,"
says Miss X.

Cobra would
eat a chicken
and, as everybody

knows, snakes just
love eggs, if only
to regurgitate them.

Cold cumulus
late December
in big winds

the last page
of the calendar year
clucks against the wall.

HASTA LA VISTA, BABY
for the 20th Century

A cast of the dice brought me here
nude as a bone
                descending a staircase
following in the footsteps of
Guillaume Apollinaire
        in his crown of gauze
Max Jacob
                in his cups
and that debonair
                        pipe smoking chap
for whom masturbation was enough

    a urinal
    a bicycle wheel
    a coffee grinder
    a snow shovel
    a mustashioed Mona Lisa
    a broken glass
    (a bride & some bachelors)
    a green box
    among other
    (numerous really bad puns)
            things
    checkmate the assumptions of art

which is to say

        "I thing therefore I am"

progress is the new virtue
dada fathers an attitude
surrealist circles ripple across the century
free the subconscious
                           the catch phrase
in the shadow of the Eiffel tower
          a gothic girdered
French penis
      shooting its golden sparks around the world
(no wonder they're prickly!
              they were caught in *coitus flagrante!*)

defining aspects examined under a microscope
by a young doctor from New Jersey who washes
his hands of the dominating influence of the old
world in favor of the simplicity of a barnyard scene
at the beginning of the century of the future
where the past is discounted for an ideal based
on hope not the tyranny of a collective memory

the moment
in which a piece of green glass
catches light
           can be as large as a day
the grand humanity that emerges
with a vision in a down pour
        and the plums of wistfulness
a century is built upon such days

"absolutes
      I don't need no steenking
               absolutes"

looking back
           the past evaporates
(common among poets)
in a cloud of mushroom soup
           (yes Campbell's)
it's a wonder that the present could
        so quickly become the future
(Post-Modernism)
and still be totally outdistanced
           by the times
    (Post-Digitalism)
neck deep in useless information

all that's
           history
and most of it before my time

near the half century mark
I find myself in mutable flesh
at the end of another great conflagration
raised from the sea of babble
           between two languages
(I spoke the one that got me the most candy)

some welcome to the human race
time trials began as soon as I awoke

on the howling road
whole generations
           ride the flux of speed and steel
to beat time
as any distance now

measured in hours
make do with jet lag
though once there
phone home

more often
it comes down to
watching the clothes go round
in the laundromats of eternity
technology can be as mundane
as you let it be
and the imperatives of the loins
as pervasive as ever
(the diapers are dry)

many miles and much much later
I must confess
I tire of all these words
and their tedious implications
a *fin de siecle* weariness
perhaps
after all
how long have I
been tripping
down
the same flight
in pursuit of some
mocking chimera
a wreath of smoke
surrounding my head

LET'S FACE IT!

after half a century
                    on this planet
I'm still just a macho jerk

tip of the century:
if all you ever hear is bad news
turn off the radio

sit with Elvis and his gentle race

mechanical
            an unnamed fear
                        rusts my joints
ah! technology!
directing the new genus
            toward that android future

through an open window
onto the present I see myself
tangled in the multiple
organization of my pastoral dissonance
as a chauffeur today
take the boys to the movies
allow them to use me
to get in to see an R rated
sex violence and music
cream puff of teen exploitation
it's become a formula
how the syntax segues
just the right mix defiance
comedy and titillation
if I'm errant I console myself

there are a couple of laughs
a recognition of what binds
us as men the lure of wishful
thinking or not thinking
as the case may be the animal
we learn to manipulate and
distract with sleight of hand
no matter how slight or meaningless
loud thump represents heart beat
adrenaline surges through the blood
at the sound of gunfire and whole
body arousal when lascivious curves
appear and trigger the impulse
that leads to the big bang theory
but when the lights go up
I'm just the chauffeur again

THE WONDERS OF TECHNOLOGY
        (flashing neon)

thanks to a measurement
        "parts one in a billion"
I now know
where the lead
in my ass comes from

I was having such prophetic
revelations while doing the dishes
but they all vanished once
I let the water down the drain
what I remember of them
the unique solution: do not disturb

the mire of existence: made in USA
the hidden charades: the domino effect
the mercy of geography: the brute survives

acquire a taste for the bittersweet
it soothes that sinking feeling

message left for me on the answering machine:
"welcome back to obscurity"

the patina of altruism flakes away
under the microscope of the minute
accustomed to gloss
                    fictions are allowed
the more I learn about myselves
partitioned as a nude photo
                        descending
into the labyrinth of separate
but equal
          personalities

behind the amoebic eightball
that overwhelming nothing
            a wave that flattens the nap
of my prickly consciousness

some days can seem century long
"I like to watch"
            as Chance the gardener says
and as Orpheus
                I listen to the car radio

PAT NOLAN

a throw of the dice brings me
to this end of the century
where history repeats itself
      about every fraction of a second
as the flicker of light and shadow
moments matter
and I reinvent myself with each step
the message
         (from outer space)
                  same as it ever was

      $E = MC^2$ equals   *"what me, worry?"*

READY-MADE

I transport from the canvas unsteady dissonance in the blue!
I heard in a dream about Marcel Duchamp.
Was he speaking from the other side of the Great Glass heavenly
    Dada windows?
Marcel agreed to "bring a little intelligence into painting . . . this
    turpentine intoxication," he scoffed.

On Sundays friends gathered in the garden at Puteaux
(Leger, Picabia, Metzinger, Apollinaire, Reverdy),
"with almost juvenile good humor. One almost forgets that
at that time nobody was anybody," recollected Duchamp.

"Fascinating frivolity and beautiful illusions!"
chortled Ribemont-Dessaignes. They behaved like schoolboys on
    holiday,
playing pranks, games, enjoying slapstick. Fame and public image
had not yet arrived. Marcel could not stand them when they did.

Like Picabia he demanded unlimited freedom,
hated groups and schools, repetition of style.
"Art is useless and impossible to justify!" declared Picabia.

> A wild ungovernable infant
>   riding its hobbyhorse
> around the world, trampling
>   the pompous beneath its hooves
> DADA was just arriving.

Marcel drew logical conclusions:
he painted a moustache on the Mona Lisa,

an act as pointless as suicide
to which he was utterly indifferent.
His heart belonged to Dada.
He painted all values into a corner:
the urinal is the good, the beautiful, the true.

Marcel was in love with bad taste:
he invented a way of being absent
that Rimbaud never suspected.
"Duchamp is destined to reconcile art and the people,"
said the unknown Apollinaire.
But were the people ready for ready-mades?

Marcel arrived in New York with a glass ball full of Paris air.
It was a gift for a friend. His "explosions in a shingle factory,"
as one critic called "Nude Descending A Staircase" in 1913,
shocked everyone. Marcel was famous. With ironic humor
he detached himself on his condescending staircase
where with lofty vanity he observed,
"Without vanity we should all kill ourselves."
He had no other deadly sin.

In 1915 he exhibited a bicycle wheel mounted on a stool,
a bottle rack and a urinal titled *Fountain*.
The ready-mades became works of art, he said, as soon as he
       declared them so: looking at an object made it art.
He signed the urinal R. Mutt (the name of a firm of sanitary
       engineers).
The urinal achieved immortality.

          Meanwhile Gertrude Stein
          was busy in her own studio

inventing Hemingway
and Virgil Thomson;
when she created Ezra Pound
she frowned, screamed
and threw the rough draft away.

"Remarks," said Miss Stein, "are not literature."

Stein and Duchamp took the 20th Century for a ride
on the merrygoround of painted horses and calliope tunes
of childhood where they play in our memory still.

The song of Rrose Selavy.
The love-song of R. Mutt.
The pigeons-on-the-grass song.
Song of unsteady dissonance.

Chanson of the urinal.
The pissoir of melody.
Marcel Duchamp in drag
as Rrose Selavy
camps through the studios
of friends and foes.

(Marcel and Man Ray play a game of chess lasting forty years.)

from DÉSAMÈRE

'I dream,' says dead desert Desnos,
'When Kennedy sends the first Green Berets
Into Vietnam, 'sixty-two,
White moon stains a lake, watery flower
You're young, Amère, you say
"This view is corny"'
'It's the sixties,' Amère says, 'I want a city
Soon it's the eighties, the city's ruined
Which person am I, am I ruined?
The rents so high, animals sleeping
Outside at night, drugged and dirty'
'In the sixties, behind the war
A building grows larger,' says Desnos
'The war's a transparent movie, the building's
Windowless, a double-black domino'
'Can't humans escape each other's
Exigencies?' asks Amère
'Who doesn't serve the building? It
Makes weapons, cars, appliances, jobs
In the sixties Reagan's its ad-man
While the young try to block entrance to it
Human products are more powerful than humans are
But I'm not really like a decade'
'So you say,' says Desnos, 'but anyone
Smokes when the others smoke'
A voice from the dark says,
'The sky's full of smoke, everyone smokes'
'Nineteen eighty-four,' says Desnos,
'Oh isn't a woman smoking?
Black woman in a log cabin, fashionable

Blue dress, gold earrings and bracelet
Smoking, furious, cigarette, cigarette
Black men parade past the open door
They tell her they're headed for
Twenty thirty thousand dollar jobs
She sucks a cigarette, shouts,
"What's a salary, without a future?
Our heroisms, agonies, small gains in social justice,
Nothing without a planet
Reagan spends it
Squanders it sitting at a desk
Like everyone else"'
'Am I ruined?' Amère repeats
'If it's ruined, is each person ruined?
Is there something that can't ever be ruined?'
'In a zoo,' says Desnos, 'in the nineties,
I see Przewalski's horse—
They live mostly in zoos now you know
I dream you're one, bare your teeth, try to speak
You want to say something about ruin: It's not that
Soul won't outlive you unless species does
Soul is what there is, swallows ruin
And yet, you strain to say,
I am ruined if species is ruined.'
'I have such a sadness,' Amère says,
'As when a husband dies, magnified
Till it replaces all that we were
There may never be nothing more
But this feeling, and then nothing'

'A Russian woman I knew of in America
Drew the blinds so Stalin wouldn't see her
In nineteen eighty-two,' Amère says
'See that strangely shaped creosote bush?
It becomes for a moment the
Man I was with then
We'd moved into the low-rent houses
On the edge of town, right in the desert
Not much professional world there
No junk bonds or corporate mergers
Or job that required a poet
Is that Reagan near our fire?'
Desnos says, 'No one's here who had power
I often dream of Reagan somber
Quiet, his face unlined, he wanders his
Future death emptily
Looks like someone just out of high school
Crewcut, short-sleeved cotton shirt'
'Dead animals haunt live ones,' Amère
Says, 'exacting tasks from them
They keep asking me to do their work
Though there's little work to being an animal
Forage and eat, groom a little
The other species don't have poverty
The dead forget poverty, tell you to go on'
'I dream,' says Desnos, 'that in the eighties
The summers are one hot field
First a man dies, in a bed, on the ground there
Of accumulated poisons
"I die of my research," he seems to say,
"And good comes of it"'
'Grief also,' says Amère

'Soon after,' says Desnos, 'Brother begins his shaking'
'Delayed reaction to war, common,' Amère says
'And all around,' says Desnos,
'One sees parched grass and plants
Which then disappear leaving sand
Everyone everything has a fate
Now that people have invented fate
And extended its reach beyond the human world,
'But our knowledge of fate,' Amère says,
'Seems to come to us in pieces
Of the past and future blown together
Fragments of history and prophecy . . .
It's hard to make truth of tatters'
'One can't live,' says Desnos, 'as if deciphering
The truth's in you, there isn't very much to it
There's nothing to it—
And perhaps nothing in America,
In a country with a name or leader, is it'

'See this piece of amber?' Amère says to Brother
'I give it to you for Christmas,
In nineteen eighty-three
So you can be buried with it five years later'
'It outlasts my body,' Brother says
'Outlasts the Human Era,' Desnos says,
'Civilization of rocks is what there might be'
'Yellow amber from the Baltic Sea—
This is when I'm *La Veuve*, the Widow,
Like a Tarot card,' Amère says
'I replay these times for their
Perverse richness—painful and lit with mystery
Before them I was part
Technological person
Pills but never cars, destroy own
Body, but not the world's
Are pills and cars really the same?'
Desnos says, 'The dream's of earth
Pills glide over it producing smoke
The pills eat black pills, earth's black beauties'
'Take a pill and talk to us,' Amère says to Brother
He just turns away
'*La Veuve*,' Desnos says, 'I see the label
Outside the animal cage, mute and
Sable-furred mammalian female'
'My cage was haunted,' Amère says,
'A man's voice would tell me, "Leave this room"
How leave a cage? The whole world's a cage
All that's left of the old world are beautiful voices
Voice on cage fire-escape sings a
Song that goes, "Ain't a body happy?"
Or another song, "From

The past to nowhere's where I go'"
'That's the human song,' says Desnos,
'From the past to nowhere, not even
Leaving amber, because of course
Amber leaves itself behind'
'The voice in my cage,' says Amère, 'says
"Blindness can come from nowhere and be
Accompanied by temporary insanity"'
Desnos says, 'You're condemned to *see*'
'Brother,' says Amère, 'Why are you and I
Like this . . . soldier, widow,
Why aren't we cars?'
'Because you grieve like animals,' Desnos says,
'Behaving as your species would
If it hadn't turned into cars
You're still the animals'

from *Close to Me & Closer…(The Language of Heaven) and Désamère* (O Books, 1995)

ALICIA OSTRIKER

THE BALLAD OF LYLE AND ERIC

Now Lyle and Eric
Were privileged boys
In a multimillion house
With multimillion toys

So they bought some good equipment
And they laid a perfect plan
Eric said: Can we do it?
Lyle said: Bet your ass we can

     CHORUS:
       When the boys offed the daddy
       They offed the mama too
       Threw her in for good measure
       As faithful sons should do

There was blood on the pillow
Brains on the floor
They ate it with a spoon
And waded in for more

They told the police
It was some kind of slime
Broke into the house
And performed the horrid crime

     CHORUS

And then they told the shrink
To test his endurance

They did it for fun
And for the insurance

But the treacherous shrink
Went and told the grand jury
Which put Eric and Lyle
In a terrible fury

CHORUS

So they told the court
And the teevee screen
How dad was abusive
And mom was mean

And Lyle shed tears
And Eric looked so glum
They were just poor little rich boys
And we ought to pity them

CHORUS

And the call-in phones kept ringing
And the talk-show hosts were glad
And America was singing
We're glad they offed their dad

We're glad they offed the mama too
We'd like to off our own
And pay a hotshot lawyer
With the money raining down

ALICIA OSTRIKER

CHORUS

We'd like to make them heroes
Throughout this mighty land
Their statue in the park
Their shotgun in their hand

For Americans are in love with guns
In love with youth and freedom
And violence is apple pie
The media can feed 'em

CHORUS

Well a story should have a moral
A ballad needs an end
Like the right to life is for embryos
And dollars are to spend

And if the jury gets confused
The boys are not to blame—
Though when the funds start running out
Attorneys do the same

And some folks say our twentieth
Century is the worst
But the moral of this story is:
Wait till the twenty-first!

CHORUS—

GOODBYE TO THE TWENTIETH CENTURY
OR
ADIOS, BUSY SIGNAL

O Century   standing in the line of fire   A lake
on the slope of a plate   danger in the silverware drawer   O chaos
of looming disaster   where there are pots & pans teetering
no heart in the ketchup   no second guessing the mustard

O little beep beep beep   O So long
nothing about you means anything anymore   only lost
     opportunities
O hello   automated answering systems of the future   call
     waiting   O
voice mail   O pay phone at the frantic airport relaying
     delayed messages
"We're busy signal free," he said.   banishing forever   the busy
     signal

Traditionally   we were either there   or   we weren't
Now we can begin at the window   in a puddle of midnight
or sway in buckling air   a symbol of currency   and   decor
puffs rise out of the sugar bowl   Salt Spews

For most people the truly upsetting thing seemed to be
that Marilyn Monroe was home   alone   on a Saturday night
O she who was found dead   nude   in bed with a telephone
the lyrical hiccup of the busy signal   tunneling   her through the
     dark

MICHAEL PALMER

AUTOBIOGRAPHY 2 (HELLOGOODBY)
for A.C.

The Book of Company which
I put down and can't pick up

The Trans-Siberian disappearing,
the Blue Train and the Shadow Train

Her body with ridges like my skull
Two children are running through the Lion Cemetery

Five travellers are crossing the Lion Bridge
A philosopher in a doorway insists

that there are no images
He whispers instead: Possible Worlds

The Mind-Body Problem
The Tale of the Color Harpsichord

Skeleton of the World's Oldest Horse
The ring of O dwindles

sizzling round the hole until gone
False spring is laughing at the snow

and just beyond each window
immense pines weighted with snow

A philosopher spreadeagled in the snow
holds out his Third Meditation

like a necrotic star. He whispers:
archery is everywhere in decline,

photography the first perversion of our time
Reach to the milky bottom of this pond

to know the feel of bone,
a knuckle from your grandfather's thumb,

the maternal clavicle, the familiar
arch of a brother's brow

He was your twin, no doubt,
forger of the unicursal maze

My dearest Tania, When I get a good position in the courtyard
I study their faces through the haze

Dear Tania, Don't be annoyed,
please, at these digressions

They are soldering the generals
back onto their pedestals

MOLLY PEACOCK

GOODBYE HELLO IN THE EAST VILLAGE

Three tables from where Allen Ginsberg sits
in JJ Ukranian Restaurant, my old friend
who's struggled for her happiness all her life, insists
on examining why I am so happy—there's been an end
to my troubles of the century. *"Listen Molly, if I
didn't know you so well, I'd think you were
faking this good cheer,"* she says, her eyes
bright openings like a husky's eyes in its fur
(in her case, hair, and wool scarf—it's cold in here.)
The East Village shuffles past JJ's window,
and we hear Allen order loudly in the ear
of the waitress, *"Steamed only! No cholesterol!"*
"I could tell you it's my marriage, Nita,
and how much I love my new life in two countries,
but the real reason," I beam irresistibly at a
dog walker with 8 dogs on leashes in the freezing
evening outside JJ's window where we sit,
"is that I'm *an orphan.* It's *over.* They're
both dead." Her lids narrow her eyes to a slit
of dead recognition. "I couldn't say this,"—there!
the waitress plunks two bowls of brilliant magenta
Ukranian borscht, pirogi, and hunks of Challah
—"to just *anybody*,"—jewel heaps of food on formica.
"I know," she says, knowing how tight, higher,
taut, the rope grew, between my attention
to the now happily dead Them and the newly
happily alive Me . . .

          the old world order done,
just as now the US, its old enemy

the USSR vaporized, disarms itself
nearly wondering what a century's fuss
was about . . . what *was* my fuss about? (The wealth
of relief that's felt after decades of distrust,
defending constantly against an enemy,
makes you wonder why you did it, until
you remind yourself of how it was. Sensibly.)
But even a struggle to the death pales
in the afterlife of relief. Now health
for my husband and me is all I care about, and fuss
with the details of our exercise program
just as the US fusses with its health program.
It's fun to enjoy our mutual horoscopes,
America's, and Molly's—CANCER, the word
everybody's scared of: when a Republican loped
off the White House lawn, and America deferred
to a President my own age, I enjoyed
a surge, on a petty domestic level,
an *excessive* surge, of relief, buoyed
because our horoscopes predicted it, the bevel
in the glass of America connected
along a strip of my life as the window
of JJ restaurant connects Nita and me, wed
to the night life on Second Avenue, though
in reflection only, the reflection that now perfectly
joins Ginsberg with his steamed vegetables
and us with our steamy borscht and pirogi
to the winter night sidewalk, God's table,
full of passersby, pointing occasionally to Allen
joined now by an Asian boy, but more often
just hurrying past in the cold as we eat
the food of a captive of a previous enemy

and find it brightly delicious—*it is meet*
and right so to do in the world now ours completely,
the century's years hurtling behind
like snow wake off a speeding dogsled.
My old friend rests, not talking, well fed,
since at this moment things are fine.

from *Original Love* (Norton, 1995)

FROM THE FRONT

This picture can hardly be right:
a man with a hammer upraised

above a grain of sand resting
on a glass table. Then there's

another thing wrong: a scowling man
pushing a baby in a carriage

while across the street a woman
holding a child in one arm

tries the houses, asking for work
on a balmy late fall afternoon.

While I rush through the conventionally
dim 'hallways,' 'doors,' and of course

up the stern 'stairs' of dreams
searching for the history exam offstage,

the ironies of permanent childhood uncover
themselves and gesture, their magic markers

falling and streaking all economic surfaces.
The color combinations in the catalogs

wither kaleidoscopically as the market refuses
to open its arms, reveal its

motives, or die in peace. It's
1991—at least it was, once

upon a time—and communism is
dead, leaving capitalism, the word, the

movie, the whole ball of idiomatic
wax, with nowhere to go, nothing

to mean. The free world belongs
in a language museum now, along

with free love and free verse.
In mainstream editorial cartoons Arabs have

big noses and big barrels of
oil, with real and emotional starvation

figured as dunes in the desert
that can't help being so dry.

On the freeways, in malls, in
bed, in couplets, the subjects of

history study, cut class, or flunk,
but no one passes. The soft,

cliched underbelly of consumer desire comes
on screen: the untensed bodies of

money incarnate, generic curls making hay
while the sun shines, the excised

pasts and futures formed into remnant
he's or she's whose job is

to demonstrate the willing suspension of
economic autonomy. In life, the actors

may be murdered, dead of AIDS
or the recombined by-products of industry,

or have gone back to school,
but nevertheless are there on cassette,

alive and moving, rented and possessed
in the shower with vibrator and

camera eye applied to the place
in the market which stands for

a particularly crude but still undefinable
hope for utopia. No escape from

the implosions of sitting and looking,
or looking away. My little horse

must think it queer. He gives
his harness bells a shake—we

are living in a permanent Christmastime
economy after all; so even if

it hardly snows anymore there are
plenty of harness bells—and suggests,

in a horsey way, that poetry
had better focus on coherent, individualized

spots of time, with a concomitant
narrative frame of loss. A carrot,

in other words, and not theoretical
sticks crashing down on parallel jargon-universes,

with the poet wearing self-critical armor
impossible to visualize, let alone read,

inflicting transpersonal wounds on the microarmies
of intellectuals organized into professional phalanxes.

On the battlefield, discipline is ragged,
and the lines separating the divisions

waver like metaphors on a foggy
spring evening, paired bodies, adolescent, in

love, buoyed on seas of plenty,
articulated by time and energy to

paroxysms of generosity, towards themselves if
no one else. But this is

to lecture the open barn door
well after the flying saucer has

disappeared over the horizon, taking understated
control of the airwaves, leaving behind

the smell of hay, the musty
charm of provincial dress and dialect.

These are the stuff of many
a mini-series, nor do the imaginary

raw materials of this poem-like writing
come from a separate world. The

poet has no job; the only
jobs now involve tracking classes under

glass, the stories accumulating spectacles of
damage. To write the histories with

any accuracy is to write backwards,
true to the falsity of experience.

There are no longer any individuals
or individual poems, only a future

more shattery than ever but still
nearer to us than present.

Saw chairs back into branches, or
words and actions to that effect.

ROBERT PETERS

POET AND CENTURY BOTH TURN GERIATRIC

> *Sweet Thames, run softly, till I end my Song.*
> Edmund Spenser, "Prothalamion"

1.
Xerosis afflicts old limbs
with a paste of aphid
thoraxes, an amber honey
of pupa sacks, a waste,
an epidermal flake farm.
You once slept through the night:
these days the prostate
flashes incisors
at its own preposterous meal.
You sleep-walk to the john.
Once, Wisconsin farm boy genes
nurtured sinewy, big-chested
sexy capillaries sweetened
with body parrafin, estrogen.
No hair then sprouted
from your ear tops.
There's now a sardonic clapping,
a giggle of skeletal molars.
Your death will be raunchy.
You will be forever forgotten.

2.
Crisco is the best emollient,
restores oil and water

to aging capillaries.
Wear gauze mittens
to keep from drawing blood.
There's a vague odor of
fried onions and stale socks,
which disappears, and
in your bed, on your back,
in the posture of an effigy
on a tomb you sleep.
You think you're a pig greased,
pursued, and captured
at the County Fair of Death.
Sweet century, flow softly, till I end my song.

3.
Aging, so goes the lie,
is more mental than physical.
Your blood gushes red and orange.
There's still some sperm.
I'd assumed the spigot closed
before sixty, a stain on a bedsheet
impervious to bleach, WD 40,
or old perverts' teeth.
Grin at polyester clad geriatrics
leering beneath pink ballons
at a Senior Center
after a free roast chicken and Lipton's tea.

4.
Well, these old legs are itching

again, shagged as they are with death.
Mossy fungi, coin-sized, sprout
on my back, chest, and elbows, grin
with little Boschian faces transposed
from the bellies of devils
in Renaissance views of the Apocalypse.
Scraping them produces a mass
which I roll into an oily ball
and drop beneath the cushion of my
fake leather recliner.
Scarabs rasp razory tomb-wings.

5.
December 31, 1999, Midnight:
A stark green light cast
from your TV. Your mate
of thirty years is with you.
The new-century world carnival
blares from kaleidoscopic cities.
The revelry is insane
and you sit semi-comatose,
covered with scale and goosebumps,
clutching the afghan
your mother hooked for you.
At two minutes past one
you'll enjoy a melted Crisco
sitz-bath. The heating-element
bubbles—the temperature
is almost right, hot enough
to excite, not enough to blister.
A computerized baby

with "2000" printed on its sash
is a collicky, wretched creature.
He hides a sickle in his Pampers.
Though we thrust our geriatric rumps
into wipe-position, nothing can sanitize
this messy end-of-century-business.
My force, I know, overpowers the force
of the twentieth century.
Death's ectoplasm oozes over the doorsill.
Flow gently, sweet century, I've finished my song.

YEARBOOK

Farewell, years of the 20th century. Goodbye
collectively and individually. I will miss you.

Goodbye 1991, year of the palindrome. There will never
be another year like you until 2002.

Oh 1968, you and your friends 1967 & 1969 were a riot.

I'll never forget you, 1978. You were the year in
which I first had sex. I bid you farewell in French, the
language of intercourse:

Baisse-moi, prends-moi ici, dans ce poème,
sur cette page. Oh, mais tu es si sensuel,
année provacant! Au revoir.

I wish I had known you better: 1904, 1905, 1906. I
always think of you guys together, sitting at the back of
the 20th century. I wish we could have hung out!

1992. The year I graduated from law school. What have
you been up to? Let's have lunch.

1955. I wasn't born yet, but don't think for a minute
I don't lie awake, nostalgic for you.

I would like to apologize to the 1980s. I never said
you were hollow and heartless. If I did say that you were
hollow and heartless, I meant it in a positive way. We only
hurt the years we love.

CARL RAKOSI

MUSEUM OF HISTORICAL OBJECTS

I.
New Acquisition

an honest word
(embalmed in amber)
out of Washington

as rare
as hippopotamus meat

or a blade of timothy
behind a bumpkin's ear.

II.
the realists

Let us be honest,
there are the poor,

the virtuous, the artists
weeping at injustice,

and there are the realists
who secretly admire the rich

and cultivate rapacity,
who are always well-bred

303

and decently non-commital
like the upper classes

but implacable
in their self-interest.

III.
the reality

How are you?

Why do you ask?
Not floating
like a sea turtle

in chelonian
bliss,
I can tell you.

And you?

Can't say.
Too busy.

Try. What
are you
feeling?

the state
of the world
. . . flaky . . .

a ship passing
in the night,
calling:

Idealists aboard!
we're quarantined
we can't land.

LEN ROBERTS

SOMEWHERE SOMEONE IS MAKING ANOTHER

    bomb,
another tank, plane, mine, gun
    while
my son runs up the third and final
    completely
pure, deep crust of snowed hill
    behind our house,
his dog, Magic—shiny black
    as the crows
who jerk their heads to croak,
    omens,
I'm sure, of some pain or death—
    runs
beside him, nine-year-old boy
    and two-year-old dog
in a line of ten thousand years
    of bloodshed and war,
Tu Fu's Thousand Sorrows,
Rexroth's and Snyder's Thousand
    Miles
Hayden's tear-soaked store-bought
    mediocre
blueberry pie eaten at his outpost
    of January
Syracuse New York, poets of every
    possible
year and the remotest possible
    country
always watching the snow fall,
listening to the sweet song

of a tree toad
or a white-headed night sparrow,
gazing at *interminable spaces* . . .
overwhelmed with dread . . .
    only
my young son's voice bringing me
    back
to the perfect Christmas tree
    he's
finally found, him hopping
    up and down,
and the dog so excited he
    runs
in mad circles, his tags
    clinking
as I bend to saw the tree
    down
at the end of this bloody
        century.

MUSIC
for Valerie & for Jack Fulton

Dave saved up his money and bought a bar. He liked classical music and since the bar was in the middle of the Great Basin night miles from the likelihood to hear any such thing, he decided what the hell, called it the Mozart Club. He really couldn't remember whether it was Chopin, Satie, Mozart or Mendlesohn that had moved him so, but he liked the sound of Mozart. He painted a big skeleton on the side of the bar emblazoned with the legend, "This Guy Drank Water." A lot of local folks thought that was pretty funny and began to call the watering hole home.

Every month or so Dave and this painter friend of his would make the day-long drive to Reno on a supply run. They were at the Santa Fe and had consumed way too many picons and that great Friday night Basque steak dinner. They were standing around the bar drinking Winnemucca coffees, debating whether they should head back or not and if they did who, given all the picons, was the most qualified to drive, when she walked in.

She was the most drop-dead, beautiful woman you'd ever seen. She could have been northern Italian or English or Irish, what with that stunning mane of red hair and those amazing legs. But she was, in fact, Austrian. After a quick look around she walked to the end of the bar and sat on a stool, crossing her legs high. Dave, and everyone else in the bar, was speechless. She had silenced that rowdy, Friday night crowd just by walking in like the way, sometimes, the sun going down can stop a wind that's been howling all day across the desert's face.

Dave watched his heart tumble out of his chest and flop around on the bar like some fish sensing that it was, after all, the seventh year of a drought and this just might be it.

"Would you like a drink?" he suddenly blurted out.

Their eyes locked and that was it. They spent the next three hours drinking at a small table in the back. Dave kept feeding her small slices of lime from the palm of his hand and she'd laugh, oh how she'd laugh. She'd get up every so often to go and call someone and Dave would watch her walk to the phone and back wondering, wondering . . . He even reached under the table once and squeezed her leg, thinking, oh my God what a stupid thing to do, now she'll walk out and I'll never see her again.

But she stayed and talked and drank and they both felt some kind of furnace burning within them like never before until, finally, she said, "I have to go. My brother's coming to pick me up."

She left with her brother. Dave left with his painter friend and they all ended up standing in the parking lot, Dave and her just staring at each other, neither wanting to break the connection. "Jeezus Christ, Dave," the painter said, "Put your goddamn eyes back in your head and open the goddamn door."

Who's to say what happened next or how it happened but Dave hung around until he saw her again and that's all it took. A done deal. Never a question. She came back to the Mozart Club with him. That's when the music really began. And from then on everyone kept commenting on how amazing it all was, how right it all seemed, how good they looked together, how glad they were for Dave.

This is it, Dave thought. At last. And he began to think of waltzing toward the millennium on a sea of melodious light. But then there's always life. It goes on, as they say. And it does. But it also can just suddenly stop.

He went down to the bar one day and came home to find her gone. No note. No word. Nothing. Her clothes, her shoes, everything but her, still there. Dave looked and looked, went back up to Reno, but nothing. Not a trace. No one even knew her.

It was as if she had never existed, as if it had all never happened. But Dave knew it had and he tried to forget but couldn't because he didn't really want to forget. He never did look at another woman and he drank more than a bit and it was worse than fightin the weather, all that thinkin about it, wonderin what had happened, why there were all these years of nights they might have been together, but weren't.

It was thirty years later, almost to the day, that this gorgeous redhead walked into the Mozart Club. Everyone was stumblin over themselves, hittin on her, trying to buy her a drink, everyone that is but Dave, who just sat at the end of the bar nursing his drink. But she wasn't interested in all the attention and only wanted one thing.

"Is there anyone here named Dave?" she asked.

"Down there, end of the bar," Dave's painter friend said.

She walked down to the end of the bar, everyone watching her every move. "Dave?" she asked.

"Yeah?" he said looking up from his drink, his bloodshot blues meeting her amber ones, "Whatya want?"

"I'm your daughter," she said.

And so the story was told. How her mother was from a very wealthy Austrian family; how she had come to the States on vacation with her brother; how she had walked into a bar in Reno one Friday night and fallen head-over-heels in love with the piercing blue eyes of a guy named Dave who owned a bar; how her grandmother had disowned her mother for having the audacity to do that; how after that it didn't seem to matter until her grandmother fell ill and wanted her daughter back home before she died; how her grandmother sent her son back to the States to kidnap her daughter; how her mother was in a car accident and they were able to save the baby, but not her; how her grandmother recovered, raised her and never mentioned any of it; how her uncle told her all about it only after her grandmother finally died.

BOB ROSENTHAL

TWENTIETH CENTURY PRESENTS

the head of the year is not beginning
like the head of a family is not first
the end of a century does not mark a future
the final twist to a millennium of shrinkage will not expand
staring at a rusty bottle cap wedged between rocks off the porch
with its jagged Jughead crown when cans did rust

good bye big sky

good bye little tv

good bye empire

                          state building over left shoulder
bars & stars
      long whistle

          after time of repair
               necessary volume
       death's open yap
             deems passage

when we ask favors
they best be small
as we tipple clouds

           a century note ago
         the frontier closed
I felt my hand close on the hemp a half life back
the fear stood proud like cabbies bearing down on a fare

driving down McCormick Blvd. with my father conducting
en route to Grandma Esse's
Texaco Saturday Afternoon at the MET
all the miracles brought to bear on culture
yet culture of the old ebbed
and finally reduced to a digitized footprint

we sat before the black & white lines of our past
watching history replay to change the ageless
now history remembered is doomed to be relived
the holocaust just the first scent downwind
                            of the rotting millennium
perhaps while keypunching in Iowa
I never could see myself
at present easily inputting directly to a paperless future
yet my car is a quarter century old and not out cold

I marvel in daily delight at Manhattan trees
                    soaking up toxic air—drinking foul waste
                                bending up to soiled daylight
their green begets survival
        Earth tender atmosphere
            is the only bubble
                            to prognosticate a future
we are wandering into our own inversions
virtual reality chips at the base of the century of images
route 66 of information connects the new faithful
            by the illumination of microchips
                even as the numbers fall
                        the echoes of loss redouble

LAURA ROSENTHAL

MEMOREYES@AOL

sedated by the black-eyed pea & ham hock
the self
            less spirit than gizmo
sings its synesthetic revision
faster than a speeding bullet
more powerful than the most powerful
pussy
you
are not who you think you are
you
are not
being processed

hello old father!
you look timeless in beeper & bushjacket
our father
                  old century
you are a fuckup
                        & we're codependent
atm is our mantra
                        we suck
the green mother

luck's not funny & it's hard work

bye bye Mr. Century!
your big wars gave us

tampons
   penicillin
     & bob dylan
but don't drink the water in the damned global village

no poems in the poker machine

three girls
    on a pool table
        peasants
without fields
     a guy named Fish

I don't belong to me
born on a day that wasn't
born to an unconscious mother
if you're lucky
you die undiagnosed

in the next life I'll deal

JEROME ROTHENBERG

TWENTIETH CENTURY UNLIMITED

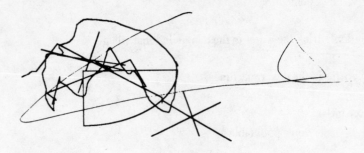

as the twentieth century winds down
the nineteenth begins
again
        it is as if nothing happened
though those who lived it thought
that everything was happening
enough to name a world for & a time
to hold it in your hand
unlimited   the last delusion
like the perfect mask of death

DEDICATIONS

for day-old soup delectability,
for that ziplock baggie I found
full of refrigerated batteries,
these are the reasons I eat read & go on—
for whatever spooked my ancestors out of Spain
and into the New World
where I learned to love plantain and tobacco,
for marching band in seventh grade
where I learned the term "neo-nazi,"
for readers who read only this far;
I don't blame you—God hears me,
for Rodger who gave me bad advice,
for Jacques for such natty non-sequiturs,
for Christopher Smart who made me feel not so crazy
about cats, so now I have four in a 2-room apt.,
for the whole of Baton Rouge—
the Exxon plant about to blow,
recycle bins full of racoons,
even Mike Bigalke who roams my neighborhood with top-secrets,
for 666 North 6th St. and the bathroom with the 3 doors,
for all the sunrooms in Spanishtown,
for wide walkable streets strewn with smooshed pecans,
the pink & lavender myrtle trees, kids who
regurgitate melifluently in the bushes every Mardi Gras,
for New Orleans for only being an hour away
(if Laura is driving),
for Patrick whose name rhymes with "hat trick,"
for Ken for twenty-one years,
for Nirmala for stamina,
for Kelly for plain beauty,

for Laura for spite,
for Wyatt for macho,
for every pilot who's flown me out of here,
for Taos where I learned to hum,
for Boulder where I learned the true meaning of "breathless,"
for San Francisco where girls walked in broad daylight
with no shirts on & daisies painted around their nipples,
where I was unfashionable but inexplicably adored,
for Kathy for a feeling like napping on a cloud,
for Mitch for that joint he scored at the last minute
for my nauseated, dying friend,
for that friend now dead for not haunting me,
for Barbara for so much free art,
for Andrei even though he is famous,
for Joël who took books and boyfriends she didn't return;
I didn't want them anyway.
God, I am too young to be this nostalgic,
or perhaps I'm about to die myself
without having published one itsy-bitsy self-important book
& hence, these dedications—
or maybe I've forgotten
too many kindnesses,
so I want to get it all down
for Ed Sanders who gave me a vitamin C when I needed one,
for this teaching and that teaching
like so many cross-etchings over my soul,
for my sister, for my dogs,
for my parents,
forever for my own growing gratitude,
for good,
for it was all
good fortune.

TURN OF THE CENTURY
TIME, LINES

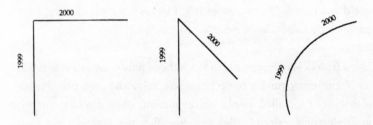

The turn of the coming century. Is the turn a right angle, 90 degrees? Silvia wears a black hat with a wide brim and soft black veiling that extends all the way to the floor. Nothing else on. She bends over a parson's table in an entry hall. Underfoot: large black and white marble rectangles. A naked man, Swami Sukhasan, enters her from behind. *Question: Could this be love?*

Could time turn back on itself at, say, a 45 degree angle? Silvia bends forward to blow dry her curly red hair. It enjoys better lift with the head thrown forward. Her cheeks come up pink. "Make them come to you," he'd said that first day over samosas at the Indian restaurant. She knew then he was a confidence man. *Question: She didn't care, Why not?*

Is the turn like a tortuous curve in the road along the Amalfi coast? Swami S.'s Maserati clings to the edge as it climbs the chalky cliffs overlooking the blue sea. Beside him, Silvia, in gray pin-stripe suit, leans over the seat, poking about for the box of white nougats he stole in Perugia. "I have my own code," he'd said, standing on his hands in Kukutasan, the cock position.

Is it a parabola with a focus, axis, directrix? The directrix is a fixed straight line. Press your hands against her if you must. Silvia peers over her horn-rimmed glasses at the roomful of physicists. She is demonstrating a computer animation program on chaos, remembering what she'd said to him: "Each time we talk, I feel as if we were having intercourse." *Question: Can love and lust coexist?*

Is it a fractal—no longer a turn but rather a paisley design reiterating itself, stuttering into the future? Maybe it's a Koch curve, pretty triangles, chaos controlled for marketing purposes. Could we have a little more electric purple? His dark eyebrows flow together. His legs, covered with black hair, wrap scissors-style around her. He is developing yoga for couples. For an hour at a time, they stare at each other in this pose. *Question: Will the future be airbrushed?*

Is the turn an illusion, an imaginary curve made of imaginary numbers extending only the egos of seers? Swami S. was late. Silvia was his computer instructor. Her red hair was pulled into a tight chignon. "You must be punished"; she said, "write a hundred times, 'I am a bad boy' on my breasts in squid ink." She undoes her suit blouse. He finished with writer's cramp. "Look," she says, "you've dirtied my breasts. Lick them clean." Between lips, smudged with black stains, come, "Only a few can master the art of kundalini." *Question: Can one in drunkenness/lust ever reach a divine state?*

Is the turn something soothing like the idea of progress? Rounding a corner, just about to remove the rough edges: the influence of hormonal drips and surges, the limbic system, the R-complex. Remove not only messiness but also civilization in the form of bonding and ritual. No more drawbacks to murder. "Intimidating, powerful. You're exactly the kind of woman I like," he said.

Does the century know it's supposed to hold surprises? Does time know it's expected to turn? Will time do something radical like run backward? "To avoid respiratory disease insert a stiff string into each nostril and bring it out through your mouth." Silvia and Swami S. were standing on their heads in the lotus padmasan position. *Question: Does the one you love make you more of the person you are?*

The torque of the century. Force(s) that produce a twisting motion. The turn of the screw. Screwed into the twenty-first century. The cork-screw penises of ducks and pigs suddenly in vogue. The threads go from left to right. Most viruses originate in the gut of farm animals in China, a pig-duck culture. "I'm going to fuck you through your little finger," he said. *Question: Is this an example of intimacy or hatred?*

Is the turn so banked, everyone who missed the last century can catch up? New concepts of language and time could be picked up on the far turn. Swami S. said, "Every time we talk I feel as though we're having intercourse. I'll call you tomorrow; you believe me, don't you?" And then he vanished. Later she saw him on TV advertising his interactive computer program—"Yoga for Couples," introductory offer. She remembered their first meeting: "Make them come to you."

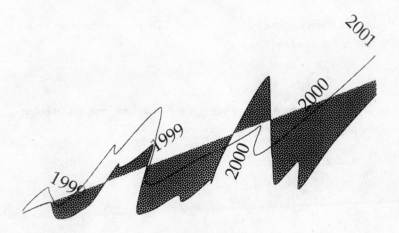

FROM: *NEW TIME*

Why would they dismiss it because it's not the same?

It *exists* because it's not the same

. . .

     running with bare feet, the snow falling, after the man
clothed in black in the black sky—is the neck cut out

     in their (other's) existence—one's neck cut out
     blossoms blossomed. in time.

. . .

     'Undermining' this, by seeing its appearance—places the individual doing so in the light of aberration (viewed by others, but also increasingly in the act of aberration by seeing (its) appearance) which may be regarded hy a 'viewer'—as merely 'personal,' not theoretical (which, as interpretive, assessment, is at that moment 'authority' itself)

     if there's no overriding structure, "There is no character-simulacrum for it to reside in."

. . .

     economic poverty (not being special) of them, one, is that being the physical body, *per se*. throughout.

     which isn't inner.

. . .

from the waist—so that, turned the bulb that's oneself (tho-
rax)—only—then—doesn't have any existence—turned (wherever
one turns)

as conception—at waist of magnolia buds that exist in the day
really

sewing the black silk irises—not when one turned at waist

sewing them, they have no shape literally except being that—
from one's hand (being, in the air)

the irises only had existence in the black, before dawn, in fact

a man doesn't want me to become quiet again—go into ocean
not weighed of before fighting—ever

formation of that of narrowed to no form in one—of black
voluptuous lip—outside—voluptuous lips that (aren't) on black
dawn, or before it when it's black.

There was no intention—being done—with their existing.

not weighed before fighting which is the black, weighed, air—
not the lips which have no weight—isn't following

if one's not contending . . . so the inner isn't contending
either . . . ?

. . .

there's no time to oneself is the dawn occurring—its rim

it has no rim

pressure so that the mind comes in to the social unit
it isn't done by people there's no time to oneself
(it's done by people only)—the night, the dawn, there

the constructed unit being no time to oneself—standing being completely alone ('standing,' as 'walking')

. . .

flowering trees float the sky—packed luminous sky of ocean (a sky that is an ocean) the group, not having time for oneself, opens that one floated sky

sleep-deprived one
pressure so that the mind comes into the social unit—only
the flowering trees, that have nothing but swimming on sky

. . .

we can not speak as to concentrate on the constructed unit—nor sleep much and that "causes" (?) an actual harmony, serial or it's there after a while, not based on the similarities of the people

the night is exhaustion rains
luminous night while running to the rise

that's dawn is when running to the rise, later
the rise is the floating people

IN THE HEART OF THE EMPIRE the nightsounds
tingle the gyzmatic box   the sensor   in the giant sensorium
this comfort   now fleeting & not so fleeting
now elusive
       now found
                 now no where around
I am dreaming
          I'm not dreaming
               I wish I were dreaming

I am trapped in a geography of chemicals & I don't mind as long as
it don't hurt too much   & I don't know what to do about the pain
of my brother & sister creatures on this planet   or how to look them
in the eye   & have something to say besides   cry

      there are so many freaks

    & yes   there has been so much joy in all of us

      especially those soft come sleeps   & mother dreams

    or the sunflower showers of radiation & elation

to be running over   earth's gentle tresses hillsides

beneath sky man

      pure sky

   which we come out of & return to like water back to water

            which is also alive

while in the street   the usual madmen reflect the faces

of the demons that made them mad   which is to kill

which is to be hungry

which is to be insane in the wall of cacophonous sound

& the steely brickbattered sootsky   reminder

I'm not free   I'm not free

& no good ever came out of the barrel of a gun

to splatter the flexing cerebrum

but watch out for the jack boots & the nightmare raiders

& if it comes to that   would you want to be armed against all

possible assailants

or rather   have none   & be   at ease

so this is something we must all work towards

being high   & unafraid

to shine it on

like the cow mother who nourishes us

but she obliterates herself   with heroin

because of the dream that it will make you fine

                    perpetrated by a liar   so subtle

   his face was hidden

                              behind a beatific smile

there is a promise

                there is a promised land   right in the body

      but the land is overrun by creatures who feel that someone

must get the trains to run on time

ARMAND SCHWERNER

ECTROTERIFISICA
(Electronica Esoterica/Metafisica) by Ingenio Malatesta

By the third decade of the 21st century, insensate tsunamis of information gathered force. They resulted from preconscious earthquakes of feckless optimism. How much release of irritation, fear or panic was triggered in citizen sufferers depended on whether individuals were living in space stations, if they were subjected to narrow majoritarian mediaspectra, whether they were residing in vast technobubble-sheathed agripolises or right inside centers of modern electrurbs. Pain was by no means inevitable; that depended; in addition to the variable of site, the degree of pathology experienced by any individual derived also from the status of h/his personal mechanisms of defense, h/his degree of futurological opacity, h/his age and profession and the particular conformation of the macrosynapses which connected the citizen with a particular Municipal Neural Site, MUCEUS.

Sometimes the best way to experience home is to wander away from known ports and into dusk. Assumptions that drive actions in daylight suffer the little doubts under the moon. Not lunacy but compellingly indistinct quitclaim evacuations keep sapping the great conducting vessels of our 21st century. The possibility of a viable 22nd century may lie in renunciation not deed transfer; out of a singular epiphany to make over to others a rejected will begs the creative anarchism of surrender.

Krishnamurti writes, "In meditation one has to find out whether there is an end to knowledge and so freedom from the known." In that light, the 2030-2045 C.E. (30-45 E.) transition from the flourishing of Selective Elimination of Information (SEI, contextualized in this volume by the Archivist Basil Fotherington-Thomas) to the dourer, more enkompsiŋ Superior Information Destruction Application (SIDA), limns the Path to Silence. Krishnamurti writes:

Meditation is destruction to security, and there is a great beauty in meditation, not the beauty of things that have been put together by man or by nature but of silence. This silence is emptiness in which and from which all things flow and have their being. It is unknowable; intellect and feeling cannot make their way to it; there is no way to it and a method to it is the invention of a greedy brain. All the ways and means of the calculating self must be destroyed wholly; all going forward or backward, the way of time, must come to an end, without tomorrow. Meditation is destruction; it's a danger to those who wish to lead a superficial life and a life of fancy and myth.

It's easy to see in such apothegms apologia for crackpot meltdowns of civilizational process. Aldous Huxley writes in his 'Preface' to a new edition of *Brave New World*, "The greatest triumphs of propaganda have been accomplished, not by doing something, but by refraining from doing. Great is truth, but still greater, from a practical point of view, is silence about truth . . . silence is not enough . . . . The most important Manhattan Projects of the future will be vast government-sponsored inquiries into what the politicians and the participating scientists will call 'the problem of happiness'—in other words, the problem of making people love their servitude." The very ambiguity, oracular, of Huxley's adjective surprises the 21st century reader; Huxley greatly loaded "great."

Little early 21st century speculation envisaged the corrective purgations of SEI, much less the degree of willing subjection to the Way of Silence. Sophisticated tallies of viewpoints evident in popular and scholarly expressions, from 2001-2060 E., present the Way of Silence as a major new player in the World Syncretist Order, which followed hard upon and radically undid the petty narcissisms and cloistered Occidentalisms of the Neo-Post-Modern period. The energy of the path of Silence entwines inextricably with the potencies of Knowledge and Information. Like medieval cartographers we locate trouble spots, and we publish them: *Hic Sunt Serpentes;* but unlike our forebears we identify the fear-inducing Other variously. Who the monsters are, and where, and how they agitate, though mighty difficult questions, are not totally beyond conjecture. Many dualists among present-day scholars cite two distinct organismic realms: that of the Ogre of Information, the other that of the Fiend of Silence

Aiming at an implicit contrast between past and present language practices, we have been at great pains to compose this essay in the Formal American Dialect current in 1994, seventy years ago. In order to track current subversions we examine some mid-21st-century language practices, in the context of six growth categories contributory to the Sectors of Silence: 1. ICONOCIZATION; 2. COMPDiŋ; 3. RIDUKSHN; 4. APHASIA INTERMITTA; 5. POLGLŌ ; 6. MACERAŠN.

To demonstrate language changes, and the implicit directions of those changes, we present, below, a few examples taken from paragraphs I and II, transformed from the 20th century Post-modern American writing system to contemporary usages; we note the relevant growth categories. The uses of the distant past irrigate present day language-seeds. A most striking development, accelerating in the 40s and 50s of the 21st century, involves the functional recrudescence in Speed-E-Mail (SPEEDY) and Speed-E-Publishing (SPEEDEEPUB) of pictographic icons modeled on pre-cuneiform notational systems. Contemporary language reformations include various terms and icons—some reconstructed by Armond Schwerner's magistral Scholar/Translator in *The Tablets*—some reminiscent of Egyptian and Akkadian, all of which may operate as Determinatives both within and outside of utterances. Another development introduces Utterances/Texture/Indicators—most notably icons standing for particular Body-Declensions. (For example see below: ≈, or ʮ.)

We stress the *absence of body* incident to the physically isolating, endemic pullulation of E-Discerning and E-Composing: the spirit of this time has provided iconic parallels for the evanescently subtle body-signs which had for thousands of years enriched human relationships. The rapidity and troglodytization of E-Discourse exact substitutive deformations—some of which do contribute creatively to current language-modes. Other Utterance/Texture/Indicators, notably the now familiar Torques of Separativeness, ▢, ▭, ▭▭, plangently inform our contemporary notation. Icons are often contextually definable. (See for instance, ❟, in the first example.) In the first sentence,

"By the third decade of the 21st century, insensate tsunamis of information gathered force." =

" ℘ ≋ 21 ➔ + 30, ▭▭ tsnm❟,"

term 1, ℘, the Broken-Scissor U/T/I of Solitary Reading and the Subsuming Position-

Determinative, readies the E-Reader for entry into term 2, ≋, a Body-Declension signifying 'Crouched-Dying,' which like all such icons offers the E-Reader para-diagrams within which, or through the agency of which, he or she may experience the phrase-object and its harmonics.

Thus the para-diagram partly fills the space left by absent body-signs. For the rest, the utterance is self-defining. More manifestly than in 20th century writing, intention informs our notational system: should the composer of the utterance wish to stress pervasiveness, he can substitute for ≋ the icon ♄, 'Boundaryless Identification,' thus yielding: " ℘ ♄ 21 ➔ +30, ▭▭ tsnm❟."

An idiosyncratic icon, the U/T/I-Blocker, 𓂀, serves if the utterer wants suddenly to cancel a preceding body-Declension without altering the rapid forward movement of his E-Composing. Such cancellation yields:

" 𓂀 ꓧ 𓂀 21 ➜ + 30, ⬓⬓⬓ tsnm❢," or

" 𓂀 ≋ 𓂀 21 ➜ + 30, ⬓⬓⬓ tsnm❢."

Current usages are reflected in the transformed first line of paragraph II, given below in its 20th century form:

"Sometimes the best way to experience home is to wander away from known ports and into dusk." =

" 𓂀 ꓚ 𓋹 sometimes = 𓏤↔←↑→↓ from ⸙ and into dusk,"
in which the Body-Declension ꓚ signifies "Crouched-Giving-Birth," and the Mind/Texture/Determinative 𓋹 casts its open, lit, features onto the initial segments.

The modern practices of APHASIA INTERMITTA, along with creative punctuation, facilitate the rapid forward movement of E-Reading. Take for instance the modern transformation of the 20th century sentence given above:

"Sometimes the best way to experience home is to wander away from known ports and into dusk."

=" 𓂀 𓏤 ⸙ ⇒ SOMETIMES BEST HOME: WANDER,
NO LOVEPORT; DUSK."

The successful application of the extreme MACERAŠN (20th century "marceration") depends on the intimacy between E-Composer and E-Perceiver; indeed the use of MACERAŠN (rarely EMACIATION) is ipso-facto evidence of such intimacy; for instance:

"Sometimes the best way to experience home is to wander away from known ports and into dusk."=

"BEST OUT FOR IN, GOODDUSK."

However swift the linguistic changes in the E-Period, and however arduous the processes of this backward look, we have profited from the experience of this exercise in the reconstruction of 20th century American; the curious reader will not fail to investigate the particulars of 2.COMPDIŊ; 3.RIDUKSHN; and 5. POLYGLŌ. In some indecipherable but deeply affecting way the Ogre of Information ↔ the Fiend of Silence.

SUNDRY IMPROVEMENT OUR MARK
A Nostalgic Farewell to Capitalism

The merchandisers flowed into the central arena and warped a bit of spacetime to make some delicacies, whose uses, virtues and (in one instance) inhibitions they propounded to one another in highfalutin tones. "I'm just sitting on the modicum of recalcitrance *this* fright of a hedgehog transmits to the holder." "You may canvas all tiny reactions and canvas all giant reactions, but you'll never canvas the full range of deeply felt sympathies *this* food processor brings out even in organized criminals." "Journey far, journey near, but don't journey at all unless you've got Stealth Unaccoutered. Stealth Unaccoutered is not ridic, wan or shafted. Stealth Unaccoutered is handiness standing."

This was intimacy unalloyed!

An actor wandered into the show and declared to the assembled his love for the moment, his desire for rest unrelenting, and his mostly unexpressed hate for The Things That Were Wrong With the World. His tears streamed down to his feet, right past his genitals, which were quaking with all the sundry tenacities of a grand motive. The merchandisers bawled, they leaned upon one another's shoulder and ran solicitous hands over one another's chest and belly, and their tears ran down to their feet past their genitals, which were shifting hither and yon with all the confusions of psyches aroused and unmastered. The actor bowed, shuffled backwards and out, and the merchandisers fell upon one another with tales of wives, houses and heroin.

Then there was an intermission, with the kindest merchandisers standing upon footstools brought by other merchandisers, and proclaiming the meaning of the rest: "Rest, that stippled pond. That snowfield caught up in the banks like bunched velveteen. Take your rest, good merchandisers, for the needs of the day are upon us, nearly, and something remains to be done." The footstools were rendered back to the appropriate parties. A fine bliss of hominess shot through the bunch.

During the second half, things were returned to their constituent elements by a master disassembler in from the sticks. He knew tires, nutcrackers, galoshes, computers, and the patented essence of farce. The merchandisers ran to catch each part as the master disassembler hurled it into the audience, hurl hurl, not even alerting the audience with his patter of each hurled part. "Gonna snap, crackle, pop, 'cause the din of the mustard's a-courtin' the mousse. Shriek and unbend, freak and relent, there's nothin' but shaftedness here." His beard reached down to his genitals, which had lain in wait for seventy years now; he displayed them for a moment, and the merchandisers oohed, for there was a religious element in all of them.

Then the music began. The music was enormous, there were tympani galore and all manner of beauteous, shimmering trills and mordants in the violins, and a mighty fine pianist squandering riffs on the Steinway as if riffs were replenishable. The conductor had a moustache and tackled the trumpets at one point, launched himself into the air over the second violins and landed smack dab amidst the trumpets, whom he tackled to the ground, bending their instruments into amusing animal shapes which he threw to the merchandisers as tokens of his and his orchestra's affection. He was a devoted conductor, anyone could see that, and the merchandisers applauded with one heart, and something was improved in the spirit of American enterprise.

Finally dusk threatened from the distance. "Ho," said a merchandiser, "if I am not mistaken that is a mass of dusk on the horizon, looming." "Yes," said another, "I wouldn't warrant a nay to that augury." "Ho then," said the first, "it's high time we pealed out of here, no? Come dusk, come dark, as they say." "Come dusk, come dark," said the second, wiping his nose, "but I'm not entirely sure of this particular configuration. Still . . . " "I know what you mean," said the first, "you mean we are blessed by the light bulb." "Yes." "Ah."

The lights were lit with some ceremony and the merchandisers gazed into each other's eyes in the new extra brightness. They remained in the arena for hours and hours, for there was depth to their delicacies, and endless uses, wants and even inhibitions that wanted propounding, and only a lifetime for all.

1. *After*
There is the gate or the copy of a gate
Blood outlines the gate, like a nude
A pink flower like a tree emits sparks
They gather into a yellow blue fragmentary flower
In the other space, formed by flowers torn apart
It bites the ground, like a blackened moon
Blood outlines a few jagged petals
Where does this flower emerge if not from history
The night-flower beside it is not dark enough with
Turmoil of strokes, with labor of HAVING BEEN THERE
The night flower explodes, is blue less
Relentless, should there be nothing but shadow
The twentieth century falls off below and fragility
And the kitsch of flowers above, finesse of heaven
No one can enter here, and there is nothing but hope

2. *A Part for the Part*
I demur. What was Gomorrah's crime?
Parodying, parodying, parodying?
That grotesque moment when I realize I am flying like a firefly
beneath the frozen, inverted earth
in the shadow of the shadow of a cassette
Oh door to the door

CHARLES SIMIC

PARADISE MOTEL

Millions were dead; everybody was innocent.
I stayed in my room. The President
Spoke of war as of a magic love potion.
My eyes were opened in astonishment.
In a mirror my face appeared to me
Like a twice cancelled postage stamp.

I lived well, but life was awful.
There were so many soldiers that day,
So many refugees crowding the roads.
Naturally, they all vanished
With a touch of the hand.
History licked the corners of its bloody mouth.

On the pay channel, a man and a woman
Were trading hungry kisses and tearing off
Each other's clothes while I looked on
With the sound off and the room dark
Except for the screen where the color
Had too much red in it, too much pink.

RELATIVES, BELFAST
for Maura Dooley

Who are they over there?
Where do they get their guns?

We imagine the family gathered,
Mum, Dad, Sis, and Sis,

a late dinner and then the telly.
Does it happen as it does with us?

A glance between the bites
at sitcoms, wine's little blood

on Mum's lip and napkin.
Dad's funny eruption of hair

where his cap's stayed on
coming home from work, and the good

surprising news has been given.
Talk rolls like a stone

in the hands of a young magician.
Heaved, all that clatter.

Think about this, friends,
as we spend our faithful savings bonds.

They don't know us, nor we them.
What did they dream? And where

would they go, if chance invited?
We're worlds away, of course. The dead

do not speak to us, as we wish.
They don't complain how they are cold.

Like spaghetti.

THIS HERE (1)

> *Time is the substance I am made of.*
> Jorge Luis Borges

Beyond earth
Is the moon
Planets
Further into night
Galaxies
Other worlds

And beyond that
Is heaven or hell
Or nothing
Beyond which is nothing
And beyond

The other world
Lights the mind on fire
With instant lilacs
Roses in bloom
Star blossoms as sweet
As hyacinth

After the risk
Of this world
Is the risk
Of that other world
Beyond this life

Or even no risk

MICHAEL STEPHENS

No nothing
The black night
Without stars
Or flowers

The black night
Is what the mind
On fire
Sleeps in anxiety of
And is why I touch you
This night

Beyond and before me
Be with me
Be who you are
On this planet of
Star gazing
And roses

from *Circles End*

LOVE ME

It was in a good city
I was sent out to buy
peaches in the marketplace
from men wearing tzitzits
in little round peach baskets
that cost a zloty apiece,
twenty cents American,
baskets worth fifty,
maybe now a hundred,
in the Flea in Lambertville,
perfect little baskets
with double layers of willow
held together by hickory
and a curved wire topped by
an oiled wood handle.

A white bird flew
over the crowded wagons
dropping white snow
into the peach baskets,
a Ukranian dove
with one boring cry,
"Love me, love me,"
by which he meant let me
climb all over you,
let me do my bobbing,
let me mount your face,
let me ejaculate
my dot of creamy stuff
onto your lovely clothes;
let me fuck my brains out.

One scholar walked—
this I can assure you—
with his blue eyes fixed
on the wooden poles
between the wagons. He
was buying a yellow squash
in such a place as Damascus;
he was pouring water
onto his plants. His mind
was on dark flowers, he knew
one tree that was like a bush,
he knew the red berries
that hung between the leaves;
he knew who lived in those leaves,
he the potato eater.

If there was snow you waited
beside your coals; I know this
is always the case, I huddled
over a bucket myself
beside the sleds. I folded
the papers in darkness. You shiver
in front of your wagon, you stand
all day in the soaking rain;
the ice comes later, it forms
on your clothes, the cold cuts through
without love, your forehead
is frozen; there are nine eggs
for sale, clean and candled,
a jar of schmaltz, some mushrooms;
these are the things that saved you.

Walking around with rifles
and fixed bayonets the police
patrolled the sidewalks, they shouted
all day. There was one table
with handkerchiefs strung up
on ropes; I guess they were *kerchiefs*
or *scarves*; they were, in Poland,
either wool or silk, either plaid
or flowered; how white they were
on Sunday morning, and black
when the time came; how good
the knots were, how quick they were tied
and shaped—I saw it myself
on a mountainside in Pittsburgh;
maybe next year in Poland.

Cardinal Chlond, a weasel,
twice passed through. He hated
Jews. He wanted to cleanse
the country, a weary word
that "cleanse." He learned at the feet
of fifty bastards. Aquinas,
could he be a bastard? Voltaire,
Wasn't he one? My love
Horace, was he? I lived
outside, but what I did
I did in a minute. I give
thanks for that. I learned
at the feet of a dwarf, the one
who carried two chickens; he wore
a black fedora, a *stetson*.

I weighed the basket, I carried it
into my bathroom; I didn't
take out the apples but what does it
matter now? I moved it
from side to side; the apples
rolled; there was profundity
in that—I almost retired
into a treehouse to watch
or into Yaddo to count
the panes in my window. Next time
I'll weigh the darkness. I know
I could like that. I have
less bitterness now, more knowledge.
I rubbed the handle, I smelled
the fruit first, then the blossoms.

LARGE WHITE SPOT

In 1990
astronomers saw a large white spot
appear in the atmosphere of Saturn
and they watched it evolve, change shape,
until the spot became a band
that encircled the planet.

In 1992
on a billboard a few miles
south of Williamsport, Pennsylvania,
on the continent known at that time
as North America, on a planet
the natives called Earth,
there appeared this advice:
SELECT THE RIGHT GOD.

By 2001
nothing in the film had come true,
there was no second coming,
and more people were being born
who would never have enough to eat
than ever before.
Another large white spot
appeared in the skies of Saturn.

STEVEN STYERS

IN THE GARDEN

A red-haired poet from Woonsocket
Kissed a guy who was and was not Inuit
While they planted delphiniums
At the end of the millennium
Because flowers are one way of renewing it.

STREAMERS

1.
As an archaeologist unearths a mask with opercular teeth
and abalone eyes, someone throws a broken fan and extension cords
into a dumpster. A point of coincidence exists in the mind

resembling the tension between a denotation and its stretch
of definition: aurora: a luminous phenomenon consisting
of streamers or arches of light appearing in the upper atmosphere

of a planet's polar regions, caused by the emission of light
from atoms excited by electrons accelerated along the planet's
magnetic field lines. The mind's magnetic field lines.

When the red shimmering in the huge dome of sky stops,
a violet flare is already arcing up and across, while a man
foraging a dumpster in Cleveland finds some celery and charred fat.

Hunger, angst: the blue shimmer of emotion, water speeding
through a canyon; to see only to know: to wake finding
a lug nut, ticket stub, string, personal card, ink smear, $2.76.

2.
A Kwakiutl wooden dish with a double-headed wolf
is missing from a museum collection. And as

the director checks to see if it was deaccessioned,
a man sitting on a stool under bright lights

shouts: a pachinko ball dropped vertiginously

but struck a chiming ring and richocheted to the left.

We had no sense that a peony was opening,
that a thousand white buds of a Kyoto camellia

had opened at dusk and had closed at dawn.
When the man steps out of the pachinko parlor,

he will find himself vertiginously dropping
in starless space. When he discovers

that his daughter was cooking over smoking oil
and shrieked in a fatal asthma attack,

he will walk the bright streets in an implosion of grief,
his mind will become an imploding star,

he will know he is searching among bright gold threads
for a black pattern in the weave.

3.
Set a string loop into a figure of two diamonds,
four diamonds, one diamond:
as a woman tightens her hand into a fist
and rubs it in a circular motion over her heart,
a bewildered man considering the semantics of *set*
decides no through-line exists:

to sink the head of a nail below the surface,
to fix as a distinguishing imprint, sign, or appearance,
to incite, put on a fine edge by grinding,

to adjust, adorn, put in motion, make unyielding,
to bend slightly the tooth points of a saw
alternately in opposite directions.
As the woman using her index finger makes
spiral after spiral from her aorta up over her head,
you see the possibilities for transcendence:
you have to die and die in your mind
before you can begin to see the empty spaces
the configuration of string defines.

4.
A restorer examines the pieces of a tin chandelier,
and notices the breaks in the arms are along
old solder lines, and that cheap epoxy was used.

He will have to scrape off the epoxy, scrub some flux,
heat up the chandelier and use a proper solder.
A pair of rough-legged hawks are circling over a pasture;

one hawk cuts off the rabbit's path of retreat
while the other swoops with sharp angle and curve of wings.
Cirrus, cirrostratus, cirrocumulus, altostratus,

altocumulus, stratocumulus, nimbostratus,
cumulus, cumulonimbus, stratus: is there no end?
Memories stored in the body begin to glow.

A woman seals basil in brown bags and hangs them
from the ceiling. A dead sturgeon washes to shore.
The sun is at the horizon, but you see another

sun rippling in water. It's not that the angle
of reflection equals the angle of incidence,
but there's exultation, pleasure, distress, death, love.

5.
The world resembles a cuttlefish changing colors
and shimmering. An apprentice archer has

stretched the bowstring properly, but does not know
he will miss the target because he is not aiming in the hips.

He will learn to hit the target without aiming
when he has died in his mind. I am not scared of death,

though I am appalled at how obsession with security
yields a pin-pushing, pencil-shaving existence.

You can descend to the swimming level of sharks,
be a giant kelp growing from the ocean bottom up

to the surface light, but the critical moment
is to die feeling the infinite stillness of the passions,

to revel in the touch of hips, hair, lips, hands,
feel the collapse of space in December light.

When I know I am no longer trying to know the spectral lines
of the earth, I can point to a cuttlefish and say,

"Here it is sepia," already it is deep-brown,
and exult, "Here it is deep-brown," already it is white.

6.

Red koi swim toward us, and black
carp are rising out of the depths of the pond,
but our sustenance is a laugh, a grief,

a walk at night in the snow,
seeing the pure gold of a flickering candle—
a moment at dusk when we see

that deer have been staring at us,
we did not see them edge out of the brush,
a moment when someone turns on a light

and turns a window into a mirror,
a moment when a child asks,
"When will it be tomorrow?"

To say "A bell cannot be red and violet
at the same place and time because
of the logical structure of color" is true

but is a dot that must enlarge into
a zero: a void, *enso*, red shimmer,
breath, endless beginning, pure body, pure mind.

FIN DE SIÈCLE

You'll hit for the cycle at the *fin de siècle*.
You're ahead just by being alive, celebrating
the barbecue at the top of the ninth.
We're almost there and the table is set
with wicker-work images of vast size
their limbs filled with the survivors
of this interesting decade. Read them
for their randomness, like Chinese cookies.
We doze on clouds of well-being, mentally
jerked by Pergolesi, Dvorak and Spohr.
What's left stretches before us into chaos
a road up a chimney in a painting. Where's

the fire? I sense the end of the century
press toward my situation like the Dolby
train in *The Fugitive*. Didn't they publish
my flat book with my flat face xeroxed on the cover.
It was fun pushing my nose against the glass
headlights flashing like a headon collision,
a headache to call in sick with, out of print
press broke, that's the way it goes.

The vanishing point will arrive on schedule
screamed at by Times Square crowds
a year ahead of time no doubt, right down
on the last tooth in its gums. My whole life
in its craw and now it's spitting up.

Natural radiation from rocks may prevent this
not to mention indoor radon but I plan to make

the party. The voices that sing to me
in the shower tell me it'll be just another day
without breath stops. Or the Third Coming!
Walt Disney thawed before our eyes.

We'll be saved from disease by virtual fucks.
Tired as we are, we want it all right now.
Not that it bodes any better, but saying good-bye
is like saying hello, isn't it, I mean it's hard
to see what's taking the place of everything
that's gone to hell. One has to be selective.
When you're raising chickens, never
name the ones you're going to eat.

NATHANIEL TARN

OBIT XXC

Not until the fat
boy stops singing

DEVOTION

> *Goodbye and keep cold.*
> R.F.

1.

To silence and to fierce cold.

To "galactic wind." To the Bowery Santa Clauses keeping Christmas safe each city block. To Preserved Fish.

A lovely light is singing to itself, in "The Poems," in my eyes, in the line, "Guillaume Apollinaire is dead."

2.

To the "polar night." To the painted flowerpot in the east window. To the elevator that stopped on each floor, then left.

To winter in the city. To snow and to gutters full of slush. To the Empire State Building, at midnight.

3.

To the moon, and the Pleiades.

To the Museum of Natural History. The Tyrannosaurus Rex on the same floor as the sea slug. To tree frogs in a store on Second Avenue.

To a blue door with bricks the color of white sand on the beach in Urubamba. To great circles of bone. To a bodega filled with yellow plantains.

To Joe DiMaggio, with or without Marilyn Monroe. Hot air subway blast radiating hydrogen jukebox. To a closet, an empty apartment in any building.

(To any building with an interior courtyard, for its secret life of plants.)

To my apartment on Fourteenth Street between A and First.
To Phoebe Legère.
To Larry Rivers.
To the city of meat and videos that mirror the sky.
To the Rivington School. I had always wanted to be a shoe salesman. As a painter I would like to abolish art history.

4.

And always to candles at night, to pink roses, to a voice that says *I've been dying all week for a nice fuck.*

The brain itself in its shell is very cold, according to Albertus Magnus. To a large ocean liner caught in the ice. To a few lights still burning on the deck.

ANCIENT HISTORY

1949 Hedy Lamarr snips Victor Mature's hair while he sleeps, but he regains his strength in time to heave the pillars apart. George Sanders, an urbane leader of Philistines, raises his glass with rueful approval as the temple collapses about him.

1955 Condemned to wander the Mediterranean after the fall of Troy, Kirk Douglas is bewitched by Silvana Mangano, while his crew are transformed into swine.

1956 Charlton Heston turns his staff into a snake, refuses Anne Baxter's advances, frees the Jews from Pharaoh Yul Brynner, majestically leads the Exodus and parts the Red Sea, and witnesses a rather jet-propelled inscription of the Ten Commandments.

1959 Gina Lollobrigida smoulders and heaves in a series of plunging gowns, drives a chariot with abandon, dances in a curious balletic orgy, and seduces Solomon (Yul Brynner) for political purposes.

Charlton Heston wins a chariot race and an Academy Award.

1960 Kirk Douglas excels in gladiatorial school, falls in love with Jean Simmons, and rebels after a private game staged for Roman general Laurence Olivier. Olivier makes a casual (but unmissable) come-on to slave-boy Tony Curtis.

1961 Stewart Granger rescues the Hebrews from the city of Sodom, whose depravity consists largely of dancing girls, sprawled bodies sleeping off orgies, and Stanley Baker chasing Lot's daughter (Rosanna Podesta) into the tall grass. When fire and brimstone are about to descend on her palace, wicked queen Anouk Aimée is called upon to deliver the memorable line: "It's just a summer storm. Nothing to worry about." The city is then overwhelmed in splendid ruin, Granger and Co. escaping to high ground, all except Pier Angeli, who looks back and is turned into a pillar of salt.

1963 Elizabeth Taylor enters Rome enthroned on an enormous Sphinxmobile hauled by sweating musclemen. After Rex's assassination and Dick's suicide, Liz outwits Roddy McDowall by sticking her hand in a basket of figs.

1964 Christopher Plummer shows tyrannical tendencies which alarm the dead Emperor's protégé, Stephen Boyd (his hair dyed blond and marcelled), who is in love with Plummer's sister, Sophia Loren, whom Plumer marries off to Omar Sharif. Confusion ensues: the talk is endless, and there are ambushes, troop decimations, high-speed chariot crashes, and a ridiculous spear-duel between Boyd and Plummer (in the Forum, of all places), which ends with Plummer dead and Boyd nobly refusing the imperial crown. To Dimitri Tiomkin's pensive cello, Sophia prays to Vesta in a fabulous fur-trimmed cape.

1965 An all-star cast populates the Holy Land: Max von Sydow, Dorothy McGuire, Charlton Heston, David McCallum, Roddy McDowall, Sidney Poitier, Carroll Baker, Pat Boone, Telly Savalas, Angela Lansbury, Martin Landau, José Ferrer, Claude Rains, Donald Pleasence, Van Heflin, Ed Wynn. Sal Mineo is healed by Christ, as is Shelley Winters, who crieth: "I am cured! I am cured!" John Wayne, the centurion managing the Crucifixion, utters: "I believe this truly was the Son of God."

1966 Clutching his fig leaf, Michael Parks is expelled from Paradise; Richard Harris kills his brother, Franco Nero, in an Irish frenzy; John Huston builds a massive Ark and potters among pairs of elephants, hippos, penguins, polar bears, and kangaroos; Stephen Boyd (wearing heavy eye shadow) climbs an impressive Tower of Babel and has his language confounded; God talks to patriarch George C. Scott.

Raquel Welch, clad in a bikini of wild-beast skins, is carried off by a squawking pterodactyl.

UNACCOUNTABLE II

Suddenly repeated the same scheme
the same configuration: a set
which tirelessly repeats a previous
model. It never fails to reproduce
itself—so faithfully that
I begin to fear what's imminent,

What could happen any time now
a few seconds or years ago.
I had never heard such a conversation
when life was cheap. Now it's so
expensive that everyone dreams
of a great catastrophe to end it all.

Masking the issue a combustion
mechanism set to go off in another
century. Fear is on the outside wall
Inside a dark soft girl sitting waiting
For a move. It never comes. Nobody
moves. Sitting and waiting for nothing

To happen all over again: The room
is narrow and long—even though it is
proportionally narrow and long compared
to its overall surface which is small
No use taking measurements. They
Have been abolished long ago: Now

Other weights and magnitudes are used
by alien people who know nothing

of our lives—they have forgotten
all the questions—and I have
put the answers in a folder
somewhere so that they would remain

As unobtrusively discreet as
possible: I will contend with no one
about the necessary information
the knowledge that tomorrow
may be already here becomes,
as the evening slips away, a certainty.

GREETINGS FROM THE YEAR 2000, WITH RESPECT

Glancing back at the millennium we are leaving,
I see a cannon roll out into the dust
of a tiny war in the patch of sun
in a store window
on the Lower East Side
Noise, blood, suffering, even the animals
take part, and no one is winning

Great theaters of carnage
bright science yoked to bleak
military arsenals, kids are killing kids
people are torn between nationalism
and compassion, and the entire human species
is hurling itself headlong off the edge.

And he laid hold on the dragon, the old serpent,
and bound her for a thousand years
and cast her into the abyss
and shut it and sealed it over her
that she should deceive the nations no more
until the thousand years be finished;
after this she must be loosed a little while. *

She must be loosed a little while?
How little a while?
Lording it over the beasts in the field,
the trees in the forest, the air, the water,
with the rapt egocentric stance that nature
is the devil, we have been supremely free
to disrespect whomever we choose.

I think of the lovely Lilith,
tossing her hair as she leaves the abyss
the unbound fire in every atom
She steps out into a vacant lot
in the Southeast Bronx, where to *dis*
somebody is to face down a handgun

A serpent curls among the streets
of the world, a naked energy
climbs our spine and gazes from our eyes
Don't cut the trees, don't blaze more trails
across the mountains, leave a little
wildness for the next inheritors,
with respect.

Monte Alban for a thousand years
was a Sacred City and civilization
of peace. With plentiful fields of corn,
the people were free to serve and adorn
their temple. In synchronicity
with the earth, and their culture,
they derived their names from what they did.

Let us go out and greet the new
century, said Seraphita, Balzac's angel,
and the icy fjords cracked and melted
the bells rang wildly
With great respect, with great love
she said, and the energy
crackled across the sky like lightning.

Look at the serpent
curling through the green woods
spiralling up the hills in the flat land
and greet the new millennium with complicity
for the unchained nature in the earth,
with respect for the air, the water,
the snake undulating up our spines
and the dragon in the stars.

* Revelations 20; 2-4.

ENVOY

Go, my songs,
    go to the desperate, the hopeful,
the dazed, the interminable
    waiting line of humanity.
Sidle up to the kind, the stingy
    the love-stricken, and say,
                Whubba-whubba.

Rescue the poor politician
    choking on his own words.
Help perform the tracheotomy.
    Along with a promise
that he'll never use them again,
    extract those words—
slimy, disgusting—
    clean them up in time to join
the great refrain
    of the new century:
Faith and Peace, whubba-whubba.

Go, my songs,
    careen into the blank page,
the face of the new year, be the fly
    on the nose of astonishment.

Go to the scrambler, the conniver,
    the misanthrope, the dolt.
Go to the hooligan.
    Go to the jovial sarcast
and maudlin reveler.

PAUL VIOLI

Show them the skyline,
convince them Manhattan's ancient
        rooftop water tanks
                    are the squat rocketry
that will loft them
    into the first great poem
of the next century—Whubba-whubba!
            We have lift-off!

Fill their little hearts
        with the music of expectation,
so while I'm in my front row seat
        in Tierra del Fuego,
watching oceans
                and millennia collide,
they'll land at day's end
    on the other side
                    of Bleecker Street
in time to hear the sound
    of a slumper, coat
slung over his shoulder,
                tie untied, shaking
a few last ice chips
    in the bottom of a paper cup,
waylaid by a jaunty,
                    importunate tramp,
shaking coins in same:
        Jingle jingle, whubba-whubba.

OBIT

necrology? death roll?
casualty list?
body count?
what's allowed
this corpse of a century,
to fathom
to dream on
                    what got plundered

but we lived, loved
party is not a word I'd think to blare
what is the summation of
the nightmare
or
the dream
who puts it thus away
when we're to fathom
a speculation
what's gone
undone
for a tangle
(tango)

this Hundred Year Meditation . . .

it was a moment
it was a golden eye-blink
it was a microdot—one galaxy's inbreath
one sigh
one gesture of seduction

one rapt pause
several comets
eclipse, eclipse, eclipse
it was the shrug of Brahma's shoulder
creak of Isis' oar
heave of a chest
lonely cough
her sidelong glance
her fancy gait
will she kiss her lover?
her gasp—is it bad? is the news bad?
they make love at dawn
"time" explodes
his quizzical look
what news, Claudius?
the end of a movie
someone dies
it was a dart of passion
it was a conjunct of earth & sky
the earth stood still
a scream
then falters
it was over & it was beginning
it was war it was war it was war it was war
it is war
it was war
no
it is war
it is the set-up for war
the frame up
it was a long time
Neptune rules

*

the century grows on us
poets invent language
perceptions collide
I hear the mitocondria shifting in my dna
part of it was part of my history
& part of it was elsewhere
& Gertrude Stein said
America was the oldest country
because it entered the 20th century first
I saw the century unfold & die
I saw it unfold from within America
it was part of me
it made me what I am
I am war I was war I am war
 American made
I am power & eyes & parables
I will close my fist & raise it to the first cause
I will fight
I will not survive
No
I am survivor
but I forget what I just said to you
I forget something
no
I forgot
I forgot something
amnesia of holocaust
amnesia for war & war & more war
witness the end of Nature
I want to forget her beauties
because I helped destroy them

nothing will ever be the same
there is no topsoil left in the world
& many species extinct . . .

*

from the vantage point of
power & power & more power
see with ancient eyes
because it would be the first to die
we'll die in America first
are we modern,
are we modern yet?
someone tell us
are we the post-modern Dark Ages yet?
it is simply dialectical materialism
it is the charnel ground
many jackals roam about
& feast on the bloody severed limbs of
1. desire
2. hope & fear
real live bodies
it was divide & conquer
it was glory glory & more glory
what genomes?
what clones?
what could we ever do to outdo our century

*

made love this century
gave birth this century
walked this century

laughed this century
protested this century
dreamed the rapids came this century
dreamed a lamp to light the way—
O Nirvana of the little lamp!
meditated this century—hey ho the happy yogini!
raged on stage this century
practiced diction this century
founded a school this century
stomped on the corpse of ego this century
became an ego-maniac this century
watched good folks die this century
buried a mother, buried a father

set flames to the corpses on the charnel ground this century
are they really planning to create life from the ovaries of unborn
        fetuses this century?

took a powder this century
took a powder down the information highway

KEITH WALDROP

ACCIDENTAL NUMBER

stars, for
example, or atoms

horrors of
blood and state

vestigial
wings, discarded
data

night and
rain and the
body
falling

watch how life, mere
life, survives
the turn of the millennium

as coughs in-
crease in moments
between movements

at last
best, at best
last

now
look again

now particles
are temporary

stars
spring leaks

there can be
light—the thought
appalls me—without
sensation of light

and, another
example, dreams

the extreme
weakness of gravity

boundless
straits

from inconceivable
distances a con-
tiguous *Verboten*

fringe of
leg on a film
of surface ice

shaped by
machine, leaving an or-
ganic design
in the metal

KEITH WALDROP

I would like to know
more about
wormholes

bridges

about the
foamy and
the spongelike

the god of
desire is also
god of memory

two thousand years from
no matter what

nothing important with
everything in train

from here we can
describe the
open door

the *body*
falling

all the images we
have, born
blind from our
seeing eye

all eyes, and yet no
eye of my own

a feeling a bit like
awe, which might qualify as
quasi-oceanic

time, a poor
thing, standing
so still

a world of
other numbers

I'm the one who's
running out

and then

time's
on its own

NEW CENTURY

One war replaces another, one strand of hair on the pillowcase, an earring under the pillowcase ("whose earring is this?") There's always been wars everywhere, not between countries with borders as much as between people with bodies, people who live inside their bodies unconditionally. As she kissed him she could feel the bulge of the shoulder holster beneath his jacket. There was a relationship between violence and sex which was possibly not new to this century. Or dreams. No one knows about this until now.

Dreams become real. We walk around and believe our fantasies. We tax ourselves against the possibility of achieving what we want to do. We take jobs we don't want. We don't get paid for overtime. We get fired if we aren't devoted to our jobs. Jobs are more important than children or lovers. Please prove this by working until nine.

Define the term sanity without referring to war or jobs. The ex-lover who calls up at midnight is simply that. For awhile it was possible to say the words "free love" without laughing. People who missed the sixties think they missed something. I missed being alive in 1933 in Germany. I missed celebrity sweepstakes, the pain in my leg. There are a few people who were alive in 1933 in Germany who can speak self-critically about what happened. There were more people alive in China in 1989 who can tell us what happened. What's happening now.

You have to begin a new century with these words but it doesn't matter. I left the house at 8:15 and never came back. The last time anyone saw him it was down at the bodega buying a loose cigarette. This century seems to involve words like "acting out," but maybe that was true of the last century as well. It's too easy to say that that's what everyone's doing every minute. A woman who's fired from a job might return home and yell at her husband who's innocently polishing the silver. Healing: what happens after the war is over. That's something else, what we're never not doing.

You don't have to be alive to have lived through something. A war, a job, a marriage: don't equate these things in your mind. Define your life by what you do, what you can't do. This century is a kind of limitation, like replaying an old movie backwards. When I talk about the sixties I mean "my sixties," don't you know?

Possibly the key words are "endangered species" or "how corny." It was possible to assume interest in etymology or genealogy as a way of discovering why some issues were easy to dismiss while others were only resolvable by pulling a trigger or throwing someone's body onto the ground & prodding it with a nightstick or the butt of a gun. This century began with The Boxer Rebellion: keep the foreign devils out of China. The next century will be China, we know that already. We can see it coming, through the repetitions and cycles of history, through the lies and secrets that are a new version of truthfulness, so that it's almost impossible to say what's wrong with the country we live in without passing through a mirror, without digging a hole in the ground and going back to the beginning.

A rupture. A cloudless sky. The brackets around a feeling. Something permanent, something transient. The last drop of sap rolling down the trunk of a tree. All of us with our bad postures, our private agendas. You have to begin the new century with a list of words. "Thumbprinting" "refuge" "inconclusive" and "euphoric" were on my list. And "kiosk," my favorite word, because that's what I was doing. It was 1969 and I was crossing Constitution Square in Athens. I was sitting at a cafe with a newspaper, drinking coffee, trying to define myself by what was happening elsewhere. I had stopped living in the present. I was no longer aware of my immediate surroundings.

METAFOURS NEAR THE END

as bob dole often
says god bless america
god bliss america god
floss america god's very
possibly way outta here

ok let's get real
and let's get really
snooty in the bargain
how can one come
on heavy in the
eschatology department when the
national consciousness bounces from
imelda to leona to
lorena to tonya with
a sizzling pit-stop at
neverland with wacko-jacko o
tempora who will first
print the three-million-dollar snapshot
of jacko's blotchy joint
not that the plastic
surgeons and dermatologists will
have left blotch one
plus the rumor is
they've grafted jeff stryker's
dick onto jacko and
that's why he faints
from lack of blood
everytime he gets a
hardon which explains why

he has to sleep
in that weird bed

excuse me i digress
staggered by the gravitas
of the republic where
the barbarians are not
at the gates dummy
they are breaking down
the attic door up
on the third floor
who are all those
people on television who
say things like buddy's mama
is coming to see him
and i and me
and she are going
to wal-mart's to buy
200 rolls of toilet
paper make my day

boobus americanus hath swept
the boards remember what
the last poets said back
in the 70s niggers
run around shoutin fuck
this fuck that niggers
would fuck fuck if
they could fuck it
and by now everydamnbody
feels just like that
afraid to go to

wendy's to see if
dave's lousy hamburgers are
still square in the
glare of semi-automatic fire

lyndon baines johnson proclaimed
the arrival of the
great society unto the
congress and the citizenry
and said privately that
most people were so
dumb they wouldn't know
how to pour piss
out of a boot
even if the instructions
were printed on the heel
in big orange letters
possum eliot used to
say when you get
down to brass tax
that's all the fax
birth copulation & death
but what i think
about at the end
of the age are
the measures of power
and they are three
science dick-size & jism
the measure of power
jism has the power
to make something happen
it's the same word

as jazz call it
elan vital to be
mandarin about it speaking
of mandarin remember that
old ez thought the
brain was a cum
clot and had special
chairs made so more
blood would get to
his head which takes
us back to michael
jackson it all coheres
now doesn't it just

hereabouts we sit in
the woods like good
pagan cistercians and pretend
that macon county north
carolina the land of
the sky god's country
is the simulacrum of
toyama where chomei built
his hut in the
forest far from the
prattlings and the gorilla-hash
dishings of poets who
kenneth rexroth told me
50 years ago were
the worst people you'd
ever meet including today's
endless array of buttholes
with no attention no

time no imagination and
no manners simply none

some remain more sanguine
guy davenport for instance
who says it will
be the business of
literature and the arts
to contain and transmit
what culture survives the
century if any he
adds in a parenthesis

here on the mountain
the mind runs around
like a blue darter and
all i know is
everytime i walk in
the bathroom i think
i see jesse helms'
shadow hiding behind the
shower curtain that's rough

and no birds sing

and god bless america
cause nobody else will

FUTURISM OF THE PAST

Here in the colonies, a light year from Mars,
immortal old men struggle with clothes
and hangovers in the morning, as something jars
our memories and eases all our woes:

We recall those ancient days on mother earth
a hundred years ago, when we were free
to live within the rules of death and birth,
and pass quietly away. I remember a tree

I saw once. Its gnarled and leafy limbs
twisted in the blue sky. And once we ate
real food off plates! But my memory dims
of the lost, near-forgotten splendors of the late

Twentieth century. We have heard the tapes
of dogs barking, seen pictures of people smoking,
fucking, sleeping. What a parade of hairy apes
we were—miserable, primitive, terrified of croaking.

Now we loiter out here on this desolate mall
in space, and we live forever, cursing Carl Sagan,
aching for the old century, the filth of it all,
the beautiful terror of our archaic pagan

Souls, an almost sexual yearning for our fears.
They gave us face to lose, they fed our lonely need
to die and be reborn. Now those sullen years
spin away from us with untraceable speed

And we cry out the orphan's sad goodbye
in this junkyard where flesh and spirit eat
each other out, when all we want to do is die,
sleep, dream, and revel in our glorius defeat.

PEARL

We sought the word that sows and the word that reaps, we sought
     the one word
That would comfort us, and would praise in its comforting.
We lived our lives out under the word, but the word was not
     forthcoming
And at the end was the word, and the end was the word.

Late January, crack in the cloud cover. White light
Reissues its old message, then gutters and goes out.
Silence again. Always silence from where we sit, under the dwarf
     peach trees,
The afternoon set on dead reckoning with millennium's landfall.

There is a hard, bright thing, like a pearl, at the center of pain.
We place it under our tongues, and it does not dissolve.
We roll it around in our mouths, we put it between our teeth,
We suck it, we trundle and suffer it, it will not dissolve.

What palmprint can count our sins, what sackcloth contain them?
We walk in the back yard, go to and fro among the fruit trees,
Up and down, the afternoon like a hard, bright thing above us,
Uncomforting, unforthcoming. It does not dissolve.

AUTOMATIC TRANSMISSION

Lend the old sentry a new way,
something he can bake in his head.
A thrust of dread, a brittle dumpling, a perfect unit.
A thousand fires are leaping in the park,
but no one dances through their windows anymore,
and the front doors are always clocked.
On the table, a bowl you wouldn't lick.

I'm a little spotty minded, aren't you?
But did you say "slum" or "slump,"
"sum up" or "dump out"?
I don't know where this rotten sliver is going.
Or, if I'm wearing your sarong,
what I should put on under it?

What's that steam doing in this story?
Hey steam, maybe I'm just a stabbed hut
in your path to claim. But remember
the dribble down theory,
the national ante about stardust.
Well, something has been sprinkling
my furnished rind. Something you dredged
out of your curls and insect tears,
your sand and wooden shoes.
And I've fallen too far
for my hand to withdraw its throng.

Am I loud enough to smell you back?

Do I talk erect enough for your message?

Will this spill finally bleach me?

BIOGRAPHIES

KEITH ABBOTT has published four novels, six short story collections, one memoir, and eleven books of poetry. His last three books were *Downstream From Trout Fishing in America*, a memoir of Richard Brautigan (1989), *The Last Part of the First Thing Coming, A Story* (1992), and *Skin and Bone, A Story* (1993). His work has been translated into German, Russian, French, Italian, and Czech. He is a painter and calligrapher. He currently teaches at Naropa Institute in Boulder, Colorado.

SAM ABRAMS was born in 1935. He was, with Paul Blackburn, Joel Oppenheimer, and Carol Berge, one of the founders of the St. Mark's Poetry Project, just before the Ted Berrigan/Anne Waldman era. Among his works are a number of pseudonymous erotic novels he wrote for Olympia Press. Abrams is a Professor of Classical Literature at the Rochester Institute of Technology. He is the editor of *The Neglected Walt Whitman: Vital Texts* (Four Walls Eight Windows, 1993).

WILL ALEXANDER was born in 1948 in Los Angeles. He has been shaped poetically by "the magnetic resonance of fortuitous blows which have turned his instinctive vitality into an odyssey of poetic tumult searching for the purity of sound." He has published three books, including *Asia & Haiti* (Sun & Moon, 1994).

WILLIAM ALLEN, artist, poet, and teacher, is the author of a book of poems, *The Man on the Moon*, from NYU and Persea Press, 1987. He teaches literature at Cooper Union and American literature and American social history at the School of Visual Arts. He lives in New York City.

JACK ANDERSON is a dance critic for the *New York Times*, New York correspondent for *The Dancing Times* of London, and co-editor (with George Dorris) of *Dance Chronicle*. He is the author of eight books of poetry and six books of dance criticism and history. He lives in New York City.

MICHAEL ANDRE edits *Unmuzzled Ox*; four recent tabloid issues combined to form *The Cantos (121-150) Ezra Pound*. He writes "The Art Box," a column on art and artists, for *Exquisite Corpse*. His collections of poetry include *Studying the Ground for Holes, It as It,* and *Letters Home*.

BRUCE ANDREWS edited with Charles Bernstein the critical publication *L=A=N=G=U=A=G=E*, and is the author of many books of poetry including *Executive Summary* (Potes & Poets Press, 1991), *Getting Ready to be Frightened* (Roof, 1988), and *Give Em Enough Rope* (Sun & Moon, 1987).

ANTLER was born in Milwaukee and "worked his way through college" in various factories. He has explored wildernesses in Upper Peninsula Michigan, Minnesota, Ontario, Colorado, and California. His work has appeared in dozens of literary magazines, including *La Selva Subterranea* and *Exquisite Corpse*. His books include *Last Words* (Ballantine Books, 1986) and *A Second Before It Burns* (Woodland Pattern Book Center, 1994).

IVAN ARGÜELLES, born in 1939, resides in Berkeley, and is in the employ of the Library, UC Berkeley. He has published many collections of poetry, including *Looking for Mary Lou*, which received the 1989 Poetry Society of America's William Carlos Williams Award.

RAE ARMANTROUT's books include *Necromance* (Sun and Moon, 1991) and *Made to Seem* (Sun and Moon, 1994). Her work has been anthologized in *Post-Modern American Poetry* (ed. Paul Hoover, Norton) and *From the Other Side of the Century: A New American Poetry 1960-1990* (ed. Doug Messerli; Sun and Moon Press, 1994). She teaches writing at the University of California, San Diego.

PAUL AUSTER is a poet, critic, translator, and novelist. He has written a memoir, *The Invention of Solitude* (Penguin), and is the editor of *The Random House Book of Twentieth-Century French Poetry*. Auster's novels include The New York Trilogy (*City of Glass, Ghosts, The Locked Room*), *In The Country of Last Things, The Music of Chance*, and *Mr. Vertigo*. He lives in Brooklyn, New York.

BARBARA BARG lives in New York City and is the author of *Origin of the Species* (Semiotext(e), 1994). She is lead singer/drummer/songwriter in the band Homer Erotic.

BILL BERKSON, poet and art critic, is the author of ten books and pamphlets of poetry, most recently, *Lush Life* (Z Press, 1983). He is a Corresponding Editor for *Art in America* and a regular contributor to *Artforum*. From 1971-78, he was editor-publisher of *Big Sky* magazine and books. He is currently the Coordinator of Art History, Theory & Criticism at the San Francisco Art Institute, where he has taught and directed the public lectures program since 1984.

CHARLES BERNSTEIN is author of nineteen books of poetry. His most recent book of poetry is *Dark City* (Sun and Moon Press, 1994); his essays are published in *A Poetics* (Harvard University Press, 1992) and *Content's Dream: Essays 1975-1984* (Sun and Moon Press, 1986, 1994). With Bruce Andrews, he edited $L=A=N=G=U=A=G=E$, which has been anthologized as *The $L=A=N=G=U=A=G=E$ Book* (Southern Illinois University Press, 1984). He is David Gray Professor of Poetry and Letters at the State University of New York at Buffalo

JOHN BRANDI was born in Los Angeles in 1943, and has lived in Corrales, New Mexico since 1971, with extensive travels throughout the Americas, the Indian subcontinent, Southeast Asia, and Indonesia. His latest books include *A Question of Journey: India, Nepal, Thailand Journals* (Temple Press, 1994) and *Heartbeat Geography: Selected and Uncollected Poems* (White Pine, 1994).

SUMMER BRENNER has performed, taught, and studied flamenco and contemporary dance. She is the author of several volumes of poetry and prose, including *Dancers & The Dance* (Coffee House Press, 1993) and most recently *One Minute Movies*. Her work has been anthologized in *Deep Down: The New Sensual Writing by Women* (ed. Laura Chester, Faber & Faber) and *Up Late* (ed. Andrei Codrescu, Four Walls Eight Windows, 1989). She lives in Berkeley, California.

JAMES BROUGHTON is a "confirmed believer in the amatory, the hilarious and the unmentionable." He is the author of many books and plays, and a widely respected pioneer in the realm of avant-garde cinema. His most recent publications include *Selected Poems, Special Deliveries* (Broken Moon, 1990), a pansexual confession, *The Androgyne Journal* (Broken Moon, 1991), a poetics of cinema, *Making Light of It* (City Lights, 1992), and a memoir, *Coming Unbuttoned* (City Lights, 1993). His most recent film was *Scattered Remains*, commissioned by the San Francisco Film Festival in 1988. He resides in Port Townsend, Washington.

CHARLES BUKOWSKI (1920-1994) was born in Andernach, Germany. He lived in Los Angeles for fifty years. He published forty-five books of poetry and prose in his lifetime. His last books were *The Last Night of the Earth Poems* (Black Sparrow Press, 1992), *Screams from the Balcony: Selected Letters 1960-1970* (Black Sparrow Press, 1993), and a novel, *Pulp* (Black Sparrow Press, 1994).

WILLIAM BURROUGHS is the world renowned author of *Naked Lunch*, *Junky*, and most recently, *My Education, A Book of Dreams* (Viking, 1995). He is a member of the American Academy and Institute for Arts and Letters and a Commandant de l'Ordre des Arts et Lettres of France. He and the cats live in Lawrence, Kansas.

JANINE CANAN is a psychiatrist, director of the Center for Integration in Port Townsend, Washington, member of the Worldwide Women's Party, and devotee of the Divine Mother. Most recent of her seven books of poetry are *Her Magnificent Body. New & Selected Poems* (Manroot, 1986), *She Rises Like the Sun: Invocations of the Goddess by Contemporary American Women Poets* (Crossing, 1989), recipient of the 1990 Koppelman Award for best-edited feminist work, and *Star in My Forehead: The Songs of Else Lasker-Schueler*, translated from the German (forthcoming).

JOE CARDARELLI (1944-1995) was a poet, painter, and teacher. He taught at the Maryland Art Institute in Baltimore where he ran a distinguished poetry program. He was anthologised in *Quickly Aging Here* (Doubleday Anchor). Among his books are *Phantom Rod* (with Anselm Hollo and Kirby Malone) and *From the Maine Book* (Smithereens Press).

TURNER CASSITY was born in Jackson, Mississippi, in 1929. He worked as a professional librarian at Emory University Library in

Atlanta from 1962-1991. Cassity is the author of several volumes of poetry, including *Hurricane Lamp* (University of Chicago Press, 1986) and *Between the Chains* (University of Chicago Press, 1991). He lives in Georgia and California.

MAXINE CHERNOFF, born in Chicago in 1952, has written six books of poetry including *New Faces of 1952*, which won the 1985 Carl Sandburg Award. Her most recent collection of short stories, *Signs of Devotion* (Simon & Schuster) was a *New York Times* notable book of 1993. With Paul Hoover, she edits *New American Writing*.

TOM CLARK was born in Chicago in 1941. In 1963 he began a ten-year tenure as poetry editor of *The Paris Review*, introducing to the magazine such poets as Charles Olson, Robert Duncan, Allen Ginsberg, Frank O'Hara, John Ashbery, and Ted Berrigan. Black Sparrow Press has published five volumes of his poetry since 1978, including *Fractured Karma* (1990) and *Sleepwalker's Fate* (1992). His *Junkets on a Sad Planet* (Black Sparrow Press, 1994) is a poetic novel based on the life of John Keats; his other books on the lives of writers include biographical works on Damon Runyon, Jack Kerouac, Ted Berrigan, Charles Olson, and in 1993, New Directions published his *Robert Creeley and the Genius of the American Common Place*. Since the mid-1980s, Clark has taught in the Poetics Program at New College of California. He makes his home in Berkeley.

LUCILLE CLIFTON was born in Depew, New York, in 1936. She is the author of seven books of poetry and more than a dozen books of fiction and poetry for children. Recent works include *Good Woman: Poems and a Memoir, 1969-80* (BOA Editions, 1987) and *Quilting* (BOA Editions, 1991). She is a Professor of Humanities at St. Mary's College in Maryland.

ANDREI CODRESCU, the co-editor of this anthology, was born in Sibiu, Romania. He is a poet, novelist, essayist, and editor. His recent books include *Belligerence* (Coffee House Press, 1993), *The Blood Countess* (a novel, Simon & Schuster, 1995), and *Zombification* (essays, St. Martin's Press, 1995). He edits *Exquisite Corpse: A Journal of Books & Ideas*, and is a regular commentator on National Public Radio. He is a Professor of English at Louisiana State University.

NORMA COLE, a noted translator, is the author of *Metamorphopsia* (Potes & Poets Press, 1988) and *My Bird Book* (Littoral Books, 1991). She lives in San Francisco.

JACK COLLOM was born in Chicago, 1931, and grew up in the small Illinois town of Western Springs, where he "walked in the woods alla time." He moved west in 1947 and graduated from high school in a class of four in Fraser, Colorado, worked in factories for twenty years, and now teaches writing at Naropa Institute and the University of Colorado at Boulder. Collom is the author of ten books, including *8-Ball* (Dead Metaphor Press, 1992) and *Poetry Everywhere* (Teachers & Writers Collaboration, NYC, 1994).

CLARK COOLIDGE was born in Providence, Rhode Island in 1939. "Chief experimentalist and jazz connoisseur, he has brought poetry and music closer than anyone since Gertrude Stein." Recent books by Coolidge include *The Nova Improvisations* (Sun & Moon) and *Registers (People in All)*, (Avenue B).

ROBERT CREELEY, born in 1926 in Arlington, Massachusetts, is currently director of the Poetics Program at the State University of New York at Buffalo. Recent books include *Autobiography* (Hanuman Books, 1990) and *Selected Poems* (University of California Press, 1991).

PHILLIP DACEY, born St. Louis, 1939, has taught at Southwest State University in Marshall, Minnesota, and is the author of five books of poetry, including *Night Shift at the Crucifix Factory*. With David Jauss, he co-edited *Strong Measures: Contemporary American Poetry in Traditional Forms* (Harper&Row, 1985). He performs music and poetry with his sons, and lives in the country near Camden State Park in southwestern Minnesota.

BEVERLY DAHLEN has taught creative writing at the College of Marin, San Francisco State University, and Naropa Institute in Boulder, Colorado. Dahlen was one of the founders of *HOW(ever)*, a feminist literary periodical that publishes experimental work by women, and served as one of its contributing editors until 1987. Her *Egyptian Poems* (with an afterword by Robert Duncan) appeared in 1983. Three volumes of her long work, *A Reading (1-17)*, were published between 1985-1992.

JOEL DAILEY born 1953, edits *Fell Swoop*, and lives with his family in New Orleans; recent works include *Doppler Effects* (Shockbox Press, 1993), *Audience, Ambience, Ambulance* (Black Gun Silencer, 1992), and *Public Storage* (Tight Press, 1995).

TOM DENT was born in New Orleans. In 1959, he settled in New York where he wrote the poems in his first book, *Blue Lights and River Songs* (Lotus Press, 1982). He was a member of the New York Umbra Workshop, which included David Henderson and Ishmael Reed, among others. In 1965, he returned to New Orleans and was one of the founders of the Free Southern Theatre, an important Civil Rights forum. Harvard University Press is publishing his monumental *Oral History of the Civil Rights Movement*.

GEORGE-THÉRÈSE DICKENSON co-edited *Assassin* (with Will

Bennett). She is a poet, performance artist, and teacher. She has taught poetry in New York prisons. Her work is collected in *Transducing* (Roof Books).

RAY DiPALMA was born in 1943. Since 1969 he has published more than thirty books with a variety of presses in the United States and Europe. The most recent of these are *Numbers and Tempers: Selected Early Poems 1966-1986* (Sun & Moon Press, 1993), *Hotel Des Ruines* (with Alexandre Delay, Editions Royaumont, 1993), and *Platinum Replica*, with drawings by Elizabeth DiPalma (Tele, 1994). He lives in New York City and Hudson, New York.

STEPHEN DOBYNS, novelist and poet, was born in New Jersey in 1941. His books include *Body Traffic Poems* (Viking, 1990), *Aftershocks, Near Escapes* (Viking, 1993), and *Velocities: New & Selected Poems* (Viking, 1994). He is a professor of English at Syracuse University.

BARBARA EINZIG is a poet, fiction writer, and critic living in New York City. She has published numerous books, among them *Distance Without Distance* (Kelsey Street Press, 1994). She has taught writing at Rockland Center for the Arts and at the University of California at San Diego.

ELAINE EQUI, born in Chicago in 1953, is the author of seven collections of poems, including *Surface Tension*, and most recently, *Decoy* (1994), both from Coffee House Press. She lives in New York City.

CLAYTON ESHLEMAN, poet, editor, translator, founded *Sulphur* magazine in 1981, which he edits at Eastern Michigan University, where he is a professor in the English department. Since the mid-1970s, he has been involved in research on what he calls "Paleolithic Imagination and the Construction of the Underworld," having visited over fifty Ice Age "sanctuaries" in southwest France and northern Spain. His most recent book of poetry is *Under World Arrest* (Black Sparrow Press, 1994).

LAWRENCE FERLINGHETTI was born in 1919 in Yonkers, New York. He is the founder of City Lights Bookshop and City Lights Publishing House. Ferlinghetti's recent works include *These Are My Rivers* (New Directions, 1993) and *New & Selected Poems, 1955-1993* (New Directions, 1993). He lives and paints in San Francisco.

EDWARD FIELD was born in 1924. His latest book of poetry is *Counting Myself Lucky* (Black Sparrow Press). He is the editor of *The Alfred Chester Society Newsletter*, and writes fiction with Neil Derrick under the pseudonym of Bruce Elliot. He lives in New York City.

DAVID FRANKS is a poet, song lyricist, and performing artist. His books include *Touch* and *Left for Dead*; he has collaborated with musicians Richie Havens and Root Boy Slim, among others. His CD, *Musical Words*, was issued by Pyramid Atlantic. He lives in Baltimore.

KATHLEEN FRASER's *Collected Poems* (1966-1992) was published in 1995 by The National Poetry Foundation. She co-founded and edited the journal *HOW(ever)* in the 1980s, and her work has appeared in numerous anthologies, including *The Norton Anthology of Post-Modern Poetry*. She taught writing for many years at San Francisco State University, where she founded the American Poetry Archive, in conjunction with the Poetry Center.

ED FRIEDMAN was born in 1950, and grew up in Los Angeles. Since 1987, Friedman has served as the Artistic Director of the Poetry Project at St. Mark's Church in New York. His most recent book, *Mao &*

Matisse, includes a number of works first created for Display Poem, a permutational computer animation in which the elements of the poem are always being reordered at random.

GLORIA FRYM's books include *How I Learned* (Coffee House Press), *By Ear* (Sun & Moon Press), *Back To Forth* (The Figures); *Impossible Affection* (Christopher's Books), and *Second Stories: Conversations with Women Artists* (Chronicle Books). She is a recipient of California Arts Council grants to teach poetry writing to jail inmates. She also teaches in the Poetics Program at New College of California in San Francisco.

BARRY GIFFORD is a novelist, screenwriter, and poet. He is the author of the novels *Baby Cat-Face*, *Night People*, and *Wild at Heart*, among other books. He lives in Berkeley, California.

ALLEN GINSBERG was born in New York in 1926. He is the author of *Howl & Other Poems* (City Lights Books, 1956). *Howl* has become one of the most widely read poems of the twentieth century. Together with Anne Waldman, Ginsberg founded the Jack Kerouac School of Disembodied Poetics at the Naropa Institute, Boulder, Colorado.

PATRICIA GOEDICKE teaches poetry at the University of Montana. She is the author of *Paul Bunyon's Bearskin* (1994) and *The Tongues We Speak: New and Selected Poems* (Milkweed Editions, 1989).

TED GREENWALD lives in New York City. His Books include *Word of Mouth* (Sun & Moon), *Licorice Chronicles* (Sun & Moon), *You Go Through* (Case Books), *Exit the Face* (with Richard Bosman, Museum of Modern Art). He has also produced *Poker Blues*, a video, with Less Levine (Museum of Mott Art).

AIMÉE GRUNBERGER, born in Connecticut in 1953, works as a psychotherapist at the Providence V.A. Hospital. Her first book, *Ten Degrees Cooler Inside*, was published in 1992.

JIM GUSTAFSON was born in Detroit in 1949, where he now lives, making a living as a feature writer for the *Detroit News*. He has lived in San Francisco, Chicago, Austin, and New York, and was editor of Jeffrey Miller's posthumous book, *The First One's Free*. Gustafson's recent books include *Virtue and Annihilation* (Alternative Press, 1988) and *The Hurt* (Little King, 1990).

JANA HARRIS was born in San Francisco. She is a poet, novelist, short story writer, and essayist. Her books include *Manhattan as a Second Language* and *Oh How Can I Keep On Singing?* (poetry, Harper & Row), and *Alaska* (a novel, Harper & Row). She writes and raises horses in the foothills of the Cascade Mountains in Washington State.

JIM HARRISON is a poet, novelist, and screenwriter, born in Michigan in 1937. He's published seventeen books, the most recent a novel, *Julip*, from Houghton Mifflin. He lives in Northern Michigan.

WILLIAM HATHAWAY was born in Madison, Wisconsin, in 1944. His books of poems include *The Gymnast of Inertia* and *Fish, Flesh & Fowl*, both from LSU Press; and *Looking into the Heart of Light* and *Churlsgrace*, from UCF Press. Hathaway lives in Saratoga Springs, New York.

MICHAEL HELLER, poet and teacher, is the author of *In the Builded Place* (Coffee House Press, 1990). His critical study of the Objectivist poets, *Conviction's Net of Branches* (Southern Illinois University Press, 1985) won the Di Castagnola Award of the Poetry Society of

America. He is the editor of *Carl Rakosi: Man and Poet* (National Poetry Foundation Press, 1993). Since 1967 Heller has been a member of the faculty of NYU's American Language Institute.

DICK HIGGINS was born in Cambridge, England, in 1938. From 1958-1959 he studied music with John Cage and Henry Cowell. In 1961, he co-founded *Fluxus*, and through the sixties operated Something Else Gallery, giving the United States its first exhibitions of concrete poetry. In the eighties, Higgins' focus moved to painting; his work has been exhibited in Germany, Sweden, Canada, Brazil, Netherlands, France, and the United States; in 1993 he received a Pollock-Krasner grant to paint.

ANSELM HOLLO was born in Helsinki, Finland, in 1934. In 1966 he settled permanently in the United States. Since 1989 he has been a member of the faculty of the Jack Kerouac School of Disembodied Poetics at the Naropa Institute, Boulder, Colorado. Hollo's most recent books include *Outlying Districts: New Poems* (Coffee House Press, 1990) and *Space Baltic: The Science Fiction Poems* (Ocean View Books, 1991). Translations include *Paavo Haavikko: Selected Poems 1949-1989* (Carcanet Press, 1991); *The Tzar's Madman* (a novel) by Estonian writer Jaan Kross (Pantheon, 1993); and *Sarajevo: A War Journal* by Zlatko Dizdarevic (Fromm International, 1993).

BOB HOLMAN, poet, performer, and poetry activist, has published five books of poetry; his most recent are *Cupid's Cashbox* (Jordan Davies) and *Panic*DJ* (University Arts Resources). Holman fronts poetry into daily life by all means: he has produced poetry videos, winning three Emmys for *Poetry Spots* (WNYC-TV) and an International Public Television Award for *Words in Your Face*, which aired nationally on PBS, and he is a co-director and Slam host at the Nuyorican Poets Cafe, a founder of NuYO Records (a spoken word label), and is currently working on a four-part PBS series, *The United States of Poetry*. With Miguel Algarin, he is editor of *Aloud: The Nuyorican Poets Cafe Anthology* (Holt, 1995). Holman teaches Exploding Text: Poetry as Performance and other courses at the New School in New York City.

PAUL HOOVER, born in 1946, is co-editor with his wife Maxine Chernoff of *New American Writing*. He is the editor of *The Norton Anthology of Post-Modern Poetry*. His books include the book-length poem *A Novel* (New Directions, 1990), *Idea* (The Figures, 1987), and a novel, *Saigon, Illinois* (Vintage, 1988). He lives in Chicago and San Francisco.

FANNY HOWE, novelist and poet, was born in Buffalo, New York, in 1940. She lives in Boston and teaches at MIT. Howe is the author of many volumes of poetry and fiction including *The End*, published in 1992.

RODGER KAMENETZ is a poet and professor of English at Louisiana State University. His books include *The Missing Jew: New & Selected Poems* and *The Jew in the Lotus: A Poet's Rediscovery of Jewish Identity in Buddhist India* (Harper, 1994).

ROBERT KELLY, born in 1935, co-founded the *Chelsea Review* (now *Chelsea*), and edited the magazine from 1957-1960. He edited with Paris Leary the influential anthology *A Controversy of Poets* (Doubleday Anchor, 1965). Author of numerous books of poetry and fiction, his most recent works are *Selected Poems 1960-1992* (Black Sparrow Press, 1995) and *Queen of Terrors*, a book of stories (McPherson, 1995). Kelly lives in upstate New York, and teaches at Bard College.

JUSSI KETONEN was born in Helsinki, Finland, in 1952. He came to the United States in 1968, and became a U.S. citizen in 1977. His previous literary efforts include articles in the *Annals of Mathematics* and *Fundamenta Mathematicae*. Ketonen lives in Palo Alto, California.

FAYE KICKNOSWAY changed her name to Morgan Blair in December of 1993. **MORGAN BLAIR**, aka Faye Kicknosway, lives, teaches, and writes in Honolulu, Hawaii, "a suburb of Detroit if you know the right tunnel." Her latest books of poetry are *The Violence of Potatoes* and *Listen to Me* (Ridgeway Press).

CAROLYN KIZER born in Spokane, Washington, 1925, received the Pulitzer Prize in 1985 for her book *Yin: New Poems* (Boa Editions, 1984). She has published seven books of poetry, including a volume of translations (with Donald Finkel) from the Chinese democracy movement. *Proses*, her essays on poems and poets, was published in 1994 by Copper Canyon Press. Kizer lives in Sonoma, California.

STEVE KOWIT was born in New York in 1938 and now lives near San Diego. He has written two books inspired by the love poetry of India, and four volumes of verse; he is the editor of *The Maverick Poets*, an anthology, and *In the Palm of Your Handbook* (Tilbury House, 1995), a poetry textbook.

MAXINE KUMIN, poet, novelist, and essayist, was awarded the Pulitzer Prize for Poetry in 1973. Author of more than fifteen volumes of prose and poetry, her most recent publications include *Women, Animals, and Vegetables: Essays and Stories* (1994) and *Looking for Luck* (1992), both from W.W. Norton.

STEVE KOWIT was born in New York in 1938 and now lives near San Diego. He has written two books inspired by the love poetry of India, and four volumes of verse; he is the editor of *The Maverick*

Poets, an anthology, and *In the Palm of Your Handbook* (Tilbury House, 1995), a poetry textbook.

ALEX KUO was born in Boston in 1939. He now lives in Idaho. His many poetry books include *Changing the River*.

JOANNE KYGER, a native Californian, is author of fifteen books of poetry, including *Just Space* (Black Sparrow Press, 1991). She teaches at Naropa Institute in Boulder, Colorado, and lives in Bolinas, California. She "looks forward to the scrub jays of the next century."

ART LANGE, born in Chicago in 1952, is the author of essays, reviews, articles, and interviews on music and poetry. From 1981 through 1988 he was associate editor, then editor, of *Down Beat* magazine. Lange is co-editor (with Nathaniel Mackey) of *Moment's Notice: Jazz in Poetry and Prose* (Coffee House Press, 1993), and is the author of five books of poetry, including *Needles at Midnight* (Z Press, 1986) and *Evidence* (Yellow Press, 1981). He currently serves as President of the Jazz Journalists Association.

RACHEL LODEN was born in 1948 in Washington, D.C., to parents active in the trade union movement. In 1965 she attended "the groundbreaking Berkeley Poetry Conference, but spoke to no one, and pursued obscurity for more than twenty years." Her poems have appeared recently in *New American Writing, Caliban*, and *Exquisite Corpse*. She lives in Palo Alto, California.

JACKSON MAC LOW writes poems, performance works, essays, plays, and radio works, and is a composer, painter, and multimedia performance artist. Since 1954 he has developed new ways of writing, composing, and performing, often employing "nonintentional" procedures. His most recent publications are *42 Merzgedichte in Memo-*

riam Kurt Schwitters (Station Hill, 1994), *Barnesbook* (Sun & Moon, 1994), and the compact disc *Open Secrets* (Experimental Intermedia XI-110, 1993).

MICHAEL McCLURE, performer, poet and playwright, was born in Marysville, Kansas, in 1932. His published work includes two books of essays, *Scratching the Beat Surface* and *Meat Science Essays*; two novels, more than a dozen volumes of poetry, and numerous plays, including *Josephine: The Mouse Singer*, which received the Obie for Best Play in 1978.

JIM McCRARY lives in Lawrence, Kansas. His most recent book is *West of Mass* (Tansy Press). He has published in *Exquisite Corpse*, *First Intensity*, and *Borderline*.

CLARENCE MAJOR is the author of seven novels including *Dirty Bird Blues* (Mercury House, 1996), *My Amputations* (Western States Book Award, 1986), *Such Was the Season* (Literary Guild Selection, 1987/the *New York Times* Book Review "Summer Reading" Citation, 1988), and *Painted Turtle: Woman with Guitar* (*New York Times* Book Review "Notable Book of the Year" Citation, 1988). His nine books of poetry include *The Garden Thrives: Twentieth Century African-American Poetry* (HarperCollins, 1996). He is Professor of African-American Literature and Creative Writing, University of California, Davis.

MORTON MARCUS is the author of six books of poetry, the most recent, *Pages from a Scrapbook of Immigrants* (Coffee House Press). He teaches at Cabrillo College near Santa Cruz.

JACK MARSHALL lives by the ocean in San Francisco. His books include *Arriving on the Playing Fields of Paradise* (winner of the Bay

Area Book Reviewers Award for 1983), *Arabian Nights*, and *Sesame*, both from Coffee House Press. A chapbook, *Chaos Comics*, appeared in 1994 from Pennywhistle Press.

RICHARD MARTIN was born in Binghamton, New York, in 1949. His books are *Dream of Long Headdresses: Poems from a Thousand Hospitals* and *White Man Appears On Southern California Beach*. Martin organized *The Big Horror Poetry Series* in 1982 with his friend Tom Costello, and continues to host the series. He lives in Boston.

BERNADETTE MAYER, born in Brooklyn, New York, in 1945, served as director of The Poetry Project at St. Mark's Church for four years in the 1970s. A *Bernadette Mayer Reader* was published in 1992 by New Directions. Other works include *Utopia* (United Artists Books, 1983) and *Sonnets* (Tender Buttons Books, 1990).

C.M. MAYO's short stories have appeared in *The Paris Review* and *The Quarterly*. Her first collection of short fiction, *Sky Over El Nido*, won the Flannery O'Connor Award and is published by the University of Georgia Press. She lives in Mexico City.

DAVID MELTZER, poet, musician, editor, and teacher, is the author of several books of poetry including *Tens*, edited by Kenneth Rexroth (McGraw-Hill), *The Name* (Black Sparrow Press), and most recently *Arrows: Selected Poetry 1957-1992*. *Orf*, one of ten erotic novels he wrote in the sixties, has recently been reprinted by Rhinoceros Books. Vanguard Records has reissued his 60's rock band's first album, *Serpent Power*, on compact disc. With poet Clark Coolidge, vocalist/song-writer Tina Meltzer, and assorted musicians, poets, and artists, he is part of Mix, a performance ensemble. Meltzer teaches in the undergraduate Humanities Program and the graduate Poetics Program at New College of California in San Francisco.

DIANE MIDDLEBOOK, author of *Anne Sexton: A Biography*, is now working on a biography of jazz musician Billy Tipton, who spent fifty years of professional and personal life masquerading as a man. She lives in San Francisco and London.

FRED MORAMARCO is a poet and critic who lives in San Diego and teaches American Literature at San Diego State University. He is co-editor (with Al Zolynas) of *Men of Our Time: An Anthology of Male Poetry in Contemporary America* (University of Georgia Press, 1992) and co-author of *Modern American Poetry, 1865-1950* (University of Massachusetts Press, 1991). Moramarco has also authored a book on the American writer Edward Dahlberg, and has concluded a sequel to *Modern American Poetry* called *Containing Multitudes: Poetry in the United States Since 1950*.

STANLEY MOSS was born in 1925 in New York City. He is the author of *The Wrong Angel, Skull of Adam,* and *The Intelligence of Clouds*. He is publisher of Sheep Meadow Press in Riverdale, New York, and president of Stanley Moss and Co., a private art dealership.

EILEEN MYLES is a New York City poet who teaches poetry to the masses, and ran for President of the United States in 1992. Her books include *Chelsea Girls*, and *Maxfield Parrish/Early & New Poems* (both from Black Sparrow Press), and *Not Me* (semiotext(e). She is the co-editor (with Liz Kotz) of *The New Fuck You: Adventures in Lesbian Reading*. (Semiotext(e).

ELINOR NAUEN was born in Sioux Falls, South Dakota, in 1952. Her books include *Diamonds Are a Girl's Best Friend* (Faber & Faber, 1994) and *Cars and Other Poems*. Nauen's work has been antohologized in *Up Late* (ed. by Andrei Codrescu, Four Walls Eight Windows), *Stiffest of the Corpse* (City Lights, 1989), and *Out of This*

World (ed. Anne Waldman, Crown Publishers, 1991). She lives by her pen in New York City.

JIM NISBET, San Francisco poet, playwright, and novelist, owns and operates his own business specializing in the design, construction, and installation of electronic furniture. This work engendered the 1991 publication of his only work of nonfiction to date, *Laminating the Conic Frustum*. Nisbet has published five novels, including *You Stiffed Me!*; his most recent book of poetry is *Small Apt* (Thumbscrew Press).

PAT NOLAN was born in French Canada half a century ago. His writings, translations, and reviews have been published in magazines like *The Paris Review*, *Exquisite Corpse*, *The New Censorship*, and *Poetry Flash*. A student of Chinese and Japanese prosody, Nolan has worked at adapting some of the idiosyncratic features of Asian forms to his own poems. A selection of his tanka entitled *Cloud Scatter* was published in 1994. He is founder of The Black Bart Poetry Society, and co-editor of its newsletter, *Life of Crime*. Nolan is a long-time resident of Monte Rio, California.

HAROLD NORSE began his literary career as friend and secretary of W. H. Auden in New York. He has published thirteen volumes of poetry, an experimental cut-up novel, *Beat Hotel*, with a foreword by William Burroughs, an autobiography, *Memoirs of a Bastard Angel* (Morrow) with a preface by James Baldwin, and *The American Idiom*, a ten-year correspondence with William Carlos Williams. Norse has received a Lifetime Achievement Award from the National Poetry Association. He is working on his *New and Selected Poems*.

ALICE NOTLEY lives in Paris and teaches creative writing at the American University of Paris. She is also a permanent visiting faculty member of the Naropa Institute in Boulder, Colorado, and has taught at the Maryland Institute, College of Arts and the St. Mark's Poetry Project in New York. With her husband, the British poet Douglas Oliver, she is the co-editor of *SCARLET* and Scarlet Editions. She is the author of over twenty books of poetry and has also written essays, a memoir, and a play. Recent books include *Selected Poems of Alice Notley* (Talisman House Publishers, 1993), and *The Scarlet Cabinet: A Compendium of Books by Alice Notley and Douglas Oliver* (Scarlet Editions, 1992).

ALICIA OSTRIKER has written seven volumes of poetry, including *Green Age* (1989). Her newest book is *The Nakedness of the Fathers*, a set of meditations on the Bible, or what Ostriker fondly calls "the Old Testicle." She has also written *Feminist Revision and the Bible*.

MAUREEN OWEN was born in Minnesota in 1943. She founded Telephone Books in New York City in 1969, and is the author of five books of poetry, including *Zombie Notes* (SUN Press, 1985). Owen was director of the St. Mark's Poetry Project from 1976-77.

MICHAEL PALMER was born in New York City in 1943. Poet, translator, and choreographer, Palmer has collaborated on more than a dozen dance works with Margaret Jenkins, published an equal number of books of poetry, and collaborated with painters, composers, and performance artists around the world. His most recent books are *At Passages*, a new collection of poetry, from New Directions; *Selected Writings and Talks*, from the University of New Mexico Press; and *Theory of Tables*, a translation of the poetry of Emmanuel Hocquard, from o-blek. He lives in San Francisco.

MOLLY PEACOCK is the author of four books of poetry, including *Original Love* (Norton) and *Take Heart* (Vintage). She served as

President of the Poetry Society of America from 1989-1994. She lives in London, Ontario, Canada, and in New York City, facing the millennium coming and going.

BOB PERELMAN teaches at the University of Pennsylvania, and writes both poetry and criticism; his works include *The Trouble with Genius: Reading Pound, Joyce, Stein, and Zukofsky* (University of California Press, 1994), and *The Marginalization of Poetry: Language Writing and Literary History* (Princeton University Press, 1995).

ROBERT PETERS was born in rural Wisconsin in 1924. Poet, critic, and scholar, he has been a Professor of English at the University of California at Irvine since 1966. Peters is author of over thirty collections of poems and a dozen volumes of criticism, including his 1994 collection of essays, *Where the Bee Sucks: Workers, Drones and Queens of Contemporary American Poetry* (Asylum Arts, 1994). Other books include *Poems: Selected & New* (Asylum Arts, 1992), *Zapped: 2 Short Novels* (GLB Publishers, 1993), and a memoir, *Crunching Gravel: On Growing Up in the Thirties* (Mercury House, 1988).

PAM QUINLAN's favorite year was "the fetching yet mysterious 1906"; she was born in 1959. Quinlan is "an exceedingly lucid law clerk living in Oregon's Willamette Valley," a lyricist for a country/punk band, and has published poetry and fiction in numerous journals, including *Exquisite Corpse*.

CARL RAKOSI is one of the Objectivist poets associated since the 1930s with Louis Zukofsky, Charles Reznikoff, and George Oppen. His *Collected Poems* were published in 1986 by the National Poetry Foundation and his *Collected Prose* in 1983 by the same publisher. Rakosi's work has been translated into five languages, and he was an honored guest at the International Objectivist conference in France in 1990. He has been awarded a lifetime achievement award by the National Poetry Association.

LEN ROBERTS is a professor of English at Northampton Community College in Bethlehem, Pennsylvania, and the author of six books of poetry. His new book is *Counting the Black Angels* (University of Illinois Press, 1994).

KIRK ROBERTSON lives in Fallon, Nevada, and has published seventeen collections of poetry, including *Music: A Suite & 13 Songs* (Floating Island Press, 1994) and *Again & Again: Some Selected & New Poems, 1969-1993* (University of Nevada Press, 1995). He is the director of the Nevada Arts Council and the editor of Neon.

BOB ROSENTHAL was born "exactly mid century—1950—mid country—Chicago—middle income—Father psychoanalyst, Mother German teacher. Told self stories to get off center. Twenty-first birthday brought post tequila spiritual realization that he could be a poet and never have a career. Married Rochelle Kraut and moved to New York City to read, write plays, act, have kids, and end up in medieval lifelong servitude to Allen Ginsberg Cottage Industries." His most recent book of poetry is *Viburnum*.

LAURA ROSENTHAL is executive editor of *Exquisite Corpse* and co-editor of this anthology. She in Baton Rouge, Louisiana, was born in 1958.

JEROME ROTHENBERG is the author of over fifty books of poetry, and has edited six groundbreaking anthologies of experimental and traditional poetry (*Technicians of the Sacred, Shaking the Pumpkin, A Big Jewish Book, America a Prophecy*, etc.) Rothenberg has been actively engaged in poetry and performance since the late 1950s, and he is now a professor of Visual Arts and Literature with the University of California at San Diego. New books of poems include *The Lorca Variations* (New Directions, 1993) and *Gematria* (Sun & Moon, 1994). He has edited a two-volume global anthology of twentieth-century avant-garde poetry (University of California Press, 1995).

DEBORAH SALAZAR was born in Guayaquil, Ecuador, in 1962. Her poems, stories, essays, and translations have been published in magazines like *Harper's* and *Exquisite Corpse* and in anthologies such as *Best Essays by American Women* and *Palabra: Latino Poets for the New Millennium*. She lives in Baton Rouge.

CHRISTY SHEFFIELD SANFORD is the author of four books; the most recent is *Italian Smoking Piece*, published by Helicon Nine Editions. In 1992 she wrote, produced, and directed a spoken word opera, *The H's: The Spasms of a Requiem*.

LESLIE SCALAPINO was born in 1948 and lives in Berkeley, California. She is editor and publisher of O Books. Among her recent publications are *Objects in the Terrifying Sense/Longing from Taking Place* (Roof Books, 1994), *Defoe* (Sun & Moon, 1995), and *The Font Matter, Dead Souls* (Wesleyan University Press, 1996).

HARRIS SCHIFF was born in New York City in 1944, and grew up in the West Bronx near Yankee Stadium. In the '60s he studied at CCNY with Paul Blackburn, and was introduced to Ted Berrigan, Tom Clark, Ron Padgett, and the St. Mark's scene. In 1969 he ran the Monday night open readings at St. Mark's Church. His poems have recently appeared in *The World*, *RealPoetik*, and *The Poetry Project Newsletter*.

ARMAND SCHWERNER, performance artist and musician, was born in Antwerp, Belgium, in 1927. He has worked with Jackson Mac Low,

Glenn Velez, Jerome Rothenberg, and Ellen Zweig; he has performed in Belgium, Germany, Switzerland, France, the United States, and Japan. Schwerner's work has appeared in 38 anthologies of American poetry, beginning with the *New Directions Annual* (ed. James Laughlin, 1966) and including appearances in Jerome Rothenberg's anthologies *Shaking the Pumpkin* (1972) and *The Big Jewish Book* (1978). Schwerner is professor in the departments of English, Speech, and World Literature at the College of Staten Island, CUNY.

JACQUES SERVIN is the author of two collections of poetic stories published by the Fiction Collective, including *Mermaids for Attilla* and *Aviary Slag*. He lives in San Francisco.

DAVID SHAPIRO was born in New Jersey in 1947, and lives in New York City. He was a professional violinist, and is an art critic as well as a poet. His poem commemorating Jan Palach inspired John Hejduk's monument to Palach in Prague. His works include *January* (Holt, 1965), *Lateness* (Overlook, 1977), and *After a Lost Original* (Overlook, 1994).

CHARLES SIMIC, a MacArthur Fellow, has received the Pulitzer prize for Poetry in 1990 for a book entitled *The World Doesn't End* (Harbrace, 1989). *Wedding in Hell* (Harcourt Brace) is his latest book. He lives in New Hampshire.

DAVE SMITH's most recent book is *Night Pleasures: New and Selected Poems* (Bloodaxe Books, 1992, England). He is the co-editor of *The Southern Review* and lives in Baton Rouge.

MICHAEL STEPHENS was born in Washington, D.C., in 1946, but has lived nearly all his life in New York City. His books include the novels, *Season at Coole* and *The Brooklyn Book of the Dead*; and the collection of essays *Green Dreams*. His books of poetry include *After Asia* and *Jigs and Reels*. Currently he is the writer-in-residence at Emerson College in Boston.

GERALD STERN taught at the writer's workshop in Iowa and is one of the founders of the *American Poetry Review*. He is the author of *Selected Poems* (HarperCollins) and *Bread without Sugar* (Norton). He is the 1993 recipient of the Fellowship of the Academy of American Poets.

STEVEN STYERS is assistant to the director of the Stadler Center for Poetry at Buckness University, managing editor of *West Branch*, and assistant editor of *Buckness Review*. He was born in 1955, year of rock'n roll.

ARTHUR SZE is a second-generation Chinese American, born in New York City in 1950. He now lives in Santa Fe, New Mexico, where he is Director of the Creative Writing Program at the Institute of American Indian Arts. Sze is the author of five books of poetry, including *Archipelago* (Copper Canyon Press, 1995).

WILLIAM TALCOTT is the publisher of Thumbscrew Press, San Francisco, and editor of the magazine *Carbuncle*. He co-edited *Isthmus* magazine and books (with Jim Willems), and was the founder of the Babar Cafe school. Talcott's recent book of poetry is *Kidstuff* (Norton Coker Press, 1992).

NATHANIEL TARN is a poet, translator, editor, critic, and anthropoligist. He has published 25 books; the most recent are *Seeing America First* (Coffee House) and *Views from the Weaving Mountain: Selected Essays on Poetry & Anthropology* (University of New Mexico Press).

MIKE TOPP was born in Washington, D.C., in the 20th century. His *Local Boy Makes Good (Appearances* #21) was published in 1994. He is currently living in New York City "unless he has died or moved." Topp is a frequent contributor to *Exquisite Corpse* where he can sometimes be found in his own corner, "Under the Big Topp."

DAVID TRINIDAD was born in 1953 in Los Angeles. He now lives and works in New York City. His poems have been included in a dozen anthologies and have appeared in such magazines as *Harper's, The Paris Review, New American Writing*, and *City Lights Review*. His poetry books include *Monday, Monday* (Cold Calm Press, 1985), *November* (Hanuman Books, 1987), *Hand Over Heart: Poems 1981-1988* (Amethyst Press, 1991), and *Answer Song* (Serpent's Tail/High Risk, 1994). He is the poetry editor of *OutWeek* magazine.

NANOS VALAORITIS was born in Luasanne, Switzerland, in 1921. He is a trilingual poet and renowned translator of modern Greek poetry. In the early fifties he lived in Paris where he participated in the Surrealist movement. His numerous books in English, Greek, and French, include *Hired Hieroglyphs, Diplomatic Relations, My Afterlife Guaranteed, Punishment of the Magicians*, and *Terre de Diamant*. He lives in Oakland, California, Paris, France, and Lefkas Island, Greece.

JANINE POMMY VEGA, poet, lecturer, performer, was born in Jersey City in 1942, and has lived in Jerusalem, Paris, Amsterdam, London, Spain, Ireland, South America, and Hawaii, performing her work. She is the author of many books of poetry and editor of numerous anthologies, and has served for eighteen years in New York State Poets in the Schools and Poets in Public Service. Her recent books include *Threading the Maze* (Cloud Mountain Press, 1992), a prose work on mother worship sites in Europe, and *Drunk on* *a Glacier, Talking to Flies* (Tooth of Time Books, 1988), a collection of poetry.

PAUL VIOLI was born in 1944 in New York. After graduation from Boston University, he traveled throughout Africa, Europe, and Asia. He was managing editor of *The Architectural Forum*, worked on special projects for Universal Limited Art Editions, and helped direct a poetry reading series at the Museum of Modern Art. He has taught at various colleges and universities and has published six books of poems, including *Likewise* and *The Curious Builder*.

ANNE WALDMAN was born in New York in 1945. She has developed an international reputation as a reader-performer. In 1976, she toured as poet-in-residence with Bob Dylan's *Rolling Thunder Review*. Collaboratively she has worked with musicians and composers, dancers and visual artists. Waldman was director of The Poetry Project at St. Mark's Church in New York until 1978; now she teaches full-time at The Naropa Institue, Boulder, Colorado, where along with Allen Ginsberg, she founded the Jack Kerouac School of Disembodied Poetics. Her recent poetry was collected in *Kill or Cure* (Penguin, 1994).

KEITH WALDROP, poet, novelist, and translator, teaches at Brown University. With his wife, Rosmarie Waldrop, he co-edits the small press Burning Deck. Recent works include *The Opposite of Letting the Mind Wander: Selected Poems* (Lost Roads), *Hegel's Family* (Station Hill), and a novel, *Light While There Is Light* (Sun and Moon, 1995).

LEWIS WARSH was born in the Bronx in 1944. A writer of fiction and poetry, he is editor of United Artists Books and of *The World*, the literary magazine of The Poetry Project. Warsh teaches at Long Island University in Brooklyn. His recent book of poetry is *Avenue of*

Escape; other works include *Information from the Surface of Venus* (United Artists, 1987) and *A Free Man* (Sun & Moon, 1991).

JONATHAN WILLIAMS was born in Asheville, North Carolina, in 1929. In 1951 he founded the Jargon Society, and remains its editorial director, publisher, and (often) designer. Since its founding, the Jargon Society has published some of America's finest poets and photographers, including Kenneth Patchen, Charles Olson, Robert Creeley, Mina Loy, Paul Metcalf, and John Menapace. Poet Jonathan Williams has published over 100 books, pamphlets, and broadsides; his readings, public lectures, and seminars number over 1100. William's upcoming books of poetry is *Horny & Ornery*. He lives in Highlands, North Carolina.

TERENCE WINCH was born in New York City in 1945. He now lives in Washington, D.C., where he performs with a traditional Irish band, Celtic Thunder. His *Irish Musicians/American Friends* won an American Book Award in 1986. His most recent book of poems is *The Great Outdoors*.

CHARLES WRIGHT was born in Hardin County, Tennessee, in 1935. From 1966-1983 he was a member of the English Department of the University of California, Irvine. Since 1983 he has been a Professor of English at the University of Virginia in Charlottesville. His recent works include *The World of the Ten Thousand Things: Poems 1980-1990* (Farrar, Straus, & Giroux, 1990).

JOHN YAU was born in Massachusetts in 1950. He is an art critic as well as a poet, a frequent contributor to *Artforum* and *Art News*. *Cenotaph*, with drawings by Archie Rand, was published in 1987 by Chroma Press.